Angels on a School Bus

Angels on a School Bus

HOW A COMMUNITY OF VOLUNTEERS SAVED TWO
HUNDRED GERMAN SHEPHERDS AND HUSKIES

Dr. Roberta K Ray

ISBN-13: 9781517357528
ISBN-10: 1517357527

Credits

The dog at the top of the front cover with snow on his face is Monsieur Marcel Marshmallow (a.k.a. Puff), a greeter dog at the Fragrance Vault in South Lake Tahoe and one of the dogs on the bus. The photo was taken by Jana Menard. Below Monsieur Marcel is Apollo (a.k.a. Moose) of Colorado, one of the puppies born at Camp Husky. The photo was taken by Kirby Rowe. The dog at the top of the back cover is Luci, a Camp Husky mother dog and official greeter at Seiler's Hardware in Three Forks, Montana. The photo, courtesy of Glenda Barnes and Richard Seiler, shows Luci looking down on Lake Plateau in the Beartooth Wilderness of southwestern Montana. The photo at the bottom of the back cover shows adults and puppies looking out of the back of the school bus on October 6, 2008, courtesy of photographer Adrienne Herren.

Dedication

This book is dedicated to the 120 people from Butte and other communities in Montana who volunteered at Camp Husky; to all the individuals and businesses that contributed money, services, equipment, or business space to help the dogs; and to all those who helped to find good homes for the dogs, including those volunteers who drove or flew dogs for out-of-state adoptions. Finally, this book is dedicated to all the angels on the school bus, to their puppies, and to the men, women, and children who have provided these magnificent dogs with loving homes.

The author is donating the net proceeds from the sale of this book to organizations that helped the Camp Husky dogs and to German shepherd and Siberian husky rescues.

Acknowledgments

The author conducted more than 130 interviews in writing this book. It would not have been possible to do this research without records of volunteers and their work schedules, fostering and adoption records, and other documents. I was unable to obtain any documentation from Butte Animal Services or the Chelsea Bailey Animal Shelter. Most of the information I obtained was through records kept by volunteers. As busy as volunteers were—caring for the dogs at Camp Husky, conducting fundraisers, and working to find homes for the dogs—several took time to maintain written and photographic records. I have drawn on the written documentation and the visual evidence, as well as the interviews, in writing this book. I am grateful to the many volunteers and dog owners who took time to tell me their stories. The following individuals supplied me with essential documentation, photographs, and scrapbooks: Samantha Collier, Sarah DeMoney, Cathy Decker, Katie Donovan, Barb LeProwse, Cindy McIlveen, Christy Stack, and Debbie Rossi, the owner of Thrive, a pet health-food store. Judge Kurt Kruger took time to explain how the Brode case proceeded through the legal system and the *why* behind the final settlement of the case. Paul Babb, former chief executive of Butte-Silver Bow, also patiently answered my questions about the role of the consolidated city-county government in the rescue. Finally, Lora O'Connor and her staff at the Humane Society of Western Montana in Missoula not only found homes for many of our dogs but also provided invaluable help to me in researching this book by telephoning those who had adopted and securing their permission for my interviews.

I am especially indebted to Sarah DeMoney and Christy Stack for their help with initial editing of the book and their encouragement when the task of completing it seemed impossible. Sarah set up and monitored our Facebook page (Camp Husky 2008 Butte Montana), did a super job of editing the chapters about the dogs, and designed and prepared the photo inserts for the book. Christy stepped in toward the end and helped me with typing and editing the chapters about Camp Husky when my eyesight was failing. Without the help of these two remarkable women, I could not have finished this project.

My husband, John, is the one who encouraged me to volunteer at Camp Husky, but volunteering sixteen hours on weekends, plus working my full-time job during the week, meant that all the household chores fell to him. His patience, encouragement, and willingness to listen to me talk about almost nothing but Camp Husky for the last five years are remarkable, to say nothing of getting up before five in the morning so he could proofread my latest work. Finally, there are my two Camp Husky dogs, who keep me company in the lonely process of writing. They are constant reminders of why we volunteered.

Contents

Preface

The only creatures evolved enough to communicate
pure love are dogs and infants.
—Johnny Depp

I n early October 2008, I walked into the Anselmo Mine hoist house on a hill just above the small town of Butte in southwestern Montana. As I entered that historical building and climbed the steps to the second floor, I was shivering from the cold in spite of the heavy jacket, warm hat, and gloves I was wearing. The temperature was below freezing outside and even colder in the unheated building. And then I saw them—the dogs from the school bus. There were more than one hundred of the most unusual and beautiful dogs I had ever seen. Many had fear in their eyes, as one would expect from feral dogs raised as one huge pack with little human contact on a large tract of land in Colorado. There was also an innocence and sweetness in their faces. Volunteers caring for them over the next six months would refer to them as "our huskies" and "our gentle giants." All of the adult dogs and puppies on the bus, as well as the puppies born at Camp Husky, would be given special names—often reflecting their appearances or personalities—like Glacier, the large pure-white husky; Pinkie, named for her pink nose; or Puff, who was so sweet and gentle, one thought of a cream puff.

I realized that first day that these German shepherds and huskies were unique dogs, like none I had ever seen before, and more than that, there was something spiritual about being in their presence. Later, when

I researched this book and interviewed more than thirty-five men and women who volunteered at Camp Husky and about one hundred individuals and families who adopted these dogs, I realized that I was not alone in my admiration for the beauty, intelligence, and magical quality of these German shepherds, huskies, and husky-shepherd mixes. A young woman from Boise, Idaho, adopted one of these dogs while she was a student at the University of Montana. Now in her senior year at Washington State University College of Veterinary Medicine, Casey Drummond wrote me about her "best friend," Japhy, a puppy born at Camp Husky, now more than seven years of age. Casey had encountered many Camp Husky dogs while a student in Montana and wrote of the unique and magical quality of these dogs.

Casey wrote, "I am so glad that you are writing this book. It will be a nice way for me to keep Japhy and her story with me always. While I would never wish for a rescue situation like Camp Husky to happen again, it will be incredibly sad once all these dogs have passed away. The Camp Husky dogs remind me of the mythical breed of shepherds in the novel called *The Story of Edgar Sawtelle*. I can always spot one of the Camp Husky dogs. They have a unique quality about them that I cannot quite articulate. I wish I knew what it is that makes them so special. These dogs will exist for only a relatively brief period of time, but they will have touched so many lives. I know they are affecting many lives in some very significant way; something about that makes them seem like so much more than 'just dogs' to me."

Casey's words were echoed by many men, women, and even children I interviewed who adopted Camp Husky adult dogs and puppies. I came to realize that these dogs were indeed angels on a school bus, angels who would awaken the souls of those who saved and adopted them. Young people as well as seniors told me how their lives were enriched by the playfulness and joy these dogs brought them. I had men and women tell me of the agony of losing a best friend, a fiancé, a spouse, or even a child and how a Camp Husky dog brought emotional comfort to them at a time when their grief seemed like more than they could bear. Owners of Camp Husky dogs told me stories of dogs with senses of humor or dogs that speak human language, even forming sentences. They told of other amazing things their dogs have done, and they described acts of courage, loyalty, and selflessness. They spoke of a human-animal bond like none they had ever known before. If an angel is a being sent to teach us spiritual lessons; maintain our belief in a power for good; and sustain our faith that unconditional love and kindness will ultimately triumph over ignorance, meanness, and greed, then the dogs on the school bus were indeed angels. I believe I speak for all those who have loved the dogs of Camp Husky. They touched our souls so deeply that we will never be the same.

CHAPTER 1

Reflecting, Seven Years Later

O n a military base in North Carolina, a sergeant major embraces his beautiful young wife, Erin, in a tender good-bye before boarding a plane with his fellow marines. The long separation and the anxiety for her husband will be hard on Erin, but she knows she can cope with the support of her best friend and protector, Sergeant Huck, a magnificent white German shepherd. Far away in Montana, a young army veteran is slowly healing from the physical and emotional wounds of war with the help of a playful and affectionate Siberian husky–German shepherd mix named Bella.

When ninety-five-year-old Fay walks outside to fill the bird feeder in her backyard, the retired music teacher is not alone; standing beside her and helping her maintain balance is Bucky, her 130-pound companion dog. This highly intelligent white German shepherd–husky mix is part service dog and part clown and always seems to understand what Fay needs.

Far north of where Fay lives, in the rural community of Ovando, Montana, there is a dog who was named Mylie because, as a puppy, she looked like the cartoon character Wile E. Coyote. However, her owners will be the first to tell you that there is nothing loony tunes about their German shepherd–husky mix. When only nine months old, Mylie challenged a hungry mountain lion more than twice her size, saving her owner's life.

In Colorado, a little boy named Henry and his baby brother play while their two devoted babysitters look on with concern. Honey and Fiver, husky-shepherd mixes, have been watching over them since each child was born. In Oregon, a five-year-old and her seven-year-old brother are climbing up into their tree house to play, and climbing right behind them is a 120-pound pure-white Siberian husky named Dandy. Having known only neglect and abuse during the first year of his life, Dandy found contentment when a young couple adopted him and patiently taught him to trust humans. He repays their love with devotion to their children.

In Michigan, a young couple enjoys taking their German shepherd–Siberian husky mix wherever they go in their leisure hours, whether it is a long backpacking trip or just a stroll through the farmers' market. Folks often stop to admire the unusually beautiful Ollie and ask if she is a wolf.

In New Mexico, a poet receives inspiration from his best buddy, a Belgian Tervuren named Rhett. In Montana, a singer-songwriter and her white German shepherd, Mr. Jones, make beautiful music together.

Near Seattle, a woman always knows precisely when her husband is going to arrive home from work, although he doesn't tell her. Exactly twenty minutes before his master drives up to the house, Simba, a Belgian Malinois, goes to the large bay window in the living room and stands watch. Simba's prescience is remarkable because his owner arrives home at a different time nearly every evening, depending on how far away his consulting job has taken him that day.

In a cabin on the edge of Yellowstone National Park, Bob Landis, an award-winning wildlife cinematographer, arises long before dawn so that he can prepare everything for the day's filming. Known for films that have aired on PBS and the National Geographic Channel, Landis is now filming the struggle for survival of one small wolf pack in Yellowstone. Keeping Landis company are two white German shepherd dogs with an exciting survival story of their own that has never been told.

In the Montana town of Three Forks, everyone knows Luci, a long-haired, black-and-tan German shepherd and the official greeter in the local hardware store. From Monday through Saturday, children and adults come by "just to see Luci." In South Lake Tahoe, California, a beautiful husky-shepherd mix named Marcel works as a service dog and as a greeter in a perfume shop. Three years before, this dog with an amputated front leg was terrified of people and other dogs—until he formed a most unlikely friendship with a wolf.

In Great Falls, Montana, a fourteen-year-old and her very large white German shepherd dog are having great fun in an agility competition. Bear has been Katie's best friend and protector since she was eight years old. In another Montana city, two men are about to break into the home of a man who has recently lost much of his hearing. This retired gentleman has no way of knowing the danger facing him until his white German shepherd, Bob, alerts the man and protects him until police arrive and arrest the robbers.

These are some of the heartwarming stories of the angels on a school bus who were destined to change the lives of the volunteers who saved them and the individuals and families who adopted them. These seventeen dogs were part of one of the largest and most challenging dog-rescue operations in the United States. This rescue took place in Butte, Montana, in the winter of 2008–2009, and it was unique in that the dogs did not come from Butte or even Montana but from Colorado. They arrived in Butte on a large school bus and trailer. Although there were some traditional black-and-tan German shepherds and three types of Belgian shepherds on the bus, most of the dogs were long-haired white German shepherds or Siberian husky–shepherd mixes, and most were exceptionally large—giant sized, to be precise. Their beautiful but unique appearance would prove a problem because many folks unfamiliar with white German shepherds, including some veterinarians, would conclude that they were wolves or part wolf.

There were no animal-rescue organizations coming to the aid of these dogs, which is atypical in most animal rescues. When the bus full of dogs arrived in Butte, the fate of the dogs depended on volunteers— compassionate people who looked into those eyes and saw gentle but frightened creatures. For the next six months, as many as 120 people would volunteer, and many others would donate money and supplies to the effort to save these dogs, socialize them, and find good homes for them. These were people motivated by compassion, love of dogs, and altruism. There were also people in influential positions who were hostile toward the dogs from the start. In the end, the volunteers would be justified in the faith they had in these dogs.

This is the story of how volunteers fought extreme cold, disease, and often indifferent or even hostile animal-services officials to save the dogs. It is the story of eighty-one of those dogs and the lives they changed through the love and affection they passed on to those who adopted them.

Many years ago, as a twenty-one-year-old college senior, I took a course in Medieval Latin. The manuscripts we students translated painted a picture of a time in Europe when ignorance, superstition, and extreme cruelty, often fostered by religion, were all too common. Stories of the cruelty expressed toward innocent women and the murder of a little black slave child by monks haunted me for years, but there was one inspiring story I never forgot. It was an account of what happened in a small village during the plague years, and it involved a wolf dog. This was a time of violence not only toward people, especially women, but also toward animals. Wolves were slaughtered as they are in the West today, and when women were accused of witchcraft, not only were they brutally killed but often their pet cats and dogs were too.

The true account I translated told of a small village during the fourteenth century, when the Black Plague killed nearly a third of the population of Europe. People in this small village were in shock, overwhelmed by grief and terror as more people became ill and died each day. Neither medicine nor religion could offer any protection from this hell on earth. During this turmoil, a large dog (from the description, it was either a wolf or a wolf hybrid) wandered into the village. Miraculously, no one tried to kill the wolf dog. About a week after the wolf dog arrived, people realized that there were no new cases of the plague. People were not getting sick in the village, and yet word arrived that other villages were still ravished by the plague. Why the plague ended for this village no one can say for certain, but the villagers came to believe that the wolf dog was responsible for ending the plague. The villagers came to believe that the wolf dog was an angel sent by God to save them, and they allowed the animal to live peacefully with them and even treated it with reverence. When the wolf dog died of old age, the villagers buried him and started to worship him. Whether the wolf dog brought protection from the plague is questionable, but there is no question that he brought the lesson of unconditional love to those villagers. The villagers believed that the wolf dog had saved them, asking nothing in return—not even food, since it ate rats. The account I translated was written many years after this event took place, and it attested to the powerful influence of the dog saint, as he was then called, on the villagers and their descendants. A generation after the plague ended and the wolf dog died, the villagers were still affected by the lesson of unconditional love they learned from a wolf dog.

I would often ponder that story as I volunteered at Camp Husky and looked into the eyes of those magnificent dogs. Sick and malnourished, with dirty, matted fur, those dogs offered the gift of unconditional love for those of us willing to look into their sad eyes and make a connection. As I sit at the table, writing on my laptop, two of those dogs lie near me—one was on that bus, and the other was born at Camp Husky. Like the villagers in the story, those of us who volunteered and those who adopted dogs realized that there were angels on that school bus, offering us a profound lesson about love, compassion, and connection. And like the villagers who were forever changed by the wolf dog, we were changed by the dogs on the bus.

CHAPTER 2
The Rescue Begins

Many important projects fail when good people let fear and doubt stop them from doing what they know is right, because the odds are stacked against them, or the work required is just too overwhelming. In this chapter you will meet five individuals who were responsible for starting the Camp Husky rescue. Without these five people, all the dogs would likely have died. In chapter 3 you will meet many other volunteers who played an essential role in keeping Camp Husky functioning. As a young college student, I was inspired by the words of cultural anthropologist Margaret Mead: "Never doubt that a small group of thoughtful committed citizens can change the world; indeed, it's the only thing that ever has." Selfish, mean-spirited, and even cruel individuals who inflict suffering on innocent animals are all too common in our world. Even more common are good people who do nothing more than sympathize with the suffering of animals. Good people who act are rare. The fate of the dogs on the bus would depend on these rare individuals.

The Camp Husky story began a number of years ago in La Jara, Colorado, where a disturbed man and animal hoarder named Philip Brode had purchased some property after relocating from Taos, New Mexico. Brode told folks in Butte that he had been breeding white German shepherds for thirty years, so he may have been breeding dogs when in New Mexico. Robin Jordan, reporter and currently editor for the *Butte Weekly*, supplied me with information about Brode's life in La Jara based on her interview with Diana Hamilton, director of the Valley Humane League in La Jara. Jordan learned from Hamilton that Brode kept the dogs chained outdoors without any shelter from the weather. Apparently, the pregnant females were forced to dig dens to give birth and provide some shelter for newborns on that prairie land.

Jordan learned from Hamilton that her La Jara shelter negotiated with Brode and was able to supply him with dog food in exchange for puppies that they could put up for adoption. Those puppies were badly malnourished and unsocialized. Hamilton also told Jordan that she had offered to spay and neuter the dogs and give Brode free dog food if he consented. He apparently did this only once with some dogs. "Hamilton said Brode told her he was a disabled Vietnam veteran with posttraumatic stress syndrome," wrote Jordan. That may explain why the man became a hoarder.

The information Jordan obtained from Hamilton and published in the *Butte Weekly* November 5, 2008, suggests that Brode decided to leave Colorado and head for Alaska in the fall of 2008 because he was being pressured to give up his dogs and have them spayed and neutered. Apparently frustrated with Brode's hoarding problem and the poor care the dogs were receiving, "Hamilton contacted the Colorado office of the United States Department of Agriculture, which oversees breeders and shelters for the state. Two officers, Kate Anderson and Cindy Thompson, came to cite Brode and make him relinquish the dogs. They served him with a cease-and-desist order to stop him from selling puppies in front of the local Walmart," reported Jordan. Fearing the officers would take his dogs, Brode loaded the majority of them into a large school bus. He attached a double-decker plywood trailer to the bus. The trailer was full of wire cages where many other dogs, including mothers (and sometimes fathers) were enclosed with their puppies. Apparently, Brode provided the dogs minimal food but little else. They were very large dogs, mostly white German shepherds and Siberian husky–shepherd mixes. Many of the dogs looked emaciated and many were sick as he drove away from Colorado. But this book is not about Brode or dog hoarders—it is about the dedicated volunteers and the dogs themselves.

The Good Samaritan Who Initiated the Rescue

As we labored at Camp Husky, volunteers occasionally spoke with great appreciation of "the Good Samaritan," the individual who first reported the bus full of dogs and got city officials to seize it and undertake the rescue effort. We knew that Brode's old bus had broken down on more than one occasion after he left his home in Colorado, and we knew that his plan was to drive to Alaska. In all likelihood, if Butte officials had not seized the bus on October 5, it would have broken down in some isolated place on the way to Alaska in the dead of winter, and all the dogs would have perished from starvation and cold. The dogs were already sick and malnourished when the bus arrived in Butte, and many of the pregnant females were close to term. In just a few days, the temperature in Montana would drop to below freezing. Butte was the last chance for approximately 125 wonderful dogs and puppies on that bus and trailer, and one courageous man with a big heart gave the dogs that chance at a good life.

The Good Samaritan's name was not known until I received a phone call from a man named Donald Frost after a story about this book appeared in the *Montana Standard* on October 9, 2011, for the third anniversary of Camp Husky. When I answered the phone, he said, "I am the one who called animal control and the police about the bus and trailer that broke down near the Flying J truck stop on October 1, 2008." Until that article came out, Mr. Frost had hidden his involvement from all but his family and close friends because of the treatment he had received from two animal-control officers. This is what Mr. Frost shared in an interview with Sarah DeMoney and me:

"I was employed doing maintenance work for the Flying J Restaurant at the Rocker truck stop when a man named Philip Brode first drove in and parked his old school bus and trailer full of dogs near the Flying J. The bus was leaking water when Brode drove in there. He was parked for three days doing his laundry and fixing the bus. I visited with him and even helped him with his laundry. Brode's routine was to take a few dogs at a time off the bus, feed them, and walk them. The dogs were protective of Brode when he was around; however, when he would go into the casino to warm up, I would go into the bus and pet the dogs. It really surprised me how friendly the dogs were toward me when Brode was not there. For the next three days, I would bring biscuits from home and feed the dogs on the bus.

"Brode gave me two puppies because I helped him with his laundry. He said that as he drove from Colorado to Montana, he had sold puppies whenever he stopped to buy gasoline in order to pay for the gas and other essentials. Brode had apparently sold many puppies at many stops between Colorado and Butte. The story he told me was that he was going to Alaska to participate in the Iditarod race. The man was too smart to think he would be allowed to take that bus and trailer full of dogs into Canada. I knew that people could sneak into Canada using backroads or logging roads, so I figured he would be heading toward Libby or Troy, Montana, with the goal of entering Canada via logging roads somewhere near Libby or Troy. I also knew that the bus was in no condition to make such a journey. I knew in my gut that if Brode and the dogs did not find help in Butte, they would be doomed. Brode was not a man I could reason with. I had to get help for him and those wonderful dogs.

"Brode told me that police in Dillon, Montana, had escorted him out of town." What occurred in Dillon probably occurred more than once in Colorado and in Utah as well. No one could fail to notice the dogs, but one can well understand that city officials would be reluctant to take on the burden and expense of rescuing so many dogs. It would be so much easier to turn a blind eye to the problem than to show compassion when faced with the suffering of the dogs. There were certainly those in Butte who had no compassion for the dogs or the disturbed man who owned them. Had it not been for the kindheartedness and persistence of one good man, the same thing would have happened in Butte that happened in Dillon.

Mr. Frost was concerned about the welfare of the dogs, and he knew that Brode needed help. The hoarder had little money, the bus was in poor shape, and there was obviously a serious sanitation problem. "You could smell the bus fifty feet away. It reeked of feces and urine. Even after the bus was towed away, the smell remained." What was most troubling to Mr. Frost was his premonition that Brode and the dogs would all die if he did not do something to help them. "Before moving to Butte, less than two years before I met Brode, I had lived in Florida and worked for many years in bail enforcement. That job required me to track criminals all over the United States and into Mexico and Canada. I frequently followed criminals who were using logging roads to sneak into Canada. Brode knew this would be the only way he could get into Canada on his way to Alaska. Winter was rapidly approaching, and I just knew that bus would break down on some isolated logging road and Brode and the dogs would freeze to death.

"Knowing that Butte would be the last chance for Brode and the dogs to survive, I called Butte Animal Services Department, talked to the woman in charge, and described the problem. Two animal-control officers came out, looked around, and left." Apparently, Butte Animal Services Department was going to ignore the problem as other communities had done and hope Brode would drive on. When Brode was still there the next day, Mr. Frost decided to call the police department as well as the animal services department "with the intention of getting help for Brode and the dogs." The phone call to the police department got action. Officers came out, saw the condition of the dogs, and arrested Brode on charges of animal cruelty. The police contacted Judge Steve Kambich, and he ordered animal services to seize the bus and trailer and had them hauled to the Chelsea Bailey Animal Shelter in Butte.

Apparently, the two animal-control officers were angry that Donald Frost alerted the police to this case of animal cruelty, which ultimately forced the animal services department to get involved. Perhaps they feared it would mean extra work for them. When they found out that Brode had given two puppies to Mr. Frost, the animal-control officers seized his two puppies from his truck. "Naturally, I tried to resist when they wanted to take my puppies. They were very sweet puppies, and my wife and I were quite attached to them. Those two men threatened to call the police over and implied that I might be arrested if I did not comply. Later I tried to find out what happened to my puppies, but the animal-services people would not tell me, and they discouraged me when I offered to volunteer at Camp Husky." A week after Brode had been arrested and Camp Husky was up and operating, one of the animal-control officers went to Mr. Frost's place of work to give him a bad time. "He chewed me out for opening a can of worms and giving the city a problem it was not prepared to deal with. He said I was the cause of this entire dog problem in Butte and that I made extra work for the animal-control officers." Because of the way the officers spoke to him, Donald Frost spent three years feeling guilty that he had alerted the police and very sad that he had lost his puppies. It was cruel, and possibly illegal, for the animal-control officers to take those puppies from Frost, and I can think of no reason for doing so other than to punish the man who had forced them to take action. Although the director of animal services must have had Frost's name, because Frost remembers talking with her, she never acknowledged the man who made the rescue possible in her many interviews with the press, nor did she give much credit to the volunteers who did all the work of running Camp Husky. As someone who volunteered for and donated to Camp Husky, I find it ironic that the well-paid animal-control officers would be so resentful of Mr. Frost when they personally had little extra work from the rescue, while the unpaid and tireless volunteers had nothing but appreciation for the unknown person who had made the rescue possible. The cruel treatment of Donald Frost foreshadowed a conflict that would continue between volunteers committed to saving the dogs and those who were far less committed or downright hostile to the dogs—specifically, the animal services department and our local animal shelter.

Throughout my research into Camp Husky, I often saw a stark contrast between the indifference of people in well-paid positions who were supposed to be helping animals and the strong commitment of unpaid volunteers. The passion and commitment to save the dogs set the volunteers apart from those in official, paid positions. Many officials did their jobs exceptionally well and were highly professional, but others did more harm than good. The cooperation of city officials was essential and necessary: We needed the police to arrest Brode; we needed the county attorney's office and a judge to get possession of the dogs so that we could spay and neuter and adopt them; we needed animal services to build a case against Brode and allow the volunteers to operate Camp Husky and do the work; we needed Butte-Silver Bow government to provide a temporary building to house the dogs. Later, a generous donor leased us a much better facility for virtually nothing. Ultimately, Camp Husky proved to be an excellent example of cooperation between local government and committed private citizens. The government provided the structure, legal sanctions, and a building to house the dogs; and the volunteers provided the passion, the commitment, and the hard work of caring for the dogs and raising money to cover expenses.

Donald Frost is truly the hero of Camp Husky. His compassion and persistence made the rescue possible, and this good man paid a heavy price. In my conversations with him, I came to appreciate what it must have been like believing that he was hated by the people of Butte because of what the animal-control officers told him. After volunteering at Camp Husky and interviewing many people who adopted these dogs, I was in a unique position to assure Mr. Frost that he was appreciated by the volunteers, who never knew his name, and I was able to tell him how much good he did for both the dogs and those who adopted them.

Sarah DeMoney Remembers the First Night of the Rescue

When Brode was arrested on the evening of October 5, the new director of the animal services department and the director of the Chelsea Bailey Animal Shelter were both out of town for the weekend. That proved to be fortunate for the welfare of the dogs, since it enabled volunteers to be involved from the very beginning. It was the volunteers who had the knowledge of dogs, the many skills required to run the rescue operation, and most importantly, the commitment to save the dogs. The rescue started with two local women who were called upon to help that first night, but they soon recruited a large group of volunteers from the community. Samantha Collier, a Michigan native and CEO of the Butte Family YMCA, received a phone call from Erin Wall, the director of the Chelsea Bailey Animal Shelter, asking her to drive to the shelter and assist with a dog-hoarding problem. Samantha, in turn, recruited Sarah DeMoney, a native of Washington State and the YMCA's director of development, to help as well. After learning of the plight of the dogs, both women got out of bed on a chilly Sunday night, dressed, and drove to the animal shelter, where a tow-truck driver had hauled the bus after police had arrested Brode. (Later, this man would adopt Buddy, one of the older dogs.) Samantha and Sarah were met by veterinarian Dr. Torre Lewis, who worked for a local clinic that was under contract with animal services and the animal shelter. The shelter director lived an hour away from Butte and did not bother driving in from her home in Dillon for the emergency, delegating the work to community volunteers instead.

Sarah tells in her own words how she and Samantha Collier worked to get the rescue underway that first night and how they recruited friends and family to help. "The phone rang; odd, as it was ten thirty, and I rarely got calls that late. It was Sam. I asked if everything was OK. Sam said that she had received a call from the director of Chelsea Bailey Animal Shelter, asking Sam to drive to the shelter and do what she could to help the two animal-control officers and Dr. Lewis, the veterinarian. Sam asked me to help but warned me that it would be hard physically and emotionally. She was unclear at that time as to the number of dogs involved. Without hesitation, I agreed to meet Sam at the animal shelter. I then called Janet Manchester, my good friend since our college days, to see if she would be available if we needed her help—she said yes. As it turned out, we didn't need Janet's help this night.

"Sam and I arrived at the shelter before the tow truck and about the same time as Dr. Lewis. Dr. Lewis told us that she had been to the Rocker truck stop earlier in the evening after Brode was arrested, and she explained to us what she had seen there and what she knew about the dog situation. It was well below freezing that night when the tow truck arrived. We could immediately smell the bus and trailer from twenty feet away. It was a wretched smell, almost a gagging smell. Then we heard the dogs barking, barking, and barking. The trailer appeared to be divided into twenty 'kennels,' each holding one or more dogs. The bus was overrun with dogs. As we surveyed the bus and the trailer, we began pondering how to get the dogs off and what to do with them once we got them off the bus and trailer. During this time, I began taking photos with the camera on my phone to document the state of the trailer and bus before we began any removal of dogs. It looked as though it would be easier to unload dogs from the trailer than the bus, and we saw that there were several litters of very young puppies in the trailer as well, and so, we decided to begin by taking puppies and their moms out of the trailer.

"Each of us took on a task. Sam was outside with the dogs, removing them from the trailer and then bringing them inside. Dr. Lewis was inside the shelter doing an initial exam on the dogs, and I was with her, recording her findings with each exam and putting temporary collars on the dogs with an identifying code. We named the dogs using their gender, numbers, and the alphabet. For example, Sam would bring us an adult female with four puppies—her identifier would be 'female #__.' The number would be the next in sequence from the dog previously tagged. The puppy's identifier would be gender, mother's number, and then an alphabet letter—that is, the fifth dog and her four puppies taken from the trailer would be identified as: female #5, male #5a, male #5b, female #5c, and female #5d. After each 'family' was examined, recorded, and tagged, they would be put into a kennel in the shelter with water and food." Sam believes that most of these puppies were between five and seven weeks of age, but we have no way of knowing for sure.

"The state the dogs were in was pitiful. They were completely afraid and timid, barking and growling. However, I was able to collar each dog, and Dr. Lewis was able to examine each one. We had a bowl of food and a bowl of water in the area where we were handling the dogs. As soon as they knew we were not going to harm them, they would calm down and allow us to handle them. None of these dogs snapped at us or were aggressive. Fearful, yes. Barking—oh yes, and loudly.

"The dogs were filthy. They had feces all over them and matted in their coats. They were covered with fleas. As they ate, they began having diarrhea, which did not surprise Dr. Lewis but upset all of us, knowing they probably hadn't eaten for days. Many had sores, mouth issues, missing teeth, and scars. They looked big because of their long, thick coats, but when we touched them they were skin and bones, disturbingly thin and malnourished. The puppies were pretty timid and scared—we guessed they had never been socialized with people. I think because we gave them food and water, the mothers knew we weren't going to harm their puppies, so we were able to handle the puppies without aggression from the mothers.

"I remember Sam bringing in a group of puppies with two adults—she said that they had been all together in one cage, and she couldn't tell which puppies belonged to which mother. As Dr. Lewis began the exam, she noticed that the adults were female and male. We guessed this was the father of the puppies. He was protective of the puppies, more so than the mother. But we were able to handle the puppies under his watchful eye. The interaction with the puppies and their father was amazing to witness. As we would pick up a puppy, he would wait and watch us until we put the puppy down. Then he would go to the puppy and check it out to make sure it was OK. He did this with each puppy. He then would nudge the puppies to the food and water. I called them my favorite puppy family. When they were put back in a kennel, the dad lay with the puppies and some of the puppies would climb on him to sleep. One puppy slept on his head.

"When the initial examinations and collaring were completed, and the dogs were calmed down, we put them in kennels, taking care to keep families together. At the end of this night, we had twenty-six total dogs removed from the trailer, tagged, and in a kennel in the shelter. About ten dogs were left in the trailer—all adults without puppies. After we took care of the last mother-puppy set on the trailer, we walked all around the bus trying to figure out how to take off the ninety-plus dogs crowded in there. We decided to wait until the next morning to tackle the bus because we were out of room at the shelter for any additional dogs, and we had no idea how we were going to get the bus open to remove one dog at a time. Phyllis Ruana, director of animal services, arrived as we were finishing our work.

"I got home about one thirty. I remember taking my clothes off in the laundry room as they were filthy and reeked. I threw them in the washer and in doing so, noticed tons of fleas all over my clothing. Guessing they were in my hair also, I immediately took a long hot shower. My nose and throat burned from the smell. I smelled the urine and feces and heard the barking all night, and when I closed my eyes, I saw the dogs…I tried to sleep, but it was difficult."

Samantha Collier Recalls That First Night of the Rescue

Samantha Collier had started working for the YMCA as a college student in Michigan and had been the organization's youngest CEO. Having successfully built up YMCAs in Ohio and Virginia, Sam was recruited by the Butte YMCA. Because Sam was an active community member and dog lover, the Butte shelter director naturally phoned Sam for help when the dog emergency arose at ten at night. Sam recalls the sequence of events that night: "Shelter director Erin Wall phoned me about ten. As I understood it, the police arrived in response to a phone call from a concerned citizen. Seeing the terrible condition of the dogs, the police officers took immediate action. The hoarder was arrested, and city judge Steve Kambich was called. Kambich, in turn, ordered the animal-control guys to seize the bus and arrange for it to be towed to the Chelsea Bailey Animal Shelter. A phone call was made to Director Erin Wall at her home in Dillon. Erin then called me and asked if I would go down and help out with whatever needed to be done. When I arrived, no one was sure how many dogs were involved, but they knew it was more than one hundred! As I recall, Sarah, veterinarian Torre Lewis, and I did all of the work that night. The two animal-control guys stood around outside but did not help me get the dogs off the bus and lead them into the building. The animal-control director did not arrive until we three had done all the work that we could that night," explained Sam.

"Sarah and I arrived before Gilboy's Towing pulled in with the bus and trailer. The smell from a distance of at least twenty feet made me sick to my stomach. It was about eleven by then, and the temperature had dropped to about ten degrees. We tried to look into the bus, but the windows were steamed up, making it impossible to see inside. In the trailer, Sarah and I found very young puppies with their moms and, in some cases, their dads. We three worked well as an efficient team. I took the puppies and parents out of the trailer enclosures and led the adults into the building while I carried the puppies. Sarah gave each dog a number and temporary collar, and Dr. Lewis gave each dog a quick checkup. All together we took twenty-six animals out of the trailer, gave them food and water, and then put them in a special isolation room for the night. We felt terribly sad leaving the other dogs on the bus, but we had no choice since there was no room for them at the shelter."

Monday Morning, October 6, 2008

Rising before the sun, Sarah developed a publicity campaign at her kitchen table while her husband and three teenage sons slept. Sarah had three goals as she drew up her campaign: one, to enlist volunteers from Butte and the surrounding communities to care for the 125 dogs and puppies; two, to persuade individuals and businesses to donate money, services, and essential supplies from kennels to warm blankets; and three, to interest people in providing permanent homes for the dogs and puppies. Sarah had never been involved in a major dog-rescue operation, but she had essential training and experience in communications, public relations, and community relations. With her campaign sketched out, Sarah phoned Samantha and Janet Manchester, and the three women agreed to meet at the Chelsea Bailey Animal Shelter to check on the dogs before putting Sarah's plan into action.

Cindy McIlveen Finds a Building for the Dogs

While Sarah, Janet, and Sam were planning the day's activities, another woman got involved, and she would end up being among the most important volunteers at Camp Husky. Cindy McIlveen, a geological engineer working for Butte-Silver Bow Planning Department, learned of the dogs' plight immediately upon arriving at work because her office was next door to the temporary headquarters of the director of animal services. Cindy, a bright, attractive, energetic woman from Tennessee with an engaging smile and a strong sense of civic responsibility and compassion for animals, took the initiative to obtain permission from the planning director to use the only building the city owned that was large enough to house the dogs: the old hoist house at the Anselmo Mine, located just a few blocks from Butte's uptown area. Cindy spent the morning arranging for the water and electricity to be turned on. Unfortunately, there was no heat for the building. Not only did Cindy's quick thinking and action secure the first home for the dogs, she would also recruit her personal friends, faculty and staff from the local college, volunteers from AmeriCorps, and folks from another nonprofit she had started. Several of the volunteers I interviewed for this book said it was Cindy who had motivated them to volunteer.

No one was more committed to helping the dogs than Cindy, and without her problem-solving skills, the rescue effort might not have succeeded. No one sacrificed more to help the dogs of Camp Husky than Cindy, and many of our adult dogs would not have found permanent homes if not for her willingness to foster them. Cindy would later adopt one of the most troubled dogs at Camp Husky, and she continued to help our dogs that needed new homes long after Camp Husky closed.

Morning of October 6: Sarah, Sam, and Janet Work Tirelessly Recruiting Volunteers and Soliciting Donations

Sarah describes how she, Janet, Samantha, and volunteers from the YMCA worked to organize the rescue: "I met up with Janet at the shelter by eight—I showed her the trailer and bus. It was even more shocking in daylight. The stench was still overwhelming, and the pitiful sound of the dogs was heartbreaking. Janet was very still and quiet, and tears were running down her face as she stared at the dogs looking out the window at her. Just then Samantha arrived with the good news that we had a building for the dogs. We felt energized and encouraged by news that we would be able to use the old Anselmo hoist house building to accommodate the dogs.

"We began making phone calls to the media to broadcast the need for blankets, bowls, leashes, collars, food, and cash. The YMCA leadership staff was called to help, and they had contacts to get fencing for kennels. We also began making calls to the thrift shops for donations of blankets and bowls. I began sending e-mails to friends to spread the word of what was happening and what we needed in the way of donations and volunteer help.

"Knowing we were going to need a lot of help to take the dogs off the bus, I went to Butte High School to get my son Brychan, since he has a natural ability to relate with animals, and I knew he would be good with these frightened dogs. I then texted my son Andrew, asking him to drive to the Anselmo and help us as soon as his classes ended for the day. We needed Andrew because he was very strong, and I knew he would be adept at figuring out how to set up and arrange kennels in the building for the most effective use of space. Later, Andrew and several other highly motivated volunteers—townspeople I did not know—worked energetically, setting up the kennels as quickly as possible so that they would be ready when the dogs came off the bus.

"Janet, Brychan, and I returned to the shelter, where I introduced them to the dogs we had taken off the night before. The dogs were settled but, of course, barked when we walked by them. The puppies were snuggled with their moms and dads. Most of the dogs were not too keen on being petted, but we talked to them and smiled a lot. Brychan took a couple of dogs outside for a walk."

Now that a time and place had been set for unloading the dogs from the bus, Sarah prepared radio announcements asking the public to volunteer or bring donations to the Anselmo. (We needed food, bowls, mops and buckets, blankets, and cash.) She also contacted the television station and the local newspapers, the *Montana Standard* and the *Butte Weekly*, so they would be on hand when the dogs were taken off the bus. In addition, Sarah and Janet phoned local businesses and asked for donations. Finally, they drove around town collecting the needed supplies from the thrift shops and businesses they had contacted.

Meanwhile, Samantha had returned to the YMCA and recruited members and staff to contact businesses and organizations to obtain kennels, as well as other essential supplies, and enlist volunteers to care for the 125 dogs. Soon Samantha and her staff of volunteers were answering phone calls from folks who had heard Sarah's radio announcement and wanted to volunteer or make donations.

Sarah Describes How Camp Husky Operated That First Day

At midday when the tow truck arrived at the Anselmo with the bus and trailer, Sarah, Samantha, Cindy, and Janet had assembled a large crew of volunteers, including Sarah's sons. Thanks to Cindy's efforts, the building's lights and water were now turned on. Fencing and kennels were on hand thanks to Samantha's crew from the YMCA and some local businesses, as well as the 4-H club. Thanks to Sarah and Janet, stacks of essential supplies were on hand, including dog food, blankets, bowls, buckets, and mops. In response to Sarah's radio announcements, people arrived that day with donations of money, dog food, and blankets, and many of these folks would commit to volunteering on a regular basis. The community would continue to supply volunteer labor, services, and donations for the next six months. It still amazes me to ponder how much this small group accomplished in a matter of hours.

Sarah remembers that first day: "About noon the bus and trailer were towed to the Anselmo. People had been working to set up kennels and put bowls with food and buckets with water in each kennel along with blankets to protect the dogs from the cold cement floors. Everyone gathered together before we began taking the dogs off so that we would all know what the routine was and who was responsible for what task. Everyone set to work without a complaint; it was true teamwork. Lots of communication was going on, so we all knew throughout the day what was what, who was where, what dogs could be put together, and so forth.

"We had a check-in station where the dogs were brought immediately from the bus. The routine was like this: one to three dogs would be taken off the bus by volunteers using leashes and taken to the check-in station. At the check-in station we would give them food and water. While they were eating, we would 'name' them—same as we did the night before—collar them, and conduct a quick exam noting their gender and any identifying marks, sores, missing teeth, limp, scars, and so on. Adrienne Herren, who had worked for the *Montana Standard*, volunteered as dog photographer that day, taking a picture of each dog with the number assigned to it. Then someone would be ready to walk each dog on a leash to a kennel. After one set of dogs was through the process and in its kennel, one to three more dogs would come off the bus and the routine continued with them.

"As the dogs were being taken to the kennels, my son Andrew and others were rearranging kennels depending on how the dogs were reacting to each other. Additional kennels were being brought into the building and assembled by still other volunteers. Blankets were being draped over the sides of the connecting kennels so the dogs couldn't see each other as a measure to calm them down.

"Meanwhile, a group of volunteers cleaned up diarrhea from the kennels while another group filled and rotated bowls of food and water from an old group of dogs to a new group of dogs, since we were short on bowls. We were also short on leashes, so they were moving all around the building depending on who needed one.

"At one point, a group of dogs—about five—escaped from the bus. They went under the bus, under the trailer, and hid down a slope near the building. Everyone stopped what they were doing, became quiet, and worked together to round up the dogs. It took about twenty or thirty minutes to capture all of the dogs.

"As we got down to the last pack of dogs, we discovered that some of the dogs were chained to the interior of the bus. My son Brychan went inside the bus with bolt cutters and cut the chains so the dogs could come out of the bus. He said it was disgusting inside the bus. The chains were rusted from urine and feces. They had to be cut as the clasps no longer would move from the rust. The last few dogs that had been chained so cruelly were pretty aggressive, baring teeth. Out of all the dogs, just a few were of this temperament. Photo #2 shows six of the dogs right after they came off the bus. You can see the chain that Brychan cut to free Snowball #61.

"This was a steady routine until evening—it was dark when the last dog came off. At the end of this day, we unloaded ninety-nine dogs for a total of one hundred twenty-five dogs. During the entire time we were unloading the bus and trailer, no one took a break. Amazingly, no one lost their temper. Everyone worked, and worked hard, to get the job done. Many committed to continue working into the evening and the following days. Everyone was exhausted."

Samantha and Sarah, who worked that entire day, describe how one young-adult dog was injured. "Volunteers had used leashes to take the dogs and older puppies off the bus. When most dogs were off the bus, one remaining young dog was scared and tried to hide. About this time, the animal-control officers arrived at the Anselmo. One of them decided to go after this dog with a snare pole rather than a leash, as the volunteers had done with the other dogs. Somehow that animal-control officer managed to terrorize the poor dog and inflict severe pain and injury, ripping open and damaging both sides of his mouth. Later, the veterinarian had to sedate the dog and put in many stitches. Whether the officer's cruel treatment of the young dog was intentional or the result of poor training, it explains why this dog we called Jack became so afraid of people. It would take many months and many hours of kind and patient treatment by dedicated volunteers to overcome the emotional damage that one animal-control officer had inflicted on Jack and to convince the dog that he could be safe around some humans.

How Camp Husky Got Its Name

There was confusion from the beginning as to what breed of dog was on the bus. Since the first dogs off that day were Siberian huskies or husky-shepherd mixes, volunteers and the media started referring to the rescue operation as Camp Husky. In reality, a more correct name would have been Camp German Shepherd, since the majority of Brode's dogs were long-haired white, yellow, or apricot German shepherds, and many others were shepherd-husky mixes, usually with more shepherd than husky. There were also three types of Belgian shepherd: Belgian Tervuren, Belgian Malinois, and Belgian sheepdog, an uncommon breed in the United States. Some folks unfamiliar with these breeds thought the long-haired white German shepherds and Belgian Tervuren were huskies, but a more serious problem was that some people thought the dogs were wolves or wolf hybrids, and that may be the reason the director of the Chelsea Bailey Animal Shelter was hostile toward the dogs and the rescue operation from the first day.

Janet Manchester Remembers the First Day

Janet Manchester, a human-resource director for a local engineering firm, teared up as I interviewed her about what she saw that first day as Camp Husky was set up and the dogs were taken from the bus. "Sarah had phoned me the night before to alert me about the crisis, asking me to help, and I was glad she did. We met early the next morning outside the animal shelter where the bus and trailer were parked. Looking through the windows of the bus was traumatic—all I could see was dirty matted ears poking up, but I could sense how terrified the dogs were. It was even worse to see the dogs caged on the trailer. As Sarah and I busied ourselves collecting necessary supplies that we would need for the dogs, I never had any doubts that we could save these dogs. I realized that it would be a long process, and I hoped that we would have many people willing to help. For me, there was no choice but to say yes to helping save those poor dogs. In his defense, I don't think Brode intended to mistreat the dogs. He just could not take care of them, and he likely suffered from mental illness."

After Janet, Sarah, Samantha, and the volunteers from the YMCA had everything prepared for the dogs at the Anselmo hoist house, including kennels, the three women joined many other volunteers in unloading the dogs from the bus and trailer. "I remember vividly how very thin, dirty, and terrified the dogs were as they came off the bus," said Janet. "Some of the adult dogs had been confined by heavy chains and ropes. When the last dog was off the bus we saw a horrible sight—bodies of puppies that did not survive the ordeal." For the first six weeks of the operation,

Janet, a Butte native, would go directly to the Anselmo every evening when she left work at 5:00 p.m., work at Camp Husky until 9:00 p.m., and then lock up the place. Janet's daughter, Jessi, a college student, joined her mother as a regular volunteer at the hoist house. After a little time off to take a trip, Janet returned to regular volunteering, putting in many hours of labor before Camp Husky closed. Volunteering to help the less fortunate is an important part of Janet's life. In 2008, she used her vacation time to work with Habitat for Humanity building houses for the poor in Madagascar, and in 2014, she did the same hard labor in a snake-infested Sri Lankan jungle.

Sam Is Inspired by the Energy and Dedication of the Community Volunteers

Samantha Collier and others were impressed by the positive energy of those who volunteered at Camp Husky that first day and for the next six months. Samantha said, "From that first day, wonderful people stepped up and took ownership of the problem, and because of their enthusiasm, I never felt hopeless or even overwhelmed by this challenge facing the community." Samantha used her vacation time to work full time at the camp during the first two weeks, helping in the effort to get the rescue operation up and running. One of the important jobs Sam took on was training crew leaders for the daily shifts. After helping to organize Camp Husky operations, Samantha returned to her job at the YMCA, but she continued volunteering in her free time along with many other individuals from the community. Sam also fostered a number of adult dogs and puppies at her rural residence and provided a loving home for Gigi, one of our oldest Camp Husky dogs, who passed away in 2015 at an estimated age of fifteen.

The task of caring for 125 large dogs and puppies of all ages, as well as the many new litters that arrived starting the first week, was enormous and overwhelming. Many of us volunteers might have lost heart and given up had it not been for volunteer leaders like Sam and several others, who inspired us to keep working and believing that we could succeed. When asked if she ever had doubts about our ultimate success, Sam responded with a firm no: "I never doubted for a moment that we would be able to save the dogs and find homes for them."

Her volunteer work at Camp Husky led Samantha to a radically different career path: she started a doggie day-care service called All about the Dawg, offering day-care service, boarding, and obedience classes. At six in the morning, Sam can be seen driving her large van through Butte, picking up dogs of all shapes and sizes that will spend the day playing at her large facility (once an elementary school) in Walkerville, in the north part of the city. On the day I visited All About The Dawg to interview Samantha, I saw about thirty dogs, including black-and-white Labs, golden retrievers, poodles, bulldogs, German shepherds, a Great Dane, and mixed breeds of all sizes, as well as three of our Camp Husky dogs, all playing together under Sam's watchful eye.

Inspired by her work at Camp Husky, Sam continues to help dogs and kids. She has rescued two pit bulls—because they were too gentle to fight, they were going to be used as bait dogs. She has trained the male pit bull to assist children at the public library in a program called Reading with Paws, and she uses the female as a therapy dog.

In addition to rescuing pit bulls and turning them into therapy dogs, Sam responded to the challenges of the recession by starting a food bank for dogs and cats called Kibble Connection, which supplied over one hundred folks in Butte with free food for their pets in the first three months. Camp Husky's ripples were truly wide.

Volunteers Step Up to the Challenge

Donald Frost, Samantha Collier, Sarah DeMoney, Janet Manchester, and Cindy McIlveen got the rescue started, but from that first day they were joined by many other people who worked very hard to make Camp Husky a success. From the first day of the rescue, people from all walks of life arrived at the Anselmo to volunteer or make donations of food, blankets, or cash in response to Sarah's radio announcements, or e-mails and phone calls from YMCA volunteers. Later that week, Sarah would use the Internet to spread word of the rescue well beyond Montana, bringing in donations from as far away as Colorado, Chicago, and New Jersey.

Sarah had made certain that newspaper reporters and radio and television news crews were on hand when the dogs were unloaded from the bus. That night, people from all over western Montana would learn about the

Camp Husky rescue from their local television nightly news programs or from listening to the radio. The next morning, people from all over the state would read about the rescue in their morning newspapers. Many individuals made a decision to adopt when they saw the first television newscasts or read about the rescue. Still others made the decision after hearing a radio broadcast. Many of the younger people who adopted, including one child, told me that they learned about the rescue from the Internet. Starting two months later, folks would come from all over Montana and as far away as Seattle to adopt one of our Camp Husky dogs, but that was a long way off when Cindy, Janet, Sarah, Samantha, and many other volunteers went home that first night thoroughly exhausted. Their work had just begun. For the next six months, volunteers would do all the hard work of caring for the dogs, raising money to cover expenses, and promoting adoptions.

CHAPTER 3
Volunteering at Camp Husky

As I write nearly seven years later, I can still recall my first day of volunteering at Camp Husky. It was Saturday morning, October 11, less than a week after the rescue had begun. I was bundled up in a heavy winter jacket, hat, and gloves as I walked about a mile from my house to what was once the Anselmo Mine. The air was cold (about 38 degrees), not unusual for the second week of October. Montana is one of six states with the coldest winter temperatures, and Butte is the coldest city in Montana—one of the ten coldest cities in the United States because of our mile-high altitude. In fact, Butte has the distinction of being one of the few places in the United States where temperatures have gone as low as –50 degrees Fahrenheit. I have personally experienced –40, and it was most unpleasant.

As I approached the Anselmo Mine yard, I saw the school bus and trailer parked near the mine shaft building. I walked up wooden stairs to the second floor, where more than one hundred adult dogs and older puppies were housed, along with some moms with their newborn pups and many pregnant dogs close to their delivery dates. Later, the puppies and parents removed from the trailer on the first night of the rescue would be housed on the first floor. Over the next two months, so many females would give birth that the number of dogs would soon reach two hundred.

The structure that housed the dogs was about one hundred years old and designated as a historic building. There was no source of heat for the building, and volunteers were not allowed to use electric heaters because the Butte Historical Society was understandably concerned about fire danger in the old wooden structure. I noticed that the roof was full of holes, which allowed frigid air to flow down into the building. Soon snow would be coming down through those holes as well.

My first sensation that day was how cold I felt inside the building. Frigid weather would be a challenge for the volunteers throughout the six months that Camp Husky operated. The winter of 2008–2009 was not one of our coldest winters, but the temperature was below freezing nearly every night from when the bus first arrived in Butte until Camp Husky closed in April 2009, and we had several days with brutally cold temperatures as low as –34 degrees Fahrenheit in the daytime and worse at night. Many of us who volunteered have memories of watching the water freeze as we mopped the concrete floor in the dog kennels at the Anselmo hoist house, and I recall one Sunday walking dogs in –10 temps after we moved to our second location. The dogs had to go outside to relieve themselves and get exercise daily, but I worried about their feet. Some seemed to be able to handle that degree of cold and worse, but others would lift their paws, and you knew the cold was burning them.

After the cold, the next things I noticed that first day were the sound and the smell. The noise of one-hundred-plus dogs barking and howling in an enclosed space was excessive. Odor was also a challenge, especially for the first couple of months when most of the dogs suffered from diarrhea. The noise and stench assaulted your senses when you first stepped into the building, but after working an hour or two, you no longer noticed. Those were the challenges, but what most impressed me and others I interviewed was the large size and unique beauty of the dogs.

Although they were skinny and malnourished, most had very large bone structures. When I later interviewed one hundred owners, I asked them the size and weight of their dogs. Some were normal size and weight for German shepherds and huskies; these were our smaller adult dogs at Camp Husky. However, we had many giant-sized adults at Camp Husky, and most of the puppies have, according to their owners, grown into very large dogs. The average female weighs about 80 to 90 pounds and the average male is 90 to 100, with many of the males weighing 120 or more. The largest dog is 130 pounds! These dogs are not overweight but simply very tall, long, and large boned. I have one of those females, and her healthy weight varies between 86 and 90 pounds. She looks heavy because of her long, thick coat, but when you touch her, you can feel that there is no fat on her. The few "small" dogs range in size from 40 to 60 pounds. When one considers the challenge of caring for two hundred dogs, one must also take into consideration the size of the dogs.

Although most of them were filthy when they came off the bus, and it would take several baths to get the stink out of them, they were the most beautiful and unique-looking dogs I have ever seen. All had the erect ears of German shepherds and huskies. While the majority of dogs were long-haired white, apricot, or yellow German shepherds, many others had husky markings. Approximately a third of the dogs were dark brown, black, or tricolored. Among these were what appeared to be purebred black-and-tan German shepherds, Belgian Tervuren, Belgian Malinois, and one Belgian sheepdog.

Most of them seemed to welcome human attention, while some obviously feared people. I remember some white females who had scars on their faces. Had they been bitten while protecting their babies in crowded conditions where all the dogs were on the verge of starvation? Many of the dogs had a sadness in their eyes that haunts me to this day. Many were severely underweight, malnourished, and sick with *Campylobacter* and other bacterial infections. None of the dogs had been spayed or neutered, so one can easily imagine the fights that must have broken out over females in heat.

Looking at the dogs that first day was a painful reminder of how cruel humans can be toward animals. No sane or compassionate person would have allowed dogs to live in such horrible conditions as existed on the bus. The more time I spent with those dogs, the more I would become in awe of them. Whenever I looked into their eyes, I felt something very special that is difficult to put into words. I saw intelligence and sweetness in all of them, but many also displayed high levels of anxiety and fear—not surprising, considering what they had experienced at the hands of a disturbed man. Looking into their eyes reminded me of an experience I'd had twenty years before and could never forget. I had been in San Francisco attending a conference, and as I walked near my hotel, I saw a young, emaciated woman sitting on the cold concrete. As I reached down to give her some money, we made eye contact. Perhaps she was a drug addict or mentally ill or both, I don't know—but when I looked into her eyes, I felt as though

I had encountered an angel disguised as a homeless person. There was gentleness and goodness in those eyes but also pain. I have never forgotten that encounter or her beautiful and sad eyes—it was the very same expression I saw in the eyes of the Camp Husky dogs that first day. As I interviewed people for this book, I discovered that I was not the only volunteer to have this reaction to the dogs.

The next thing that impressed me that first day was the enormous effort involved with running Camp Husky on a daily basis, and I wasn't even thinking about fundraising and all the other behind-the-scenes tasks that some of the volunteers were already undertaking. In addition to feeding the dogs every morning and caring for the pregnant mothers and newborn puppies arriving every few days, three huge jobs were ongoing from morning until closing time. Volunteer Supervisor Katie Donovan described the jobs: "We would organize people into teams of four volunteers. The teams would tackle one kennel at a time. Two people would get the dogs out to the fenced-in yard. This was often very difficult because the dogs were so traumatized, especially in the beginning. They might freeze up or dash any which way. Two to four dogs were in each kennel, so volunteers might be walking two giant-sized dogs at one time! Those who volunteered in the first week of the rescue discovered that many of the dogs had never been on a leash or taken for a walk. The other two team members would scoop poop and then remove the food, water dishes, and plastic pallets that we used to keep the dogs off the cold cement floor. Next, they filled heavy metal buckets with water and bleach and mopped the kennel floor. Finally, they put clean pallets and a bucket of fresh water in the kennel. Because of the problem of diarrhea, cleaning the kennels was challenging to say the least and a never-ending task. After a while, the walkers had a sense of when the kennel would be ready for the dogs to return. Then the process started with another kennel and group of dogs. There wasn't any time at first to clean the filthy dogs or to socialize them. This frustrated a lot of the volunteers."

The third team did the washing in a sink outside with only cold running water. This was the job to which I was assigned that first day. When we had a stack of clean bowls or pallets, we carried them up the stairs and collected more dirty ones. I worked with a young man and woman that first day, but I never learned their names. My hands were soon red, sore,

29

and so very cold. The next day I arrived with rubber gloves, but they didn't protect against the cold. Every time I walked up the wooden exposed stairs with my arms full of dishes or pallets, I wondered how we would manage when snow started falling and the stairs were covered with ice.

Although I worked as both a waitress and a maid when I was young, I have no memories of ever doing harder physical labor or working under more difficult conditions than I did that weekend. All the volunteers appeared to be suffering from the cold that day, and it was only early October. A few hours after starting my shift, as I was carrying a load of clean pallets upstairs, I struck up a conversation with a woman making coffee for the volunteers. She had also brought homemade cookies. I can still remember how wonderful those cookies and hot coffee tasted. At the end of the day, when it was time to close up Camp Husky for the night, the cookie lady was still there, finishing up the task of folding and stacking clean blankets that had arrived from the laundry. She gave me a ride home, and I learned that she was over eighty years old. Seniors like the cookie lady would play an important role at Camp Husky, and they were among those who logged the most hours, often performing some of the most difficult tasks. Even people with bad knees, back injuries, and shoulder problems volunteered regularly.

Katie Donovan also recalls the first weeks of Camp Husky, when "the work was so very hard and that October was cold. Washing had to be done outside in the bitter cold with snow and freezing conditions, but the volunteers were incredible. We had many people who signed up for regular shifts. For example, Jennifer Sehulster was there every Monday, Wednesday, and Friday, while Sue Madison was there every weekday for the eleven-to-two shifts. Many folks with eight-to-five jobs showed up in the evenings to walk dogs. Fireman Malcom Gustafson was there regularly and very helpful. There were so many volunteers that I can't remember them all. A whole different set of people volunteered on weekends. Cindy McIlveen and folks from the Northern Rockies Outdoor Center and the YMCA would act as volunteer coordinators for the weekends."

The 120-plus volunteers at Camp Husky ranged in age from teens to octogenarians. Most volunteers came alone, but many came with friends, neighbors, spouses, or other family members. Those under eighteen had to volunteer with a parent, and in at least one case we had a married couple and their daughters all working together. We had high-school and college students, as well as many teachers and professors. Many of the students were recruited by their teachers. Among those who volunteered were accountants, an attorney, a bartender, a caterer, engineers, a fireman, a forester, a reporter, government employees, a hairdresser, high-school and college coaches, office workers and managers, a medical doctor, a nurse, small-business owners, scientists, a waitress, and many retired people. Later, men and women from the Butte Pre-Release Center would join our ranks. In other words, the volunteers were a real cross section of the community—good-hearted people who gave their time, and often money, to help their community and the unfortunate dogs.

In addition to stacks of donated food, dishes, buckets, mops, leashes, and other supplies, there were stacks of donated quilts and blankets on the second floor. The blankets were essential for "the maternity ward," a section on the second floor reserved for expectant mothers and mothers with puppies born after the rescue started. Since most of the adult females were pregnant when the rescue began, puppies started arriving the first week and continued through December. In addition to the other jobs volunteers completed daily, one group of people worked in the maternity ward. Over the next six weeks at Camp Husky, one of the biggest challenges would be keeping the mothers and newborns warm. Not only were blankets placed on the floor for warmth, they were used to provide privacy for each mom and her pups since the enclosures were so close together. The volunteers thought the mothers would be more comfortable if they could not see the families in the adjoining pens. The blankets had to be changed daily, and I learned that East Ridge Laundry made an enormous contribution by laundering those blankets and quilts for us. (This was just one of several businesses that would donate their services to help the dogs.) A few of the oldest volunteers who were not strong enough for the other jobs helped out by folding those blankets.

I regret that I could not interview everyone involved, but I did interview about thirty-five men and women who volunteered regularly at Camp Husky and were representative of the volunteers as a whole. I appreciate that these individuals were all willing to take the time to tell me of their experiences, and what impressed me most was that they all said they would do it again. No one regretted all the hours of hard work they donated.

There was something special about these volunteers, who worked week after week in spite of the difficult conditions and the emotional pain they experienced seeing the wretched state of the dogs. One might think that the constant barking, stench of urine and diarrhea, and freezing cold would make people cross, but I never heard one volunteer complain in all those months that the camp operated. The volunteers were compassionate toward the dogs, even the very few aggressive ones, and they were kind to each other. I have worked at many different jobs and been involved in many volunteer activities through the years, but I had never before experienced the sense of camaraderie and shared purpose that existed among Camp Husky volunteers. We shared the common goal of saving the dogs—that goal united us and made our individual differences unimportant.

Dr. Lewis was our official veterinarian since the large practice she worked for had a contract to provide services for the animal shelter. Dr. Lewis left Butte around the time Camp Husky closed, and although Sarah DeMoney tried to contact her, we could not reach her for an interview. I remember seeing her at Camp Husky, and I have been told that she wanted to volunteer extra hours on her days off, but she could not do so because of her employment contract. The fact that most all of our sick dogs got well is a testament to the medical skill of Dr. Lewis and the devoted care of the volunteers. I sometimes observed Dr. Lewis accompanied by a woman named Tara, who volunteered at Camp Husky and served as a kind of nurse. Cindy McIlveen said of Tara, "I think she was the most important person by far keeping everything together at the Anselmo in the early days." I was unable to locate Tara when I started this book project, but I observed how she helped many sick dogs.

Conflict between Volunteers and Animal Services

While volunteers battled to save those magnificent dogs, often our worst enemy was not the bitter cold or disease but an indifferent animal-services director and a hostile Butte shelter director.

In other animal rescues I have read about, local shelters often played a crucial role in helping the dogs or cats. Unfortunately, that was not the case with the Camp Husky rescue. The Butte shelter was more of a hindrance than a help. One of the key volunteers went so far as to tell me that "the director of Chelsea Bailey Shelter [Erin Wall] wanted Camp Husky shut down and would have had all the dogs put down if she had her way." I am inclined to believe that this might be true because in the fall of 2011, when a story appeared in our local newspaper about Camp Husky and some of the very successful adoptions, this same shelter director phoned me, expressing great hostility toward the dogs. Specifically, she told me they were all "bad dogs."

The animal services was the city/county entity most involved with Camp Husky. Its director, Phyllis Ruana, was new on the job when the rescue started. As director, she had the authority and power to make decisions, but the volunteers had the commitment to save the dogs. As a manager, Ruana rarely consulted with the volunteers who were doing the difficult work, and her management style in regard to Camp Husky could be described as arbitrary and secretive. As strange as it may seem, the impression I formed during my communication with her was that she had little appreciation for the tremendous sacrifices volunteers made to save the dogs and no interest in what they knew about dogs in general or about these particular dogs, which they walked and socialized on a regular basis.

The best example of her indifference to the welfare of the dogs, the secretive nature of her management style, and her poor communication with the volunteers can be seen in how she caused the death of thirteen of our best dogs. Phyllis Ruana decided to take fourteen of our most social-ized and adoptable dogs to a shelter in Dillon before the city had legal possession of them. She claims that Susie Brown, director and manager of the Humane Society of Beaverhead County in Dillon, requested the dogs. Apparently, this shelter was not equipped to properly care for the dogs, and they were not walked or socialized the way they had been at Camp Husky. The shelter director in Dillon decided to kill the dogs rather than find homes for them. In a telephone interview, the Dillon shelter director told me she'd had the dogs killed at the advice of her veterinarian because she and the veterinarian believed the dogs were part wolf. Her assistant told me essentially the same thing, only she stated that it was because "they were part coyote." Several of our dogs were genetically tested by their owners, and they proved to be either purebred German shepherds or husky-shepherd mixes. However, all German shepherds and huskies resemble wolves, especially long-haired white German shepherds.

In fairness to them, the folks at the Dillon shelter told Phyllis Ruana that they were going to kill the dogs, giving her a chance to return the dogs to Butte. Phyllis did, in fact, drive to Dillon with an assistant and returned with one of the Camp Husky dogs, named Phyllis, leaving all the other dogs to be killed. She could have brought those dogs back to Butte, but she chose to let them be killed. I cannot imagine a worse betrayal of the volunteers. She made an arbitrary decision without consulting with the volunteers who knew those dogs better than anyone else. She kept what she had done secret from the volunteers. That was her management style.

It was not until weeks after the dogs were killed in Dillon that Cindy McIlveen learned what had happened to them. Right after Cindy learned the truth, she encountered Sarah DeMoney at Camp Husky and told her the terrible news. "Cindy was in a state of disbelief and anger as she told me what Phyllis had done," Sarah recalled. These two women decided not to share this information with the other volunteers. For this reason, I, the author, did not discover what had happened to those dogs until I researched this book.

When Phyllis Ruana saw what I had written about her actions in this book, she placed the blame for the killing of those good dogs on nearly everyone but herself. She blamed Susie Brown for requesting the dogs when she could not properly care for them, and she blamed Erin Wall for encouraging her to take the dogs to Dillon in the first place. She even blamed Butte-Silver Bow Chief Executive Paul Babb and the Camp Husky volunteers. In one e-mail she blamed me and other volunteers for not driving to Dillon to walk and care for the dogs she took there! Of course, she never told anyone that the dogs were not well cared for and in danger at that shelter. No one who was aware of how hard the volunteers were working and the hours they were putting in at Camp Husky would dream of suggesting that these individuals drive an hour to Dillon and care for the dogs that should have been returned to Butte. Only someone who had little knowledge of and appreciation for the work the volunteers were doing would dare to make such a statement.

Samantha thought the animal-services director had "a good management style in that she set up team leaders and let them do their own thing." However, Samantha observed that Phyllis Ruana was "not good with dogs; she was afraid of them." According to Samantha, "volunteer team leaders and those under them did all the actual hands-on work of caring for the dogs."

As a city employee at the time, and someone who befriended and helped the new animal-services director, Cindy's perspective is important in telling the story of Camp Husky. In an interview and e-mails, Cindy stated that "the volunteers of Camp Husky were successful despite the establishment. We worked with what we had." Regarding volunteers, Cindy said, "Camp Husky needed every volunteer we had. We all contributed, and we all screwed up at times. Management kept a distance and was not connected with the day-to-day operations of Camp Husky. Management both removed itself from the workers and volunteers at Camp Husky and did not understand the dogs. There was not a commitment by those in management positions to save the dogs. Also, some of the veterinary establishments that were making money off the rescue operation were the least supportive. It must be noted, however, that there were some supportive veterinarians in town, such as Dr. [Robert] Cornelius."

One volunteer who worked five days a week from the second week to the very end of Camp Husky described the relationship between the volunteer workers and animal services. What she had to say was repeated by more than a dozen key volunteers whom I interviewed: "We were a tight group of volunteers, working for the welfare of the dogs. Often, we felt that animal services and the animal shelter actually worked against us in our efforts to save the dogs. In spite of hostility from the animal shelter and a lack of support from animal services, we volunteers worked together and ultimately succeeded against incredible odds to save most of the dogs." This book is not about animal services, but about the volunteers who actually saved the dogs.

The Camp Husky Volunteers

Camp Husky was a wonderful community effort, and it succeeded in spite of animal services, because of the individuals who came forward to volunteer and the many businesses that contributed supplies and services. Out of about 120 volunteers, 6 were later hired by Butte Animal Services. I can attest that these individuals, who all started as volunteers, worked because of their dedication to the dogs rather than because of the modest stipend they received. Not even a high salary would have compensated for the difficult working conditions unless you loved dogs. In fact, when animal services cut pay to ten hours a week, these individuals continued to work forty to fifty hours. The volunteers and supervisors were the people who truly cared about the dogs. I can best convey what went on at Camp Husky by introducing twenty-two of our regular volunteers and offering some of their recollections about Camp Husky.

Cindy McIlveen

If I had to name one single person who was the heart of Camp Husky, it would be volunteer extraordinaire Cindy McIlveen, a native of Tennessee. Cindy was essential to the rescue operation from the first day to the last and continued to help Camp Husky dogs that needed new owners for five years after the camp closed, until she left Montana and moved to Houston, Texas, in 2014. Cindy personally fostered several dogs and adopted Jack, one of our most troubled dogs, the one injured by the animal-control officer. I witnessed the transformation in Jack made possible by Cindy's care. In the chapters about individual dogs, you will read about six dogs that survived and moved into good homes because Cindy fostered them and found people willing to adopt them. If someone heard of a dog in trouble after Camp Husky closed, they contacted Cindy. She gave generously of her time, energy, and money to the Camp Husky dogs. She acted quickly and got us permission to use the county-owned Anselmo hoist house, and she personally recruited many volunteers.

Cindy's competence and take-charge attitude were best described in Katie Donovan's memories of her first weeks as volunteer coordinator at Camp Husky: "One day I found myself alone after the eight-to-eleven shift ended. No volunteers were showing up. How would we clean all the kennels before dark? I made some calls, but everyone was busy. I managed to work myself into a bit of frenzy while I contemplated the mess we would face the next day. Then I called Cindy. She said, 'Don't worry, Katie. I am on it.' Within the hour, I had an army of volunteers. Cindy had called the Montana Conservation Corps, volunteers from the Northern Rockies Outdoor Center, and the Butte Pre-Release Center. People kept showing up—everything got done. This was such a team effort."

Sarah DeMoney

In addition to volunteering regularly herself, Sarah played a key role in getting Camp Husky up and running. During the first weeks of the rescue, she did the public-relations work for Camp Husky, recruiting many volunteers and donors as well as folks around the state and out of state who would later adopt. I was one of those recruited to volunteer through Sarah's radio spots. In addition, she organized volunteers, set up an Excel system with their contact information, and created daily and weekly schedules with names of those committed to working each shift. Those of us who volunteered were asked to commit to a regular schedule, whether it was a three-hour shift Tuesday and Thursday mornings or an eight-hour shift every Saturday. Sarah was trying to ensure that there were always people available to do all the required tasks on every shift. With a husband, three teenage boys, and a full-time job at the YMCA, Sarah was already highly committed before the rescue began, and yet she found the time to do essential work for Camp Husky. She did the initial public-relations work and organization of volunteers while suffering from a serious back injury that often caused her severe pain, and she is the perfect example of someone willing to go above and beyond to help those in need—a quality common among the volunteers. Sarah is currently the director of Early Head Start in Butte, and she volunteers her time to teach water-aerobics classes two nights a week at the YMCA, something she has done for twenty-six years.

Samantha Collier

As CEO of the YMCA, Samantha was able to inspire many members and employees to volunteer, and she had vital connections to other organizations and businesses that contributed to the rescue effort. For example, the local 4-H club loaned kennels, and Continental Fencing and Quality Supply either donated kennels or gave us a big discount on them. Thanks to Samantha and the good folks associated with the YMCA, kennels were delivered to the Anselmo and set up before the dogs were moved off the bus. According to Samantha, animal-services employees did not help with setting up kennels or organizing Camp Husky that first day. It was volunteers from the YMCA, people recruited by Cindy and Sarah, as well as some Butte-Silver Bow city and county employees who "pulled

Camp Husky together that first day. Luckily, city officials allowed us to run with it."

Samantha used her vacation time to work at Camp Husky during the first two critical weeks. In addition to cleaning and dog walking, Samantha drew on her many years of work with the YMCA to train volunteer supervisors, or "team leaders," as she calls them.

As a longtime employee of the YMCA, Sam knew a lot more about working with children than dogs. However, Samantha liked them and was very comfortable working with large dogs because her parents raised Doberman pinschers, often having ten or more around the acreage of her childhood home in Interlochen, Michigan. Sam started volunteering at Camp Husky with a love of dogs but had no special training. Her learning took place as she worked with the dogs and tried to study their behavior.

Sam fostered some of the dogs at her home, including one mother dog and her pups. Sam believes that "all dogs have four psychological needs that are just as essential as good food, water, and shelter. These needs are exercise, mental stimulation, discipline, and love." One of Sam's regrets about Camp Husky is that "in hindsight we should have allowed small packs of dogs to run free and play together" in the enclosed yard for more play, better exercise, and mental stimulation. Animal services insisted these dogs always be walked on leashes.

Sam keeps the spirit of Camp Husky alive through All about the Dawg, a dog-focused business she never would have imagined she'd launch.

Katie Donovan

A kind and compassionate woman named Katie Donovan would also play an essential role at Camp Husky. Three days after the rescue started, Katie returned home to Butte from a trip and was immediately recruited to volunteer by her good friend Cindy McIlveen. Cindy realized early on that there was a need for someone to coordinate and train the many people who came forward to volunteer. Someone needed to make sure there were enough people to work every shift, and Cindy thought Katie would be the ideal person to take on this challenging task.

Katie, who now lives in Huntington Beach, California, with her husband, engineer Rick Donovan, recalled her work at Camp Husky in an interview: "I was out of town when the bus broke down in Butte in early October 2008. I arrived two days later and learned that Cindy was already very involved in the rescue effort, and she got me involved. Not long after I started volunteering, I was hired, along with Kacie Raybould, to organize and supervise volunteers. Sarah had done the early work of organizing the day-to-day operations at Camp Husky and had the list of volunteers and work schedules on Excel when Kacie Raybould and I started working."

It was thanks to Katie and Sarah that I had both volunteer and adoption records to use in researching this book. Building on Sarah's work, Katie and Kacie put a system into place: "We organized teams of people to work in three-hour shifts, although many people chose to work two or even three shifts in a row. The shifts were eight to eleven, eleven to two, two to five, and five to eight. We needed a minimum of six people for every shift to get the work done. We would assign volunteers to teams of four people. Optimally, we would have two teams of four people as well as two people outside cleaning pallets, dishes, and water buckets. We tried to walk all the dogs and clean out all the kennels before dark.

"Imagine dawn is breaking. It is so cold I can see my breath. As I drive up the hill toward the Anselmo, I see a dark hulk on the landscape. It is so very quiet as I drive up, but when I step out of the car, the dogs hear me and suddenly there are a hundred dogs barking in the cavernous expanse of the hoist house. *It's loud!* I grab a Y-pole and carefully patrol the kennel to see which dogs escaped from their kennels in the night. I am very wary, since I don't know the dogs yet, and some are *big*. I am alone with a hundred adult dogs. Unbelievable! Once, I found Snowflake, a beautiful little white puppy, madly trying to hide from me in a pile of clean blankets. Just her little tail was visible as she tried to burrow into the pile. One afternoon, we lost one of our oldest dogs, a female named Gigi—she somehow escaped the yard. Despite all our searching, we couldn't find her. When I drove up to the Anselmo the next morning, there she was at the door—she wanted to return to her pack.

"Working with the dogs was very emotional. Everyone tried the best they could to make things right. After hours of handling very dirty dogs, scooping poop, mopping nasty floors, you—and your clothes—were filthy. I would come home cold and exhausted, take off my filthy boots and outer clothes on the back porch, and head directly to the hot shower. Once, my husband, Rick, brought me a cold beer to drink in the shower. I think he thought that I wasn't coming out.

"We were a tight group of volunteers working for the welfare of the dogs. We often felt that animal services was working against us rather than supporting our effort to save the dogs. Cindy smoothed things over when the director upset people. We were darn lucky that we had Cindy and that she was so committed to saving the dogs. Cindy's assertiveness, diplomacy, and complete commitment to saving our dogs made all the difference. Without Cindy, we probably would not have been able to get permission from city officials to use the old Anselmo hoist house and to have the cold water turned on."

Katie and the other supervisors told me that the animal-services director created a lot of bad feelings. She recalls that the director "wasn't good with people or dogs. She did a poor job of managing volunteers. When the director's arbitrary decisions left us so frustrated we wanted to break down and cry, Dave Jordan would deliver a wonderful pep talk. Cindy was a problem solver. If we wanted something done, we talked to Cindy."

Before Camp Husky, Katie and Cindy had started a nonprofit outdoor-training school with climbing walls. That project gave them access to many people who ended up volunteering for the dogs. In writing this book I have often asked myself if Camp Husky could have succeeded without the contributions of Katie, Cindy, and all the people they recruited. I believe the answer is no; they were essential to the success of the operation and the survival of the dogs.

In December—a time when more than thirty volunteers were showing up regularly every week and working as hard as possible trying to get the work done, and Katie and Cindy were busy trying to recruit more volunteers—the animal-services director decided she did not want volunteers, and she removed Katie as volunteer coordinator. This was another example of the woman's arbitrary decision-making based on no understanding of the day-to-day operation of Camp Husky and the essential need for volunteers. It is also possible that she was intimidated by the large group of volunteers who as a whole were better educated about dogs and far more committed to their welfare than she was. "It was sad," said Katie. "However, we volunteers were needed, and thus we kept showing up to work and were involved with the dogs long after Phyllis had resigned from her job and left town [in summer

2009].″ Katie continued volunteering, and most of the others did as well, including this author. There was always plenty of work to do, and Phyllis was not there to see either the work that needed to be done or who was doing it.

Working at Camp Husky was like no experience Katie had ever had. It changed her as it changed all of us. One of the last gatherings of volunteers took place at Katie's home, when she and Rick were preparing to move to Houghton, Michigan. She held a seminar on dog training, and about a dozen of us volunteers gathered to gain ideas on how we could rehabilitate some of our most frightened and timid dogs, which were being either fostered or adopted by volunteers. During a break from the seminar, Katie served dessert and played the piano for us, accompanied by one of her beautiful husky dogs, which sang. I was so impressed that Katie, in the midst of preparing for a major move, took time to host this event. She continued to send e-mails to volunteers to keep them informed about the various dogs after Camp Husky closed and she had moved to Michigan. Without the careful records Katie kept, I would not have been able to write this book.

Barbara LeProwse

Barb was working full time for Bresnan cable television when she read about the need for volunteers in the newspaper. Although Barb and her husband had two older chocolate Labs with failing health to care for, Barb made time in her busy schedule to volunteer every weekend at Camp Husky. She started out working and supervising two shifts from eight to two on Saturdays and Sundays. Later, she had to cut back to Saturdays only. She did whatever work was needed: walking dogs, cleaning cages, washing dishes, and so forth. Barb usually felt that the task the volunteers faced in caring for the dogs was "overwhelming. What kept me going back were both the other volunteers and the dogs. I made a lot of friends at Camp Husky. If it wasn't for the volunteers, who knows what would have happened to the dogs." Barb summed up the truth about Camp Husky in one sentence: "It was definitely the volunteers who saved the dogs."

She recalls that a couple of the dogs, Jack and Glacier, ran off, and she was among those who spent "countless days searching for them." Luckily, both Glacier and Jack were found and ended up being adopted into great homes. Barb had a special way with dogs. Gypsy was one of our very timid young mother dogs. While other people, including this author, could not get close enough to pet her, Barb fondly remembers picking up the German shepherd and carrying her. I might question that a slender woman like Barb could carry a German shepherd, but I have a photo!

Barb researched ideas for helping some of our problem dogs like Jack. In addition to working at Camp Husky, Barb played a key role in promoting adoptions and fundraising. Many dogs found great homes thanks to her hard work and creativity in organizing events. Her fondness for the dogs and her appreciation for their unique personalities can be seen in the photos she took and a scrapbook she made. Barb captured the special spirits of Glacier, Jack, Gypsy, and many other dogs.

Kacie Raybould

A native of Washington State, Kacie lived in Butte and had worked in the catering industry for about twelve years. The Copper King Inn, where she worked, went out of business shortly before the rescue began. With some free time, Kacie took a road trip to visit her family and was in Spokane when Brode was arrested. Upon returning to Butte and learning of the rescue, Kacie decided to volunteer and phoned Katie Donovan to sign up. "I learned from Katie and others that there was a need for volunteers seven days a week, and it took about sixteen to eighteen hours a day from the first shift that opened up Camp Husky in the morning to the last shift working at night to get all the essential work completed. By my third day at Camp Husky, I was hired as a volunteer supervisor."

Kacie's account of Camp Husky was consistent with what all the other volunteers told me. "I was deeply devoted to the dogs, but I resented the arbitrary management style of the director of animal services. I saw management [animal services] as an obstacle preventing us from doing what was best for the dogs." A major conflict occurred over nutritional needs of the dogs. Kacie believed the dogs needed more than simply whatever dog food had been donated. Having learned a good deal about nutrition from her mother, a naturopathic physician, Kacie knew the importance of proper nutrition in dogs as well as people. She consulted Debbie Rossi, the owner of Thrive, a pet health-food store in Butte, to get advice and help with the nutritional needs of the dogs.

Kacie started cooking huge amounts of rice for the dogs at her home and bringing it to Camp Husky each day to help with the diarrhea problem. Barb, Dave, Kacie, and Katie ensured that the rice was mixed into all the dog food each morning. Not only did Debbie Rossi act as nutritional adviser to the supervisors, she also donated special supplements for the pregnant and nursing moms. "Supplements were put in the drinking water of all the moms. Considering how malnourished the dogs were when they came off the bus, the supplements were no doubt critical to the health of the moms and their puppies," said Kacie. The volunteers fed the dogs the rice and supplements without informing the animal-services director or the veterinarian. They kept supplies hidden.

"By this time," said Kacie, "I had lost all respect for Phyllis Ruana. She only showed up at Camp Husky if the media were coming, and then she wanted everything cleaned up to look good for them. Also, she tried to give the impression to the media that she actually worked there, which she did not. None of us ever saw her show up on any shift to lend a hand shoveling poop, mopping kennels, or walking dogs in freezing temperatures!"

Dave Jordan

In late October, Dave Jordan, a ski instructor, received an urgent phone call from his friend Kacie Raybould, asking him to join the volunteers at the Anselmo Mine hoist house, where by then, two floors were filled with kennels and dogs. Dave, one of three US Navy veterans to play an essential role at Camp Husky, remembers "arriving in the morning and waiting outside while another volunteer, a red-headed attorney, gave me an orientation. 'I have to do this here,' she said, 'because you will not be able to hear me over the sound of all the hungry, barking dogs.'" Dave would become very familiar with the commotion in the morning as the dogs greeted a new day and awaited their breakfast. He was to volunteer every day until after Christmas. (The author remembers working with Dave and several others on Thanksgiving and Christmas Day.) Dave remembers "the leaky roof, especially in the area where we housed the expectant and new moms and puppies. It was impossible to keep that building warm.

"Mornings at Camp Husky were sheer pandemonium. We had about 125 hungry and excited dogs—not counting all the puppies—when we opened the place in the early morning. All the cages were dirty, and the dogs needed exercise. Every morning we started over with so much work to do. By the time we left in the evening, the dogs were settled down." Dave added that when they closed up Camp Husky each night, the enormous pack of dogs started howling and communicating with each other.

"We were much better organized in our second location on Arizona Street," Dave said. "By then I was taking the early-morning shift. Starting at seven, I would let the puppies out for exercise. These were groups of puppies that had been taken from their moms. I let them run around and play with each other. Sometimes I would lie down and let them crawl around me. After thirty minutes of playtime, I fed the puppies. This was my favorite time of the day. I relished being alone with the puppies."

Dave recalls a large white female named Olive and her adult pup, Pepper. "Both were in our maternity wing with newborn puppies. I came in one morning and noticed that the latch was open on Olive's cage. She had obviously opened the latch and gone out exploring sometime in the night. The fact that her pups were all in the cage suggested that she closed it when she took her nightly break." Dave would carefully insert the latch each evening before leaving, but the next morning he would find Olive and her pups in their cage with the latch open!

Olive and Pepper went to Help for Homeless Pets in Billings in the spring of 2009 and remained in that shelter until November 2010 when both were adopted by Lisa Reimer and her daughter, Allison. Lisa, a seventh grade language arts teacher in Laurel, Montana, wrote me in April 2016, reporting that both dogs remain healthy and are deeply loved. As Lisa said, "Olive and Pepper are a true Camp Husky success story." Photo #29 shows Olive and Pepper at home with Lisa.

When Phyllis Ruana had decided to take fourteen dogs to Dillon, she had asked Dave Jordan to pick out fourteen of our most socialized dogs. Dave did not know, until I told him in August 2010, what had happened to those dogs he selected for the animal-services director. Dave thought at the time that the dogs were going to a good no-kill shelter where they would be adopted easily because they were such great dogs. I did not know that he had been the one to select the dogs when I told him that the Dillion shelter had killed our dogs. Dave was naturally very upset.

Dave told me how very special the dogs were that Phyllis Ruana took to Dillon. "They were all beautiful and friendly," and every volunteer who worked with those dogs agreed with Dave. "They were good breeding stock. By that I mean that those dogs that went to Dillon were very large and exceptionally attractive white German shepherds. They were in good health and very friendly and people oriented." At that time, no one knew the dogs and their dispositions better than Dave. Two of the dogs in particular were Dave's favorites. "I called those two white German shepherds Siegfried and Brunhilde, and I was in the habit of taking a run with the two of them daily. They were exceptional dogs in every way with friendly dispositions and all the best qualities of German shepherds." Cindy also told me that among the dogs Phyllis took to Dillon were three sisters that were very popular with volunteers because of their sweet dispositions.

"For some reason, I had a bad feeling about letting those fourteen dogs go to Dillon with Phyllis," said Dave. Samantha Collier, who drove with Phyllis to the Humane Society of Beaverhead County in Dillon with the fourteen special dogs, also had a bad feeling when she saw the facility and realized that the dogs would not be in a good space.

Neither Dave nor any other volunteer had a say in what happened to those dogs. Unfortunately, Phyllis had the power and authority to make those kinds of decisions and never consulted with those who knew and cared most about the dogs, including Dave and the regular volunteers. It still haunts me to think of how those poor dogs suffered when they went from Camp Husky, where they were walked, petted, and loved, to being confined in a small space with no exercise at the Dillon shelter, where they must have sensed from the staff's nonverbal behavior that they were in danger. It makes no sense that the Dillon shelter would agree to take dogs they were not equipped to properly care for, and it makes even less sense that anyone with any degree of compassion for the dogs or the volunteers would have left the dogs there to die as Phyllis did.

Although Dave was one of the most devoted volunteers, there every day, Phyllis apparently felt no need to tell him or any of the other volunteers, except Cindy, the truth about what she had done. "The director kept it from us," Dave said. Sarah and Cindy knew what had happened, but they did not tell Dave and the others for fear of demoralizing the volunteers. When a group of former volunteers met at my home in the summer of 2015 to go over the material in this chapter, Dave and several others agreed that "there would have been a rebellion against animal services had the volunteers found out at the time that those magnificent dogs had been killed by the folks in Dillon."

We all agreed that if one volunteer had known about the poor care the dogs were receiving in Dillon and that they were going to be killed, a half dozen or more volunteers would have driven to Dillon to bring the dogs back to Camp Husky.

On a happier note, Dave has a daily reminder of the wonderful puppies he cared for at Camp Husky. He developed a special relationship with Bucky, a puppy with a deformed leg. When he learned that a veterinarian had suggested euthanizing that puppy, Dave found the puppy a great home with his mother-in-law. Dave and his wife, Robin, get healthful exercise walking that puppy, now a 130-pound dog. Bucky's story is in chapter 5.

Andrea and Don Stierle

Shortly before Camp Husky started operating, an internationally renowned husband-and-wife research team had just been awarded a $650,000 grant for important cancer research. Not only did these two chemists have enormous research responsibilities as well as teaching responsibilities at Montana Tech, but they were also active as community volunteers. But when longtime friends Cindy McIlveen and Katie Donovan asked Andrea and Don to help out at Camp Husky, they committed to work every Saturday and two weeknights as well. Andrea described her first day: "When I entered the Anselmo mine-shaft building, I had to stop and stand still for ten full minutes because of the overwhelming odor. Even having so many sick dogs crowded together in one building could not account for that odor. Was it the smell of fear as well?"

The Stierles' first major contribution was to provide needed antibiotics for the sick dogs. Determining the correct dosage of antibiotic for each dog based on its weight was no easy task, and we were so fortunate to have two PhDs in chemistry to direct that job. The Stierles opened their laboratory on the Montana Tech campus at night so that a small group of volunteers could accurately prepare dosages based on weight and age.

Katie Donovan wrote an account of her time in the lab: "The dogs all had diarrhea for weeks. Yuck. Very messy! The veterinarian finally put together a plan after she returned from a conference. Unfortunately, we had only that one veterinarian, so nothing could be done to help the dogs when she was away. I always wondered why not a team of vets, but I questioned a lot of what the animal-services director did. Anyway, Dr. Lewis finally tested the dogs and got antibiotics for us after she returned from her conference. This was how things worked. We volunteers weighed each dog at Camp Husky. Then, working at night with the Stierles, we would go to the Montana Tech chemistry lab and weigh the correct amount of powdered medication for each dog. Then we mixed the medication into a meatball and labeled it.

"We had to be very careful to keep track of each meatball and feed it to the correct dog. We worked in the lab for ten nights in a row, and we fed the dogs their medicated meatballs twice a day! We could not have done the job without the Stierles and a dedicated team of volunteers. It took hours to weigh and prepare those meatballs. Then we drove back to the Anselmo and fed all the dogs their evening meatballs. Cindy rigged up lights at the Anselmo so that we could work late into the night, sometimes until midnight, feeding the medication to the dogs." As Katie related, it was thanks to the Stierles and a very dedicated team of volunteers that our dogs got well and the weeks of diarrhea came to an end, thus making life much easier for everyone.

Once they helped conquer the diarrhea problem, Don and Andrea showed up to mop floors, wash dishes, and walk dogs. Three volunteers Andrea fondly recalls working with during those critical first weeks were Janet Manchester and her daughters, Jessi and Kelsey. Andrea recalls washing dishes and pallets outdoors at the Anselmo location: "We had to walk down the wooden steps to carry the dirty dishes and plastic pallets to the sinks outside the building, and then we walked up the steps with clean dishes and pallets. By November the steps were icy, so it was treacherous work." Andrea noted that we were fortunate that a space was available to house the dogs even if it was inadequate in so many ways. Later, it would be the Stierles who were instrumental in securing a heated building on Arizona Street. Andrea contacted Robert Edwards, a property manager, who secured permission for us to use a vacant building owned by a sculptor named John

Richen. Thanks to a connected chemist, a helpful property manager, and a generous artist, the dogs and volunteers would have a heated building and hot water just before the coldest days of winter arrived.

The Stierles, originally from California, are now conducting their research in Missoula at the University of Montana. I was able to interview Andrea when she was in Butte one weekend a few years after the rescue ended. Andrea and Don have had an exceptional number of publications in prestigious scientific journals since earning their PhDs, secured many large grants, and received international recognition for their research. Knowing that this couple had reached a level of professional achievement that most researchers and academics can only dream of, I was rather amazed at what Andrea told me in our interview. She said, "One does not often have the opportunity to do something as special and important as the work we all did at Camp Husky. When we showed up to work our evening and Saturday shifts at Camp Husky, we always felt that we made a difference. Camp Husky was Butte at its finest; I had a real sense of community with so many people showing up to work. Don and I went home crying on more than one night, overcome by our appreciation for the way the people of Butte rallied together and cared for the dogs. Most of the dogs were just lovely, and they so appreciated being petted and walked." Andrea's favorite dog was a white German shepherd mother dog named Mia because of her "exceptionally sweet nature." Mia would eventually find an ideal home with a widow in Bozeman.

Monte and Merlena Moore

California natives Monte and Merlena Moore had been living in Butte only a few years when they read about the rescue effort in the *Montana Standard* in early October 2008. This retired couple would not only join the ranks of the regular volunteers, but the contribution they would make to the success of Camp Husky would be difficult to exaggerate. Their kindness and generosity would deeply touch many of us who volunteered alongside them.

Many people who have shared their homes with a number of dogs over many years will tell you that they loved all their animals, but often these people will also tell you that there was one special dog—their once-in-a-lifetime dog. For at least half of the owners I interviewed for this book, their Camp Husky dog became their once-in-a-lifetime dog. For Monte and Mer, as she likes to be called, that special dog was Duchess, a black-and-tan German shepherd mix. That gentle, well-behaved, and loving creature died of mouth cancer at age ten, shortly before the bus full of dogs headed toward Butte.

Reading about the rescue in the *Montana Standard*, Monte and Mer decided to drive to the Anselmo to make a cash donation, with no plans of volunteering. When I first interviewed them three years after Camp Husky closed, Monte said that his first reaction on walking up the stairs to the second floor of the hoist house and seeing more than a hundred dogs was "a feeling of being overwhelmed." Seeing the enormity of the problem facing Butte, Mer said, "Oh my God, look at all these dogs!" The couple made a generous donation and went home, but later that night, Mer told Monte, "I need to go back there and help with all the work. I need to do it for me." Monte felt the same way. With tears in their eyes, they told me that volunteering at Camp Husky was a way for them to honor that special dog that had given them so much love and happiness.

Their first day of volunteering was a Saturday morning in early October, and the first person they met was Samantha Collier. Sam asked them to help prepare the dogs' food. Monte recalled being impressed as he watched Sam lift a forty-pound bag of donated dog chow and carry it up the wooden stairs to the second floor. Katie described her own encounter with the couple: "I was opening the building early that Monday morning when a couple drove up to volunteer. Since they were not on my list of volunteers, I did not have a specific job for them. I put them in charge of the nursery—one entire corner of the building held moms and pups or females about to deliver. Monte and Mer had arrived! They continued with the husky rescue and helped in countless ways to the very end." The retired couple committed to work the eight-to-eleven shift every weekday morning, caring for mother dogs and puppies, including cleaning kennels and walking the moms. Later, Mer was one of three volunteers who came down with *Campylobacter* infection followed by pneumonia, and she had to stop volunteering.

Although he was seventy-five at the time and suffered from heart disease, Monte continued to work until Camp Husky closed. For six days a week and sometimes seven, this US Navy veteran of the Korean War would arrive at Camp Husky by seven to work the morning shift, and he stayed as long as he was needed. As a former manager at Caterpillar Inc. in San Francisco, Monte was both an adept problem solver and very good with people. Also, he could repair nearly anything, and that skill was put to good use at Camp Husky. If something was broken, Monte repaired it, and if we needed something, Monte went out and bought it. When I interviewed the couple about a year before Monte died, I asked how he was able to go day after day and work so hard in the bitter cold. This was his answer: "Yes, the work was exhausting, but the need was so great and the plight of the dogs was heart wrenching. Merlena and I were encouraged by the way folks from all walks of life worked together and became one big family." Early in 2009, the animal-services director informed volunteers that there was no more money for Camp Husky—no money for utility bills, stipends for the supervisors, medicine, or other supplies for the dogs. It would be Monte and Mer who enabled Camp Husky to keep operating for the next three months. About one-third of the dogs featured in this book would not be alive and in good homes today had it not been for this generous couple, who kept Camp Husky open and operating long enough for the volunteers to find those homes.

Laura and Bill Weatherly

Bill and Laura had been married more than fifty years and were enjoying an active retirement when they read about the Camp Husky rescue and decided to help. When they first arrived at the Anselmo hoist house in early October, they had the same reaction as the Moores: they were "overwhelmed by the immensity of the challenge. With the huge number of very large dogs, the level of noise, the horrible smell, and the cold building, the task facing volunteers seemed almost hopeless." Nevertheless, these tough Montana natives volunteered a few days that first week, and by the third week of the rescue, they were working a shift every day! As one supervisor said, "Bill and Laura were constants at Camp Husky for the first three months." I remember seeing them on the weekends and even on Thanksgiving and Christmas Day. Their dedication was remarkable considering that Bill, a veteran of both World War 11 and the Korean War, was in his eighties at the time.

Laura is from Conrad, Montana, and received her English degree from the University of Montana, while Bill is from Missoula and got his degree in geology from the same institution after his wartime service as an infantryman in the US Army. Bill earned a second degree from Montana Tech in Mining Engineering and worked as a geologist and mining engineer for the Anaconda Company in Butte and later as a minerals manager with the Bureau of Land Management. In addition to rearing two children and working as a substitute teacher, Laura had worked as a trainer for the football team at Montana Tech.

By 2008, Laura wasn't strong enough to lug heavy buckets and mops to clean the cages or walk the large dogs two at a time like Bill, so she worked with the moms and pups in the nursery and folded the laundry. In January 2009, this dedicated couple had to quit their daily routine of volunteering because Bill required major surgery, and Laura was sick with *Campylobacter* infection. She was the third volunteer to contract the same disease the dogs had. When their health returned, Laura and Bill came back to visit with the volunteers and be with the dogs. They had played a key role in helping us through the first three critical months of the rescue, inspiring the younger volunteers. Spending so much time volunteering, and later visiting, at Camp Husky, Laura and Bill saw most of the volunteers except those who worked in the evenings. When I interviewed her, Laura had nothing but admiration and praise for the volunteers with whom she worked. "I observed that all the volunteers were very hardworking and dedicated," she said.

Laura and Bill felt that they got as much back from volunteering at Camp Husky as they gave. "It was a great experience. We met a lot of good people and formed lasting relationships as a result of working at Camp Husky." The experience changed them in another way. This couple had raised a son and daughter and shared their home with many cats through the years, but they had never had a dog. Camp Husky changed that, and they ended up with a husky dog of their own. One could describe Bill and Laura as "professional volunteers" who believe in giving back to their community. Now, more than seven years after Camp Husky closed, they are still active, volunteering at the Butte summer festivals, at art, music, and theater functions, with PFLAG, and at the local soup kitchen. On Tuesdays and Thursdays, Laura and Bill serve food while their husky-shepherd mix, Niki, takes care of the emotional needs of the soup kitchen's guests.

Sue Madison

When commenting on the specific volunteers she observed, Laura Weatherly had special praise for a longtime Butte resident originally from

Oklahoma. "I was impressed by the way Sue Madison came out of retirement to haul those heavy buckets around. It was amazing to watch how hard she worked," said Laura. Sue worked five days a week for six months, starting the first week and staying until we closed up operations. She first learned of the need for volunteers in a water-aerobics class taught by Sarah DeMoney. Many YMCA staff and members helped out on the first day and during the first week of the rescue, and their contributions were significant, but most were unable to continue volunteering. Sue committed for the duration, and it made all the difference. In addition to good problem-solving skills and a strong work ethic, Sue brought a lot of dog training skills. She trained shelties and competed successfully in AKC obedience trials long before the Camp Husky rescue began. That kind of competition requires good communication with your dog, lots of patience and perseverance, as well as a high level of respect and trust between dog and owner. These were invaluable skills that Sue brought to Camp Husky.

In an interview, Sue described the working conditions in the early weeks at the Anselmo: "In the beginning we seemed to go from one crisis to another at Camp Husky. The sheer number of dogs was overwhelming. Working in the hoist house building, we lacked heat and hot water, and winter was coming on. No matter how hard we pushed ourselves, we did not have enough volunteers or time in our shift to complete all the essential work. I was washing the pallets the dogs slept on and their dishes in ice-cold water outside in the freezing cold."

She regretted that there was "not enough time and manpower to keep careful records of everything at Camp Husky. Documentation often went by the wayside because we had so much work to do each day. Katie Donovan was hired to keep records, among other tasks, and she was a big help, but she was also doing all the heavy work the rest of us did as well.

"In hindsight, it is amazing that we accomplished as much as we did. We needed more resources. We needed more money and more volunteers. I was frustrated because things didn't seem to run as efficiently as I would have liked."

Sue developed deep respect for the contributions that many of the volunteers made to Camp Husky. "Toward the end, Cindy McIlveen took over. She was totally committed to saving all the dogs. Monte Moore was another volunteer I admired. He was a real dog lover."

One of the saddest things for Sue was learning that a puppy died of illness shortly after being adopted by a woman in Butte. "I felt so sorry for both the puppy and the woman." One of Sue's favorite dogs was Rhett, who found a great home with a man in New Mexico. When asked to explain why Camp Husky succeeded in saving so many dogs, Sue said, "It all boils down to people who were willing to hold in there and work their shift." While she gives credit to many others for the key roles they played, Sue was one of the faithful, dedicated volunteers who showed up regularly to work her shift, carrying heavy buckets, mopping out dog pens, walking dogs, or doing whatever else was needed. She had two very good reasons for *not* volunteering—she was allergic to dogs, and she had severe arthritis in her knees—yet she held in there to the very end and was the epitome of a committed volunteer. Shortly after all the dogs were adopted and Camp Husky closed, Sue had to have knee replacement surgery. She may have sacrificed her knees to save our dogs.

Kay and Dr. Tony Konecny

Shortly after Kay and Tony embarked on retirement, they discussed what kind of volunteer work they might like, and Kay recalls saying that she wanted to do something to help animals. Little did she know that very soon, the opportunity to help animals would arrive in a big way. Tony and Kay were among the first to volunteer, showing up on the third day that Camp Husky opened, taking afternoon shifts every weekday. They worked the same shift as Sue Madison three days a week. When I asked why they volunteered, Kay said, "We have an absolute love of dogs." Kay grew up with dogs because her parents raised golden retrievers, and now Kay and Tony have English cocker spaniels. Like many of the volunteers, Kay had a compelling reason to not volunteer: she had a torn rotator cuff and injuries to both shoulders when she first showed up to volunteer, and yet she worked tirelessly for two months until she was scheduled to have surgery on both shoulders. Fortunately, she recovered well from the surgery.

Tony walked dogs, cleaned kennels, and washed pallets and dishes outside. Kay was exclusively a dog walker and puppy holder. "We volunteers worked with newborn puppies as well as older ones, trying to accustom them to human contact as soon as possible," explained Kay. "Those dogs were such loves! Even though they had suffered severe neglect and abuse, they were almost all nice dogs. In the early weeks, the dogs were highly stressed and very frightened, yet they never tried to bite either of us. Our goal in the early weeks was to acclimate the dogs to people and introduce minor obedience training such as walking on a leash. After only a few weeks, most of the dogs had started to learn basic dog manners.

"While many of the dogs were pure white, there were also a number with the yellow color of golden Labs. One of our fondest memories concerns two of those very large yellow dogs. This event happened during the second week of Camp Husky. Tony and I put leashes on these two dogs, but they were terrified of leaving their kennel. We had to coax them out of their kennel so that the other two team members could clean it. First, we got the dogs to stand up in the kennel, but they were determined not to step outside the kennel. Another volunteer, observing the problem, handed us a broom and suggested that we gently tap the dogs on their rear ends to encourage them to walk. It worked! A gentle tap would encourage a few steps. Slowly and patiently, we got the dogs to walk about five feet from the kennel. Then both dogs dropped to the ground, too frightened to venture out any farther. Tony and I just sat down beside them on the cold concrete floor, petting and comforting them. Although they were shaking with fear, there was no aggression in them. Looking into their big brown eyes touched our hearts. Everything seemed to scare them: the mops and buckets, the people, and just going outside. Then after about five weeks, we noticed that these two dogs, as well as the others, had overcome their fears. They now greeted us with wagging tails and happy anticipation when we opened the doors of their kennels with leashes in hand."

Working as many hours as they did each week, Kay and Tony were able to walk and observe most of the dogs at Camp Husky. "We had not been working many days when we discovered that each dog we walked had an individual personality. We volunteers could tell that some dogs were alphas, and some, especially the smaller dogs, were more passive in nature. There must have been a definite pecking order among the dogs on the bus, but they were all nice dogs," said Kay.

Like many of the volunteers I interviewed, Tony and Kay experienced some frustration with top management. "We were often confronted with what seemed like arbitrary and unreasonable decisions from animal services. We never saw the director at Camp Husky during all the time we were volunteering, and some of the directives given to the supervisors simply didn't work. We met many obstacles because of animal services, and I believe we could have done a better job of caring for the dogs if it had not been for some of the limits placed on us by management. For example, we were not allowed to use choke chain collars for walking dogs; however, one powerful dog ate through the cloth collars we were required to use for walking dogs. We had to waste a lot of time trying to catch that husky. That was an example of an arbitrary order that left us frustrated. Sue Madison did some research and found a type of collar that would have worked well for walking the dogs that pulled a lot, and we volunteers were willing to pay for the collars ourselves, but we were blocked because the director of animal services made arbitrary decisions and did not consult with the volunteers who were doing the day-to-day work of caring for the dogs and running Camp Husky."

As someone who has worked as a communications trainer and consultant for government agencies and private corporations, this author can attest that the frustration Tony, Kay, Sue and many other volunteers felt is not at all unusual. Good managers are good listeners, and they are willing to listen and learn from people at all levels of an organization. The volunteers I interviewed were in general quite knowledgeable about dogs. Unfortunately, the animal-services director appeared to have had little interest in consulting with these dedicated and very knowledgeable volunteers, who had practical ideas of how to best help the dogs.

While working at the camp and later in researching this book, I either observed or heard about little acts of kindness toward the dogs that epitomized the spirit of Camp Husky. For example, while Tony, a family-practice physician, was walking and caring for one of the smaller females, one with badly matted fur, he observed that she would be delivering her puppies soon. Dr. Tony told Dr. Lewis, the veterinarian, that he was very concerned that the young pregnant dog was suffering discomfort because of her fur's condition and that the poor creature would have difficulty giving birth and nursing unless the fur was cut away. Fortunately, the veterinarian listened to the MD, and working together they were able to remove all the matted fur with clippers.

Whitney Harris

Several of our volunteers were students at Montana Tech. Now working as a petroleum engineer, Whitney Harris was one of two students whom I was able to interview who volunteered at Camp Husky after hearing about the need for volunteers from their professor, Rick Donovan. Whitney showed up to volunteer the first week and worked two shifts a week. It was all the time she could spare from her demanding course work. "I liked going to the Anselmo and helping the dogs, but I became very angry at how the dogs had been mistreated. I felt sorry for them. I wanted to be able to be loving and affectionate to one dog at a time, but there was so much work to do that we volunteers could never give the attention and affection to individual dogs that they needed. With cleaning kennels, washing dishes, and all the other basic work that had to be done, you could not spend much time with individual dogs. The only time I could give affection to the individual dogs was when I walked them."

When she first started volunteering, Whitney noticed that being walked was a totally new experience for the dogs. "Some of the dogs were freaked out when we took them outside." Whitney recalled one young dog who was so terrified that he stopped and refused to walk. "I just sat near him and tried to reassure him for nearly a half hour. Each time I returned to work a shift I noticed that the dogs were becoming more confident."

Whitney noticed that some of the young dogs that had been puppies on the bus showed signs of having had broken legs that did not mend well. "I asked myself, how many puppies born on the bus did not survive because of the terrible conditions?" It was a question that many volunteers pondered. In spite of the difficulties, Whitney told me she was glad she had volunteered and she would do it again.

Jocelyn Dodge

Jocelyn, a longtime employee of the US Forest Service, was another volunteer recruited by Cindy McIlveen. She started working the first week of the rescue. "My heart just went out to those dogs. I was a little reluctant to go up to the Anselmo at first, knowing the condition the dogs had been in when taken off the bus. I learned from Cindy how the dogs had suffered on that bus. Many were chained to the bus and forced to lie in their own filth." Jocelyn worked weekends and filled in on weeknights when needed. She would end up volunteering until the very end, fostering one dog and helping with the dogs Cindy fostered after Camp Husky closed. "I would do it again as long as Cindy was in charge. I probably would not have gotten involved if it had not been for Cindy. Cindy was the unofficial leader of Camp Husky. People turned to her for information and coordination. She took so much responsibility and did so much work herself."

Jocelyn never knew how many hours she would work when she arrived at Camp Husky on the weekend. "I would go in the morning, planning on working for only an hour and end up working until late afternoon. Seeing how many caring people came forward to volunteer in those early weeks, I had faith that we could succeed. I was pretty amazed at the dedication of the people who volunteered." Jocelyn especially enjoyed the job of walking dogs. "They just needed exercise. They really wanted out of their pens. In the early weeks, I noticed that some of the dogs were bewildered when we took them outside. Naturally, it took a while initially to get the leash on many of the dogs since it was a new experience for them, but once we got leashes on and took them outside, they were just fine. They had been confined on the bus so long that walking was a real treat once they got over their initial fear. Walking was a way to socialize these dogs."

Meg Robbe

Meg read about Camp Husky and the need for volunteers in the *Montana Standard*. She wanted to help even though she had a husband, a son, and a part-time job at the courthouse working for Judge Brad Newman. Since she worked weekday mornings, Meg chose to volunteer for the weekday-afternoon shifts starting that first week the camp was open. She remembers receiving some training from other volunteers that first day, including being told about the diseases the dogs had. She would continue volunteering until January, when she was forced to quit because she needed surgery. When interviewed, Meg recalled a group of Montana Tech students volunteering at Camp Husky weekday afternoons—one of them had worked in a boarding kennel, and his knowledge of dogs proved quite helpful. She learned that some of these students were getting internship credit for their volunteer work.

Meg recalls feeling overwhelmed when she first started volunteering: "The sheer number of dogs needing care was intimidating. One challenge we had in those first couple of weeks was putting dogs together that would be compatible. I also observed that dogs tended to form very close relationships with their kennel mates." Meg remembers two large adult males, Mufasa and his son, Simba. "These good buddies had to be walked together because one would not leave the kennel without the other." Meg also remembered a black-and-tan German shepherd named Star that acted aggressively until a young man named Russ Wagoner took a special interest in her and helped her overcome her fear of people. (All three dogs found good homes, and their stories are told later in this book.)

Meg's kindness was evident as I interviewed her, and I could not help but think how the compassion and caring of individual volunteers must have influenced these dogs that had never been socialized and had experienced only neglect and harsh treatment before being rescued. "You had to be sensitive toward each individual dog you walked," said Meg. "Some were more afraid than others. I tried to stroke them whenever possible while walking them." Meg's fondest memories are of the days when adoptions started in December. In the new location, where we had hot as well as cold water inside a heated building, Meg was able to bathe some of the puppies before their new owners came to adopt them. "It was very rewarding to see them adopted."

Meg had a history of volunteering, including helping 4-H groups, and she will always remember her time at Camp Husky because she knows she had a direct effect on those canine lives.

Debbie Mueller

Debbie, a Butte native and school librarian, was typical of Camp Husky volunteers in many ways. With a full-time job and pets of her own to care for, she did not have much free time, and yet she came forward early in the rescue and stayed to the very end. Debbie committed to work the Sunday-morning shift, and she faithfully showed up every weekend for the next six months. When asked via an e-mailed questionnaire why she volunteered, Debbie wrote, "My emotional involvement was instantaneous when I read about the rescue. This was an opportunity to serve 'the poorest of the poor' of a species so dependent on humans."

Debbie did all the usual jobs, cleaning and disinfecting kennels, walking dogs, and washing dishes. When we moved to our second location, we had a power hose to clean pallets outdoors, and Debbie did that job as well. Because she worked the early-morning shift, Debbie began her mornings helping Dave and other volunteers feed the hungry dogs. She also made an effort to brush the dogs she walked. "Every Sunday morning, after a four- or five-hour stint of feeding and walking dogs, cleaning kennels, and hosing down pallets outside, I would come home and throw my reeking clothes and shoes into the washing machine and take a *hot* bath to warm up and get the stink off. I looked forward eagerly to the following Sunday shift and ritual bath." Later, Debbie would foster a dog named Cheyanne, one of the many puppies on the bus. Debbie and Cheyanne appeared in a KXLF television broadcast promoting Camp Husky adoptions, and later the beautiful and gentle dog was adopted by a friend of Debbie's in Missoula.

Debbie also remembers how difficult the labor was, even dangerous at times. "Working conditions were far from ideal. In the dead of winter, the walks with the dogs outside could be miserably cold. As we walked those strong dogs on a leash, our footing was often treacherous because of ice that stayed on the ground from November through April. I often worried about falling down or being pulled down. We could not let the dogs off leash for fear they would escape. We often got splashed with urine or feces while removing dogs or cleaning kennels. The cacophonous barking was deafening at times. One time I was bitten very hard by a protective mother dog when I tried to place a fresh water bucket in her kennel and got too close to her puppies."

Like many volunteers I interviewed, Debbie most remembers "the camaraderie among the volunteers" and egalitarian attitude fostered by "that one passion in common—our huskies." Dressed in warm but old clothes, the many volunteers shared the same hard labor. "I had no way of knowing if an individual I worked with on any given Sunday morning was a homeless individual or a corporate executive. This altruistic effort was community centered and supported by people from all walks of life. The only thing many of us had in common was that we valued the well-being of the dogs more than our own comfort. We were all working for the love of the dogs. I felt gratitude for everyone who was there donating time and sharing the labor." Debbie said her lasting impression of Camp Husky was "a sense of having belonged to an endeavor whose overreaching effect far exceeded the sum of each volunteer's part. I loved being part of that enormous undertaking and performing menial labor for the betterment of the dogs."

Christy Stack and Cathy Decker

Volunteers frequently showed up at Camp Husky in teams of two or more. We had many friends and several couples who chose to work together on the same shift. We had mother-daughter teams, mother-son teams, and whole families. Two regulars whom I worked with on Saturdays and Sundays were twin sisters, Christy and Cathy, from Walkerville, just north of Butte. What I did not know at that time was that these remarkable women, both with full-time professional jobs, families, and pets, were also volunteering every weeknight as well. I still marvel at the stamina of these gals, who grew up on a ranch in Waterloo, just north of Whitehall, Montana.

Christy Stack read about Camp Husky in the *Montana Standard* and drove to the Anselmo the next Saturday to sign up and start working. Christy described her first day, two weeks after the rescue began: "A volunteer met me at the gate that morning and said, 'You can start working right now.' And so that was my first day working a shift at Camp Husky. I remember that I cried a lot that first night after seeing how filthy, thin, and scared the dogs were. I was especially frustrated by the fact that we had only a relatively small fenced area where we could walk dogs, and no matter how hard we worked mopping out cages, we could not keep them clean for very long since most of the dogs were suffering from diarrhea. I knew we were all doing the best we could. Everyone there was working so hard, but it was still painful for me to look into the sad eyes of those wonderful dogs with their dirty, matted fur. I could not stop thinking about them after I went home." The next day, Christy returned to work at the Anselmo with her twin sister, Cathy Decker, and both sisters committed to working every weeknight as well as Saturdays and Sundays. Cathy and Christy would prove to be among our most committed volunteers, continuing to work until the doors closed at Camp Husky in April 2009. Each would adopt a difficult-to-place dog.

Cathy, like most volunteers I interviewed, confessed to feeling "overwhelmed by the number of dogs at the Anselmo, their poor state of health, and the fear they displayed. The Herculean task of walking, feeding, and cleaning up after about one hundred twenty-five sick dogs and puppies was daunting," she said. Luckily, the sisters often worked as a team with Dave Jordan and Monte Moore in those first months, and the optimism and enthusiasm of those two men enabled the sisters to believe that the project would succeed and that they could make a difference. "We worked as a team with two of us walking the two or three dogs in a kennel, while the other two cleaned the kennel and put a fresh bucket of water in the kennel. During those first few weeks, both Christy and I wondered if we could keep working a shift after work in the evening as well as weekends because the work was so hard physically, and the stench, the noise, and the cold assaulted our senses," said Cathy.

"Our empathy for the dogs always left us emotionally drained by the time our shift ended. During our second week of volunteering we met two women about our age who were volunteering for the first time. After they worked a full shift, they told Christy and me that it was just too hard and they would not be coming back although they felt great sympathy for the dogs. We understood how these women felt, and we wondered if we would give up like them. A few days later, I was cleaning cages with Dave, and I suddenly broke down, bawling for the dogs and what they had suffered. Dave looked at me and said, 'We will get through this, Cathy. Butte people have been through worse than this,' and I knew he was right."

Christy recalls that Monte Moore was also an inspiring fellow worker. "Monte was a very tall man, about six feet two inches with a ponytail, and he had a way of giving me confidence when I worked with him. Some of the dogs were huge, and many were so frightened of us, and frankly, I felt a little afraid to open some of the cages. It was intimidating to open a cage with giant-sized dogs I didn't know. I had to be brave, and Monte helped me with that. I remember how upbeat and positive Monte was whenever we teamed up to walk dogs. He said, 'Christy, just open the cage. They won't bite you,' and they never did. I also recall that in the early weeks when we put leashes on the dogs and tried to walk them, they had no idea what we wanted from them. They were confused and afraid since they had never been socialized. They would take a few steps and sit down. It required patience and gentle encouragement on our part to get them outside and teach them to walk on a leash. Once they got accustomed to it, most dogs looked forward to their walk time."

By the time we were in our second Camp Husky location, Cathy and Christy were old hands at all the jobs and knew the individual dogs quite well. Cathy recalls that her son came to work with her one Saturday and was initially a little intimidated by the size of some of the dogs, just as she and Christy had once been. The first dog Cathy chose to walk was everyone's favorite, old Mufasa (the presumed father of many of our pups). Mufasa stared at Cathy's son, probably curious about a new human face, but it was a bit daunting for the young man, as it would have been for anyone who did not know how sweet and mild mannered that big guy really was.

"Is this the one we are going to walk?" the young man asked his mother.

"Yes," said his mother as she opened the kennel and slipped a leash on the husky-shepherd mix. Cathy remembers with a chuckle the look on her son's face as Mufasa stepped enthusiastically toward the young man, eager to make friends with a new person and enjoy a walk.

"I remember working with so many good people from all walks of life at Camp Husky," said Christy. "And they were not all Butte residents either. I recall a high-school coach who would show up to work with us during basketball season when his team was playing in Butte or a neighboring town. I think his name was Scott, and I believe he coached basketball in West Yellowstone, but I am not sure. He would just drop in and say, 'I have a few hours. How can I help?' That was awesome!"

Both Cathy and Christy observed "a strong camaraderie among the volunteers. We had a goal of getting our dogs into good homes, and we were so joyful whenever we learned that a dog or puppy had been adopted. For example, we remember crying with joy when we learned that two of our favorite dogs, Olive and her puppy, Pepper, had found a good home through Help for Homeless Pets in Billings and that the same shelter had placed one of our sweet white puppies, Jake, in another good home with an older gentleman, and our German shepherd–husky mix, Bandit, in a loving home he so deserved with a little boy. It was days like that that made all our labor so worthwhile."

The Many Unnamed, But Not Forgotten, Volunteers

In this chapter and the previous one, I have written about 23 individuals who made the Camp Husky rescue possible, and 15 others are featured in the chapters about the dogs; however, the majority of the 120 men and women who contributed to the effort are not mentioned in this book. Some worked during the first critical week, while many more worked regular shifts for months.

One woman who had recently moved to Butte from California made a diary entry of her first—and last—day volunteering. Linda Borton was in good physical condition and was no stranger to hard work, having reared four children while working full time as a hairdresser—thus her brief diary entry gives insight into how very difficult and challenging the work was at Camp Husky.

Oct. 21, 2008
Debbie and I drove up to the Anselmo and worked from 11:00–2:00 at Camp Husky. Very hard physical work. Snowed. Bitter cold outside and no heat in the building. Poor dogs! Came home with filthy clothes, tired and sore.

Linda and her friend Debbie Knokes found the work just too difficult, and they were not alone. Many well-intentioned people came up to the Anselmo, worked one shift, and decided it was too much. But their contributions still matter, and the dogs were still grateful for their help, even if only for a few hours.

CHAPTER 4
Moving toward Adoptions

O n November 11, a story in the *Montana Standard* announced that the Camp Husky dogs would soon have a new home in what was formerly an auto-repair shop on Arizona Street in the downtown area. Butte's finance and budget director, Jeff Amerman, was quoted as saying that "a deal has been brokered for a new home for the Camp Husky dogs. It's just the perfect, ideal situation. It's basically a donation with rent only one or two dollars a month." Kacie Raybould, one of the shift supervisors at Camp Husky, was quoted as saying that the youngest dogs would be the first to be moved "since it is about to get extremely cold." We now had a new location with *heat* as well as a much larger area in which to walk our dogs, thanks to Andrea Stierle's work with the property manager and building owner. At the end of the story, the reporter, John Grant Emeigh reminded readers of the need for more volunteers.

Captain Larry T. Wyatt

One of the first individuals I interviewed for this book was Larry Wyatt, a retired merchant marine captain and US Navy veteran. Captain Larry, a Southern California native, had resided in Butte less than two years when he read about the rescue and decided to drive up to Camp Husky "just to make a cash donation." Larry explained why he ended up as one of the regular volunteers: "I had no intention of volunteering; I have never volunteered in my life, but when I saw that the dogs were German shepherds or

German shepherd mixes, I had a flashback to the Vietnam War. As a civilian employee for the military and a freelance photographer covering the war and selling photos to the Associated Press, I learned firsthand about the amazing German shepherd scout dogs. Those dogs would prevent more than ten thousand casualties before the war was over. Time and again those scout dogs sacrificed their lives to save their trainers and other soldiers. Every day they were warning soldiers of booby traps or approaching enemy troops, and they guarded the bases better than any soldier could. In my opinion those dogs were the greatest heroes of the Vietnam War. It was the memory of their courage and sacrifice that compelled me to volunteer. The work was hard, and I had some personality conflicts with a couple of fellows who worked my shift, but we always came back the next day to pitch in and do whatever work was needed because Camp Husky had *a soul*. I am not a religious man, but volunteering at Camp Husky was a spiritual experience for me."

Captain Larry started volunteering in the first week of Camp Husky, came day after day until the very end, and made a very important contribution in addition to working weekday mornings. Our new location had plenty of space for walking dogs, with about half an acre that extended from one side of the building to the back and a much smaller but adequate space for walking dogs on the other side; however, the property had no fences. Larry quickly solved the problem. He went out, bought the materials, and recruited two Native American friends who wanted to help the dogs. These men had considerable experience installing and repairing fences on reservation ranches. Larry told me that the three of them had the property fenced in one long day of labor. Thanks entirely to these three men, our dogs could safely enjoy being outdoors and playing in the snow. Captain Larry also designed and sold Camp Husky T-shirts to raise money for the dogs and promote adoptions. I still have my shirt.

Kenny, Russ, and Tim Join the Effort

Among those whom Captain Larry recruited from the Butte Pre-Release Center were three men who would make a substantial contribution

65

to Camp Husky. Kenny was a very hard worker and well respected by the volunteers. Whenever he saw me lifting a bucket or something he thought was too heavy, he would come over and help me without ever being asked. Christy and I fondly remember his kindness and thoughtfulness. Russ was another good worker, and good with dogs. Russ developed a special fondness for a very frightened young mother named Star. I can still see him petting and talking to her. Russ deserves credit for socializing Star and preparing her for the successful adoption she has had with a good family.

Tim was also very good with the troubled dogs. I remember one special day when he achieved a breakthrough with Jack, the dog that was traumatized when the animal-control officer tore his mouth. It was on a Saturday in March when someone called out for all of us to stop what we were doing and come see something. We looked out the door and saw a wonderful sight. Jack was wagging his tail in happiness and playing in the snow with Tim. Someone snapped a picture. It took weeks of patience on Tim's part to achieve that transformation. Jack's story appears later in this book.

These three men all had serious problems that had led to incarceration, but they were all very responsible, dependable, and hardworking at Camp Husky. I spent many hours working beside them, as did many other volunteers, and we never questioned their commitment to Camp Husky or their compassion for and skill with the dogs. Like so many other volunteers, I respected and deeply appreciated what all three men did for the dogs. Sue Madison remembered Kenny as "a genuinely good guy. I never saw anyone work as hard at any job as Kenny worked at Camp Husky." Sue also remembered Tim and Russ as "very kindhearted toward our dogs. Tim took his job at Camp Husky very seriously, and as long as he had that job of helping the dogs, he was able to keep his life in order in spite of his history of substance abuse. Sometimes Tim would take one of our dogs to a meeting for addicts. Tim and Kenny are decent people, and working beside them made me more aware of the difficulty in overcoming substance abuse." These three men not only made huge contributions in helping the dogs but they taught many of us an important lesson: we should judge ourselves and others not by mistakes we made in the past, but by the good we are doing in the present.

The Physical Layout of the New Camp Husky

When you entered our new location from a door facing Arizona Street, the first thing you saw was a large pen with weaned puppies and about ten kennels with moms and nursing puppies. On the left-hand side was a makeshift office where volunteers signed in and adoptions would be recorded. Dog food, biscuits, and dishes were stored in this first room. The nursery opened into a very large space where the older puppies and adult dogs were housed. To the right in this larger room was a door that opened out into a small fenced yard where two people could comfortably walk two to four dogs, not more. In the very back of the larger room was a garage door that opened to a concrete area with running water where we could use a power hose to clean the plastic pallets. Beyond the concrete area was a very large fenced yard with ample space for walking dogs, and space for keeping outdoor kennels where dogs could enjoy fresh air and sunshine. By November, the temperature was usually at or below freezing in the middle of the day, but we often had sunshine. The outdoor kennels were especially nice for the few dogs we could not walk. For example, Susie, a black-and-tan German shepherd, was one dog that we could not take outside for a walk. She was still too afraid to walk on a leash, but we could now get her outside with the help of another dog. Susie had a buddy, Glacier, a large white husky that was easy to walk and handle. A volunteer would put Glacier on a leash, open Susie's cage, and Susie would follow Glacier outside and into the outdoor kennel, where she could enjoy fresh air and sunlight with her friend. (Both dogs are now in good homes.)

Once Captain Larry and his helpers got the fencing installed, there was still one critical deficiency in our new location. There was a small bathroom, but the toilet was missing. Monte Moore came to our rescue as he did on so many other occasions. He bought a toilet and installed it himself, so it was ready for the volunteers when they moved into the new location. By Thanksgiving, the dogs were comfortably settled into their new home, and everything was running smoothly. I made a point of arriving very early Thanksgiving morning, thinking there would be a shortage of volunteers, but we had a large crew all that day. Being with those wonderful dogs and puppies made that Thanksgiving one of the best I ever had, and I was filled with gratitude that the dogs had been rescued, that we had heat, and that we had a working toilet.

Mary Ann Maguire

One of the last individuals to join the Camp Husky workers was Butte native Mary Ann Maguire. Mary Ann had left Montana as a young woman, living out of state for a number of years, but she returned in the fall of 2008 to help her father. It was about five weeks after the rescue had begun when Mary Ann landed a temporary job with animal services, helping out at Camp Husky and serving as a kind of coordinator between animal control and the volunteers. She is still employed by animal services as I write this book. Volunteer Sue Madison worked with Mary Ann on weekdays and found her to be "a calming influence at Camp Husky. She was serving as a coordinator for the animal-services director, and she did a good job."

Mary Ann remembers the extreme cold at the Anselmo location: "I worked at Camp Husky for two weeks before we moved to the Arizona Street location. It was November and very cold at the Anselmo, and when I came to work in the morning we would occasionally find that a very young puppy had died, perhaps from the cold. We used to just hope that the weather would not drop below freezing since we had no heat there."

She recalled the many hardworking volunteers who made the rescue possible: "There was Shauna Burton, a petite young woman who amazed me with her ability to handle the dogs. She could walk and control three of our large dogs at one time. Watching her taking them through the door, I thought sure they would take off running and she would go flying through the air, but it never happened. She had a gift for handling dogs and was able to gently and calmly keep them under her control. Cheryl Drew was another hardworking volunteer whom I admired very much. The Weatherlys were regulars. Monte and Merlena were lifesavers. When the city cut off funds for the project, Monte and Merlena stepped up and rescued us financially, paying electric bills and wages of workers. Without their generosity we could not have kept Camp Husky open the last couple of months. I recall that Monte worked nearly every day of the week, and when we needed medicine for the dogs, Monte went out and bought it as well." It should be noted that Mary Ann and other workers continued to put in as many as fifty hours a week when their wages were cut back to ten hours. That is only one of the reasons I consider them volunteers as well. People like Dave, Tim, Ken, Katie, and Kacie labored for the dogs, not their small stipend.

By the time Mary Ann started working at Camp Husky, a well-established routine of early-morning feeding, walking, and cleaning was in place. Mary Ann had the opportunity to work with many different volunteers, and she has a fond memory of days when things ran so smoothly that she and the volunteers could relax for a few minutes. "After all the early-morning chores were completed with the dogs all fed and settled in after a little walk, the workers were often able to enjoy a short coffee break around nine fifteen while the dogs would serenade us with howling."

Reminiscing about her experiences at Camp Husky, Mary Ann recalled one of the big alpha dogs named Mufasa. "At first I thought Mufasa was scary because of his size, but once we took him out walking, we realized how very lovable he actually was. Sadly, his teeth were damaged. Mufasa was typical of how good natured most of the Camp Husky dogs were. He had an ear infection, and Tim and I had to clean out his ears. He let us treat him and was very patient and gentle with us.

"I am convinced that some of the dogs had never been touched by a human," she continued. "We learned that before Brode loaded the dogs on the bus and trailer with the goal of reaching Alaska, he kept them staked outside on his rural property in Colorado without shelter from the harsh winter weather or summer heat. Of course, these dogs had known nothing of human affection and kindness before the rescue. The change in the dogs when they were walked, petted, brushed, and given affection was truly remarkable. They just needed kindness and socialization.

"Working at Camp Husky, I saw miraculous changes in the dogs as we socialized them. It was the first time that someone had talked to them gently, petted them, walked them on a leash or brushed them. Pinkie was one of the dogs who were especially terrified of people, and she showed sure signs of never being socialized. Volunteer Cathy Decker gave extra care to Pinkie and eventually adopted her. Like Pinkie, all those dogs really needed was to be walked and socialized. Because they had not been socialized or trained by humans, the dogs often looked to their packs for leadership and protection. We found that most of the dogs were happier and more secure when placed in a kennel with one or two other dogs."

Mary Ann fondly recalls when the last litter of puppies was delivered by mother dog Phyllis, the lone survivor of the fourteen dogs taken to the Dillon shelter. Mary Ann's eyes filled with tears when she recalled the evening Phyllis allowed her and Tim to help her give birth. It was 4:00 p.m., and Mary Ann and Tim were about to lock up and leave the dogs for the night. Tim told Mary Ann that he had a feeling that Phyllis was about to give birth, so they decided to stay and help her. "It was so special to have this beautiful dog put her trust in us," recalled Mary Ann. Because Phyllis was the last mother to give birth at Camp Husky, she was renamed Momma. She has proven to be a loving family dog.

Working for animal services has given Mary Ann a unique ability to evaluate how well the Camp Husky dogs have integrated into the community. Mary Ann noted that "Butte now has more than thirty Camp Husky dogs living with families, and many of these were among our most troubled dogs at Camp Husky. While we here at animal control get many bite cases, there has never been a Camp Husky dog among them. The only complaint we have had has been from one woman who complains that some Camp Husky dogs living in her neighborhood 'look like wolves,'" said Mary Ann.

Brode Pleads Guilty: Camp Husky Now Has Two Hundred Dogs and Pups

Many people throughout Montana and even out of state started to inquire about adoption as soon as they learned of the rescue through the newspaper, radio, television, or Internet; however, adoptions, as well as spaying and neutering, were on hold until the city got legal possession of the dogs. Finally, on December 4, Philip Brode pleaded guilty to aggravated cruelty to animals and was given a suspended sentence in exchange for signing over ownership of the dogs to the Butte-Silver Bow government. The next day the *Montana Standard* reported that the number of Camp Husky dogs at last count was 100 adult dogs (this included older puppies that had been on the bus) and 50 young puppies born at the camp. The animal-services director was quoted as saying that 40 other dogs were in foster homes in Butte. Altogether there were 190 dogs and pups. The last of the pregnant females would soon give birth and bring the number over 200.

It had been nearly two months since the rescue began, but as the *Montana Standard* article explained, everything had been on hold until the case against Brode was resolved. "The dogs—up to this weekend—couldn't be adopted out to new homes, nor could they be spayed or neutered, because of the pending court case against Phillip Brode, 60." This article described the dogs as "huskies or husky mixes," yet most of us knew the dogs were primarily German shepherd or husky-shepherd mixes. I found that inaccuracy a little surprising, but those who knew the most about the dogs and did the work of running Camp Husky were not allowed to talk to the media at that time.

Many volunteers were disappointed at the agreement reached with Brode because he was allowed to take five dogs with him. In fairness, there was not much choice. When I met with Judge Kurt Kruger in his chambers, he explained the legal process regarding the Brode case. I am convinced that both the judge and the district attorney's office had no choice but to make this compromise with Brode. Had they not given Brode the five dogs, he would not have relinquished ownership, and spaying and neutering would have been delayed.

Most volunteers formed a special bond with one or a few dogs, and many ended up adopting one or two of those dogs. Captain Larry formed a special bond with a very large black-and-tan alpha dog named Bear when he took him for daily walks. From the photo I have of Bear, I would describe that magnificent long-haired dog as a Belgian Tervuren or Belgian Tervuren–shepherd mix. Larry tells how he was initially intimidated by Bear: "The first time I walked Bear he snarled and gave out some hardcore growls as we walked between the other dog kennels to get outdoors. As we walked down the pathway, all the dogs in the kennels on both sides of us started barking, growling, and snarling very loud in response to Bear. Later, I realized that the dogs were giving recognition to Bear as the alpha dog of their large pack. This was the best part of walking Bear each day. I can still see that large, noble dog prancing down the pathway, enjoying every moment as the other dogs acknowledged him as their leader." Larry was angry and heartbroken the morning he arrived at Camp Husky and learned that Bear was one of the dogs Brode had taken with him when he left for Colorado. When I interviewed him two years later, he was still worried about Bear and what had become of that great dog.

Mary Ann told me something significant about Brode. She described him as "a mean man" based on the abuse the dogs had endured in Colorado and on the bus. Mary Ann witnessed a cruel side of Brode that she has not been able to forget. She was at Camp Husky the day Brode was released from jail. After he took possession of his bus (which had been repaired by mechanics working for Butte-Silver Bow), he arrived at Camp Husky to pick up the five dogs he had chosen to take with him. He was angry to discover that they had been spayed or neutered. Apparently, he was planning on doing more breeding. Among the dogs he took was a purebred Belgian sheepdog, the mother of the dog I adopted. Mary Ann told me that she witnessed Brode taking his anger out by hitting that mild-mannered dog. If that was typical of his behavior toward the dogs, it is understandable that many of the females like Gypsy, Star, Susie, and Pinkie were terrified of people. Was a beating the only human contact they had known when they were with Brode? We were all sad that Brode took those dogs.

Cost of the Camp Husky Rescue

In any major animal rescue there is bound to be a concern about costs. That is probably one reason that officials from other communities turned a blind eye to the bus load of dogs as Brode drove from Colorado to Butte. This author wanted to know exactly how much the rescue actually cost the Butte-Silver Bow government; however, I was unable to gain access to the records. The following cost estimates are based on newspaper articles, e-mails from animal-services director Phyllis Ruana, and interviews with volunteers.

We were told that initial money for the rescue came from the animal-services budget—specifically, monies that had been allocated to purchase a truck for use by animal control. When donations of cash and checks came into Camp Husky, or when money was obtained from fundraisers, the money was handed over to Phyllis Ruana, and she in turn gave it to the director of Chelsea Bailey Animal Shelter (Erin Wall) to deposit into a nonprofit that Erin had started to pay for veterinary care for sick or injured dogs at the Chelsea Bailey Animal Shelter. When people wanted to make a donation to Camp Husky, they were asked to write a check to Albert's Angel Fund-Camp Husky.

According to Ruana, all bills she presented to Wall associated with Camp Husky were paid out of that fund. I believe only these two women knew how much money was coming into the fund. As for how those funds were actually used, I have no way of knowing.

From the very start of the rescue, volunteers did nearly all the work of running Camp Husky and caring for the dogs. The volunteer supervisors were paid a stipend, but it was soon cut so that they were volunteering fifty hours a week and being paid for ten hours, according to my interviews with them. Individuals and businesses donated the building to house the dogs, the kennels, fencing, food, nutritional supplements, dishes, cleaning supplies, blankets, laundry services, grooming services, and printing services. The one big necessity that was not donated was veterinary care. Ruana estimated that medical costs alone amounted to over $25,000. However, she also acknowledged that donations of cash amounted to about $30,000, so donations covered those expenses. In other words, most of the essential costs of caring for the dogs were covered by donations.

One day I sat down and calculated the hours contributed by those of us at Camp Husky, excluding those who received a stipend and those who conducted fundraising and adoption events. If one uses a meager $13 hourly wage, the total would come to about $200,000. That is not even counting the individuals who donated money and supplies, or the businesses that donated space, services, fencing, and nutritional supplements. Butte and the surrounding area might well be described as poor—not in spirit but in cash—and the Camp Husky rescue occurred right after the recession hit, when many businesses were floundering, and folks had lost jobs in Butte and across the nation. There were no funds set aside for an animal emergency, or any big emergency for that matter, but it has been my observation since childhood that often those with the least are among the most generous. That was the case with the good people of Butte. In my research I discovered that many volunteers made cash donations to Camp Husky, and many other individuals from around the state and out of state donated money to help us. I was at Camp Husky one day when a note with a donation arrived from a woman in Chicago. It lifted our spirits to think that someone so far away would think of us and send good wishes.

Although donations were still coming in, around the beginning of 2009, volunteers were told that there were no more funds for Camp Husky, and that is when Monte and Merlena stepped up to pay the utility bills and the salaries of the men from the Butte Pre-Release Center (Tim and Kenny). Monte and Merlena purchased medicine and any supplies we needed for the dogs. Few of us knew of their generosity and the essential role they played in keeping Camp Husky operating during the last few months. This author does remember the couple walking into Camp Husky one day and someone showing them a huge utility bill that had arrived in the mail. I witnessed Monte taking out his checkbook and writing a check then and there. I was deeply touched at the time, but I had no idea that they were covering other expenses as well. Cindy summed up their contribution quite well: "We simply could not have made it through the last few months of operating Camp Husky without Monte and Mer."

I also learned in my research that some dogs that were being fostered at the time, to be later returned to Camp Husky, missed the free spay-and-neuter clinic. Volunteers Christy Stack and Cathy Decker were told by management that there was no money to spay these dogs. The women knew that there was no hope of finding homes for the dogs unless they were spayed, and so they took them to a veterinarian and paid for the surgery out of their own pockets.

There were two statements made to me in e-mails that I do not understand and cannot explain. Phyllis Ruana said that the "last report I had from Erin before I left, I believe there was still money in the line item for the Camp Husky Project, but you would have to ask them for the report and they do have it." If there was money in the fund toward the end of the project, why did it not go to helping with the expenses that individual volunteers were taking care of, such as utility bills and medical care? The answer may be that there was poor communication between the volunteers and Erin Wall, who had control of the money donated for Camp Husky. Phyllis stated in an e-mail, "Regarding Albert's Angel Fund, Butte-Silver Bow government really doesn't know what goes on with that account as it is a separate private fund."

In addition, Phyllis also explained that a major cost of running Camp Husky involved extra pay for the animal-control officers. She said, "A large portion of the cost for Camp Husky came from paying Charley Dick and the time that the two other ACOs logged when they did anything regarding this case (which was as little as I possibly would allow)."

This author has no idea what the animal-control officers were doing related to Camp Husky that would have involved a significant amount of time or labor. Once again, it would have been much better if animal services had maintained open communication with the volunteers and shared information about how much money was in Albert's Angel Fund, what the city was contributing, and what was being paid out in costs.

Butte Spay-Neuter Task Force Makes an Enormous Contribution

There was one expense so large that donations could not have covered it. Had we had to pay full price for all the dogs and puppies to be spayed and neutered, we simply could not have done it. We were very fortunate that some years prior to the rescue, a highly committed small group of individuals in Butte, concerned with the problem of pet overpopulation, had organized the Butte Spay-Neuter Task Force. This group started out providing coupons at local veterinary clinics for twenty dollars off their services to help low-income folks spay and neuter their pets. By 2004, these same activists had started hosting a no-cost/low-cost spay/neuter clinic twice a year. My sister Penny, a registered nurse, and I both volunteered. It was heartwarming to see how many people of all ages helped out at these important events. I remember two older women who came in one day with about five stray cats that they had been feeding. They explained to me that there was just no way they could afford to spay and neuter these cats on their fixed incomes from social security. Another memory is of a sweet golden retriever mix that had already had three litters of puppies. Her low-income family was very grateful that they could finally spay their dog. These clinics receive some financial help from the Butte-Silver Bow government but depend primarily on donations and fundraising events. People like Judy Kruzech, Phyllis Hargrave, and Noorjahan Parwana are responsible for keeping this great service in Butte. Shortly after these clinics started, the number of pets going to the shelter, dogs being picked up by animal control, people being treated for dog bites, and newspaper ads for free pets all dropped significantly.

The dedicated volunteers who operated the Butte Spay-Neuter Task Force also made a huge difference for Camp Husky by providing a clinic just for our dogs and puppies on a weekend in early December 2008. Operating a spay-neuter clinic takes a lot of volunteers. While the veterinarians and vet techs are paid for their services, many volunteers are needed to register the dogs, shave the dogs, clean and sterilize the equipment, and administer anesthetic. In addition, volunteers are needed to sit with the recovering dogs or hold puppies, keeping them warm and observing them until they recover from the anesthesia. It is a wonderful service, and I only wish that every city in this country could offer it to low-income pet owners.

On the day of the Camp Husky clinic, I arrived early to find several volunteers busy transporting dogs to the Butte Plaza Mall, which had generously provided a large space for this critical operation. Most of the regular weekend volunteers would be at the mall all day, along with a number of additional community people who were helping out at the clinic. I chose to stay at Camp Husky and make sure all the kennels were clean when the dogs returned. After a while I noticed that only one dog remained, the very timid young mother I mentioned earlier, Susie. Tim was trying to get Susie out of her cage. As I mopped a nearby kennel, I watched him gently coaxing the German shepherd. The dog was displaying fear aggression, and I felt tense and concerned for both man and dog.

When I next looked up from my work, I saw that Susie was cradled in Tim's arms. He just held her and talked to her, and soon Susie was in a truck on the way to the mall.

When I interviewed Butte-Silver Bow Chief Executive Paul Babb, he expressed sincere appreciation for the spay-neuter task-force members and all they have done to help animals in the community, most especially the Camp Husky dogs. A few days after the clinic, the *Montana Standard* published a letter to the editor entitled "Year-end Gratitude for Life in Butte," written by Andrea Stierle. Among the many things Andrea gave thanks for were the new heated home for the Camp Husky dogs on Arizona Street and the spay-neuter clinic where she and her husband, Don, had assisted:

"We spent Sunday helping the puppies at Camp Husky recover from the spay/neuter clinic. By 5:00 p.m. we were literally covered from head to foot with puppy chow and thoroughly enjoyed the day. Again, so many people spent the day helping these helpless puppies, as well as the older dogs, on the road to adoption.

"The mall provided a great space for the clinic, and Robert Edwards and John Richen stepped forward to provide a warm space for Camp Husky when the Anselmo proved inappropriate. So many people have volunteered countless hours helping these beautiful dogs since October."

Fundraising and Adoption Events

People all over Montana and beyond learned about Camp Husky dogs from newspaper and television, as well as the Internet. Volunteers worked hard to promote adoptions, but none worked harder than Barb LeProwse and a group of her friends. Starting December 6, volunteers Barb LeProwse, Katie Donovan, Lee Black, and other friends of Barb's held their first fundraising and adoption event at the Butte Plaza Mall, Kmart, and Quality Supply store. Barb's team of dedicated volunteers planned, organized, and conducted these events. Reporter Robin Jordan, wife of volunteer Dave Jordan, put a story in the *Butte Weekly* promoting adoptions as well. Pauline's Pet Boutique donated many hours of labor, grooming our puppies for these events. Later, this same small business would donate grooming services for our dogs and puppies on the day their new owners were coming to take them home.

While puppies were on display at the adoption events, Barb also displayed large collages of pictures she had taken of the many adult dogs and older puppies available for adoption. One of our black-and-tan German shepherds, Star, was adopted right after a man saw her picture and just knew he wanted that dog. Barb's hardworking committee was responsible for many successful adoptions by people in Butte and people from out of town who just happened to see the dogs and puppies while they were shopping. Many people I interviewed said that they first decided to adopt after seeing some of the dogs at one of Barb's events. About this same time, Katie Donovan made a video of the dogs to promote adoptions on the Internet.

In addition to promoting adoptions, Barb and her friends raised a good amount of money, making about $3,000 in one day alone. Barb's volunteers also raised money by selling a beautiful 2009 calendar with photos of our dogs and puppies. Once again, a local business, Insty-Prints, donated its services.

Chief Executive Reflects on the Rescue

In an interview on February 10, 2012, Chief Executive Babb reflected on the rescue. He said that Butte had three options. We could have done what Dillon and cities in other states had done: send Brode on his way out of town and ignore the problem. A second option was to euthanize all the dogs. According to Babb, neither option was considered by local government or animal services. "From the start we decided to take responsibility. We really had no idea what we were getting into when the police arrested Brode and animal control seized the dogs. Director of animal services was a brand new position for Butte-Silver Bow government, and we had only recently hired Phyllis Ruana, so she was inexperienced. Phyllis was willing to take on the project; however, it meant that other duties had to be neglected, and she would resign by the end of her first year. Our legal system was also stressed by the dog crisis."

The chief executive equated Camp Husky to a MASH unit in wartime: "Throwing everything together in one day was an enormous undertaking. I was there that first day of the rescue. I remember hearing all the dogs barking, but people were calm and worked together effectively. There was a sense that we were just going to do this thing, and, sure enough, things fell into place." Babb believes that most communities have people with the know-how to accomplish a rescue the way Butte did. "The difference is that Butte actually did it. People from local government and the community saw what needed to be done and did it. We were not paralyzed by fears of what could go wrong." Babb believes that the willingness in Butte to take on a huge rescue operation can be attributed in part to the town's history. "I think that local government and community volunteers were willing and able to take on this enormous challenge, and the city council was supportive, because risk and difficult challenges had been a way of life in Butte for many years. When miners went to work each day, they and their families knew that there was a real risk that they might not return. That willingness to risk is still a part of Butte."

Babb had heard from citizens upset that Brode was allowed to take some dogs with him. The chief executive told me that he saw Brode driving his bus into the Walmart parking lot instead of heading directly out of town after he was released from jail and had picked up the five dogs. Worried that angry citizens might confront Brode, Babb called the police and asked them to escort Brode out of town.

The Dogs Find Homes and Camp Husky Closes

After the spay-neuter clinic, the adult dogs and puppies were ready for adoption. Our oldest male dog, Wooley, a German shepherd, was adopted by the Lawrences when they were volunteering at the spay-neuter clinic and could not resist the gentle giant they cared for that day. The majority of puppies and dogs were adopted directly out of Camp Husky by individuals and families from Butte and nearly every city and town in southwestern Montana; however, a surprising number of people drove from the far north of Montana, eastern Montana, and as far west as Spokane and Seattle, Washington. A doctor drove about four hours from eastern Montana and asked to adopt our oldest female. When I was working one Saturday, a young woman walked into Camp Husky after driving more than two hours and explained that she wanted to adopt an adult dog that would be hard to adopt because of age, a handicap, or other problem. That woman's compassion lifted my spirits for the whole week!

Cindy McIlveen and Jocelyn Dodge drove to Oregon and Washington to find homes for some of our dogs. I was told that one of our cute females, Abby, went to a home with an MD in Seattle, where she was pampered, and my records show that Jackson, a very large, long-haired, dark husky-shepherd was adopted by a woman in Glide, Oregon. Our oldest dogs, our puppies, and our most socialized dogs were the first to be adopted. By April 2009, when we were forced to close up, we still had dogs that had not been placed. Volunteers either adopted them or fostered them until suitable homes could be found.

I was reminded daily of Camp Husky by the dog I had adopted. I watched a gentle but fearful young dog that had experienced all the horror of the bus trip evolve very slowly but surely into a confident and happy member of a family. Two years later it came to me that the story of Camp Husky needed to be told.

Telling the Dogs' Stories

Cindy McIlveen and Katie Donovan kept records of the dogs adopted out of Camp Husky, and those records would enable me to locate many dogs. Had it not been for the records that these women and other volunteers saved after Camp Husky closed, I could not have researched and written this book.

Shelters in Billings, Bozeman, Hamilton, Helena, and Missoula took many of our adult dogs and puppies. The largest number of dogs by far went to the Humane Society of Western Montana in Missoula, where they were well cared for, and the director of this shelter graciously helped me in my research, putting me in touch with most who had adopted. In searching for those who adopted our dogs, I was also able to obtain assistance from Help for Homeless Pets in Billings. I tried but failed to obtain information from the other shelters.

When I set out to find out what had happened to the dogs, I never dreamed that I would be able to locate so many and that owners would be so willing to share their stories with me. I was able to interview about one hundred individuals or families who adopted one or two dogs. I chose eighty-one to feature in this book.

I have an album of photos taken of the dogs as they came off the bus and were put in kennels that first day. They are filthy, with matted fur. Their faces are sweet, but fear shows in their eyes and body language. Then I have photographs of these same dogs sent to me by their owners. Dogs that were so skinny and sick have filled out and now look radiantly healthy. They have the beauty and confidence of dogs that know they are loved family members.

In researching this book I learned that three different individuals, living in three different states, are alive today because they adopted a Camp Husky dog. The vast majority of dogs went to good homes, and they are thriving now. When I started interviewing and writing the stories, two of the oldest dogs had passed away, and three other dogs had died from accidents. I shared their owners' pain as they talked about their losses. In the five years since I started collecting stories, a few other dogs have died from a variety of illnesses. As I am finishing this book, the youngest puppies are seven, and our adults range from eight to fourteen years. Nearly seven years after Donald Frost started the rescue, most of the adult dogs and puppies are thriving in great homes with people who love them. These dogs, from the oldest adults to the puppies born at Camp Husky, have enriched the lives of those who adopted them. Some, like Bob, Mylie, and Pearl, have saved the lives of their owners or a little dog or cat. Others are service dogs or work in stores, like Bella, Bucky, Luci, and Marcel. Many, like Apollo, Boons, Django, Fiver, Honey, and Sophie live with babies and young children and are very loving and protective of their little family members. Many live alone with a man or woman and are the best friend to these individuals, bringing comfort, laughter, and fun. As I interviewed those who adopted, I heard many phrases repeated again and again.

"He is the best dog I have ever had."

"Lizzie—best dog in the world."

"I don't know what I would do without her."

"I feel safe when alone because of this dog."

"He is so gentle and patient with the kids."

"He has helped me cope with a terrible loss."

"She is so smart and funny and fun to take along on a hiking or cross-country skiing trip."

"He is the best fishing buddy."

"She is my best friend."

"He protected me from two men breaking into the house."

"I would not be alive now if we had not adopted her. She saved my life."

"I am so grateful for the volunteers who rescued these dogs."

Author's note: I conducted interviews with dog owners from 2011 to 2014, with many follow-up interviews in 2015.

CHAPTER 5

Dogs with a Mission

Our Camp Husky dogs play important roles in the lives of the individuals and families who adopted them. While all dogs that are loved have a mission, in this chapter I introduce twelve Camp Husky dogs who have given special blessings to the individuals and families who adopted them.

In the first story, a young military wife tells how her dog can read her moods and help her cope with loneliness and long periods of separation from her husband. She also described the special bond she has with her beautiful white German shepherd–husky dog. Many of the owners I interviewed described this same kind of emotional bond.

In the fourth story, we learn how a dog named Shadow instinctively knew how to comfort a grieving family. An article entitled "Pets" in the May 2012 issue of *Prevention* magazine suggests that "the ability to empathize with humans may be hardwired into canine DNA. Research reveals that your dog's instinct to comfort and nuzzle you may have simply developed over time." It is also possible that the ability dogs have to empathize "may come from their wolf ancestors, who were highly social and cooperative by nature."

Sergeant Huck (a.k.a. Rocky), a Gentle Pup with a Special Assignment

While our first lady, Michelle Obama, is working to help military families, one of our Camp Husky dogs has a special mission to help one particular military family. Newcomers to Butte, Erin Lanrigan Macer and her husband, Marine Staff Sergeant Josh Macer, adopted one of our three-month-old puppies in February 2009. Josh was shopping at Quality Supply on the day that volunteer Barb LeProwse and her friends held one of several in-store fundraising/adoption events in Butte. After seeing some of our puppies, Josh phoned Erin to suggest that she drive over to look at the adorable puppies. Josh wanted a canine companion for Erin when he was away on recruiting trips and later deployed overseas. As recent arrivals, the Macers knew nothing about Camp Husky. However, Erin had had a German shepherd–husky mix as a child, so our dogs were a perfect match for her.

Erin immediately drove out to see the puppies: "I saw two little fluff balls. One of the brothers had a little spot on the top of his head and the sweetest eyes. I immediately loved this pup called Rocky; however, I was told that someone had already asked for him, so we happily decided to adopt his brother. When I got to Camp Husky to complete the adoption papers, I was told that the folks who asked for Rocky had failed to show up. The volunteer in charge told us that if I would pay the adoption fee and sign the papers right then, I could adopt Rocky. I got my boy, the puppy I felt I needed from the minute I first saw him."

When they took their puppy (now named Huck) home, the Macers thought he had been given all his shots at Camp Husky; however, only a few months after his adoption, Huck became very sick with parvovirus. It took a stay in the hospital and a blood transfusion to pull Huck through the illness. "The poor guy got really sick, and I have never been so emotional in my life, worried he would not survive. Huck is very healthy now as an adult. Additionally, we give him supplements for his joints, knowing that German shepherds are prone to hip problems." (Fortunately, no one I interviewed has reported hip problems, even with the older dogs.)

Like so many Camp Husky adopters, Erin described her dog as "the best dog I have ever had and by far the strangest, most loving, and funniest dog I have ever owned." He is also especially gentle and affectionate toward children and cats. "Huck loves, *loves*, *looooves* little kids. Whenever children are visiting our house, Huck is enthralled and won't leave them even for a second.

"As a little puppy, Huck quickly bonded with our cat, Houdini, and the two play *a lot*. Our frolicsome tomcat likes to start fights and get Huck all riled up, but Houdini is also very loving and will groom Huck's face and paws when our dog is sleeping. Huck has never once hurt Houdini. Huck understands how small and vulnerable our cat is, and he is careful when he plays with his best friend. Huck is the same with other dogs and cats he meets, playful but gentle."

Erin and Huck have a close and special bond. "I am obsessed with him, and I don't know what I would do without him. My husband is on active duty with the Marine Corps, and he travels out of town on recruiting duty and out of state for meetings and training. When we moved to Butte, I was alone a lot in a town where I knew no one. On the day we brought Huck home from Camp Husky, Josh had to go out of state for a few weeks, so my puppy and I were alone except for my cat. I believe that time alone together forged a powerful bond between us. Now, whenever Josh leaves and we are alone, I swear Huck goes into superprotective mode, alert to every noise at night while lying halfway out the bedroom door. He has been my shoulder to cry on and a body to hug when I have no family around. Huck just seems to know whenever I am having a down day, as he will come over and lie right beside me. He is my best friend and sunshine, and we do everything together. Whether I am fishing, horseback riding, or just going for a walk, Huck stays right by my side.

"While assigned to Butte, Josh and I have been living out of town, far from the nearest neighbor. One night in the middle of winter when we had three inches of snow on the ground and Josh was out of town, a man knocked on the door, and I felt frightened. Then Huck gave such a loud, deep, and intimidating growl that the man took off. I never found out what this stranger wanted, but I sure felt a lot safer that night knowing Huck was with me. Huck is a lover, and I could never imagine him hurting any animal or person unless I was in real danger. I know with certainty that if I were ever in danger, Huck would be there for me."

Erin described what she sees as unique ways that Huck communicates both verbally and nonverbally. "Huck is a talker. He talks when we wake up, he talks when he is happy, he talks when we come home, and he talks when he wants attention." In addition, Huck is adept at using facial expression to communicate affection and happiness. "He bares his teeth to smile! Some folks might find this facial expression kind of scary, but we know he means no harm. He also crinkles his ears when he is happy." These communication behaviors that Erin described are common among Camp Husky dogs, including the two this author adopted, and explain, in part, why most owners describe their dogs as distinctive and wonderful companions.

Whenever Huck is out with the Macers on a lake or river he becomes a lifeguard. "When Huck was about a year old, my eleven-year-old sister was visiting us and swimming in the lake. Although my sister could swim well, she pretended to be drowning and called out to Huck, who was watching her from the shore. My powerful white dog swam out to her, and despite her protests, pulled her to shore by holding her water shoe in his mouth. The next summer when my sister and I were out on a river again, Huck got worried about our safety and actually dragged each of us back to shore by again holding on to our water shoes. He did not give us an option. He was bringing us back to shore!

"I am so glad that the Butte community rescued the dogs on the bus and that we adopted Huck. I couldn't imagine my life without him. It is really tough being a military spouse. All my family is far away, and Josh and I have to move a lot and make new friends. Huck has been my rock to lean on while we have lived in Montana.

"More than anything else, Huck has taught me about love. I have never loved an animal as much as I love him. I understand him, and he understands me. My husband will be deploying soon, and I am OK with it because I have my dog with me, and I will not be alone. I will feel safe with Huck beside me. He is truly a one-of-a-kind dog, and I am blessed to have him in my life. I wish I could thank all the good folks who volunteered at Camp Husky and made it possible for me to have this brave, funny, affectionate, and gentle companion."

Before leaving Montana for a new assignment, the Macers adopted a buddy for Huck, a female Catahoula heeler cross named Siouxzie. This military family moved to North Carolina where Erin prepared herself to face her husband's overseas deployment. "Once again," Erin wrote, "I am so thankful to have Huck in another new place where I know absolutely no one! Thank you, Camp Husky people, for everything you have done! Oh, and Huck gets very strange looks around here, everyone is so terrified of him—if only they knew how big his heart is!"

Bella (a.k.a. Eleanor Rigby) Helps a Returning Veteran Cope with the Physical and Emotional Wounds of War

Thousands of men who served in World War II, Korea, and Vietnam owed their lives to the courage, intelligence, and loyalty of German shepherd dogs. As one of our volunteers, formerly a photographer during the Vietnam War, said, "The German shepherd scout dogs were truly the greatest heroes of that war." Currently, German shepherds and Belgian shepherds are again protecting our troops in Iraq and Afghanistan. There is a second group of canine heroes, including many Labradors and golden retrievers as well as German shepherds, who are helping returning veterans cope with both the physical and emotional wounds of war. One of our Camp Husky pups was destined to join the ranks of these therapy dogs, helping a young soldier returning from Iraq.

Theresa and her son, David, love dogs, and when David was in elementary school they adopted two Siberian husky puppies. The female became David's special companion and slept on his bed every night until David graduated from high school and enlisted in the army. This same loyal dog, although by then quite old and sick, was waiting for David in 2007 when he returned from service in Iraq with a physical injury and posttraumatic stress disorder. Losing a beloved companion dog is always painful, but it was especially devastating for David when his dog died less than a year after his return home. David was not the only one grieving; the family's other old dog, Shawn, missed the companion he had loved since they were both puppies. Theresa wanted to help both David and Shawn while they grieved, but she feared that introducing an adult dog into the home might be too traumatic for thirteen-year-old Shawn.

Then she learned there were ten Camp Husky puppies from the same litter available for adoption at the Missoula shelter. One of our mother dogs, Nellie, had a large litter of thirteen puppies, and ten were taken to the Humane Society of Western Montana in Missoula and given names from Beatles songs when put up for adoption. Theresa decided to adopt one as a Christmas gift for David. She chose a female named Eleanor Rigby, but David renamed his new puppy Bella.

Bella was only six weeks old and recovering from her recent spaying when Theresa presented the puppy to David as his Christmas present. I have a photo of the young veteran holding and admiring his adorable puppy that Christmas morning. What one cannot tell from the photo is that little Bella was sick and having trouble eating; however, with good care, Bella soon recovered and was able to devote herself to helping David and Shawn heal. Ideally, puppies stay with their mothers until eight weeks and are spayed when a little older, but with so many dogs and puppies at Camp Husky, many were adopted and spayed or neutered earlier than the ideal age.

While David and Theresa bonded immediately with this super-affectionate German shepherd–husky mix, Shawn wanted nothing to do with the puppy. However, Bella was persistent in her efforts to win the affection of the old black husky. At first, when Shawn would be resting in his favorite spot in front of the fireplace and Bella would approach him, Shawn would get up and walk away to escape her. The little puppy would then crawl slowly toward the old dog until she caught his eye. Then she would paw the air to hold his attention. Shawn's determination to remain aloof was not as strong as Bella's persistent campaign to win his friendship. After several months, Bella's efforts paid off, and David and Theresa noticed that old Shawn was warming up to the puppy and actually enjoying her company.

After Shawn passed away, Theresa and David adopted a young male Lab cross from the Missoula shelter as a companion for Bella. Bella is now the top dog, frequently reminding the very active Lab that he is at the bottom of the pack. Her favorite trick is to hide in the yard and leap out at the Lab when he isn't looking.

Asked if Bella talks, David and Theresa responded, "Oh, does she ever talk! Bella will carry on long conversations." For example, after dinner and a full work day, Theresa likes to just sit on the sofa to relax. However, Bella thinks this is her time for attention from Theresa, and she starts talking for as long as fifteen minutes. "I wish I could always understand what she is saying," said Theresa. "Bella is definitely trying to communicate something, but I often have no idea what it is. Sometimes I do understand. It might be that she wants me to brush her coat, and, in that case, she will talk to me and also point her head toward the place where I keep her brush. At other times, I have no idea what she is trying to tell me."

If Bella has a fault it is that she is too affectionate. Bella is a dog who adores people. Theresa described her as "annoyingly affectionate with people who come to the house. She likes to put her mouth around the hand of people as if to lead them into the house. She never tries to bite and shows no aggression, but she is large—eighty-five pounds—and sometimes people feel intimidated until they get to know her." Theresa and David took Bella to trainers to try to break her of being so affectionate, but nothing has worked.

As a college teacher, I have encountered too many young men and women like David, returning from Iraq and Afghanistan with wounds that don't show and are difficult to heal. In his moving book *Until Tuesday*, army captain and Purple Heart recipient Luis Carlos Montalvan described how his golden retriever service dog, Tuesday, helped him survive PTSD, a brain injury, and a painful back injury resulting from his service in Iraq. With all his emotional and physical pain, every day challenges Luis and demands as much courage as his wartime service in Iraq. Luis described how he spends every moment of his life with Tuesday beside him, supporting him physically and emotionally, and how at the end of each day when he returns to his small apartment, Tuesday curls up with him on the queen-size bed, and there is "the warm contentment of two hearts melting into one."

Thankfully, David has the support of his mother and his own therapy dog, Bella. Although Bella never had the elaborate training of an official service dog like Tuesday, she seems to know that she is a dog with a mission to heal David with her love and affection.

Bucky Returns the Love to the Woman Who Saved Him

It is often said that the good you do returns to you. One of Bella's brothers is a perfect example of that proverb. Volunteer Dave Jordan was devoted to all the puppies he cared for at Camp Husky, but one puppy named Bucky with bandaged legs was especially dear to Dave. "When I looked into his eyes, he stole my heart." Apparently, the staff at the veterinary hospital that treated Bucky thought he should be euthanized because of the birth defect that left him with deformed legs. In the words of Ralph Waldo Emerson, "People only see what they are prepared to see." While the veterinarians may have seen a "defective pup," Dave saw a loving fellow creature. Dave knew he needed to protect Bucky by finding him a good home right away.

Since he and his wife, Robin, had cats that did not like dogs, Dave turned to his mother-in-law, Fay Taylor, for help. Several years before, when Dave's father, Mark, a former police officer and later bailiff in Butte, was in the last stages of lung cancer, Fay had adopted his little Boston bull terrier. Later, when her only son died in 2002, Fay also welcomed her son's border collie into her home. When Dave told Fay about Bucky's plight, she told him to bring the puppy to her house. Bucky got a loving owner and two female dogs to mother him. That little puppy with bandaged deformed legs grew into one of the largest Camp Husky dogs, weighing 130 pounds and standing so tall his head can rest on the kitchen counter.

When I visited with Fay, the ninety-five-year-old music teacher and violinist told me how Bucky has returned the love she gave him in so many ways. When Fay walks outdoors each morning to fill her bird feeder, the faithful Bucky stands close beside her, so she can lean on him for support. When Fay notices that her border collie is not eating her dinner, she asks Bucky to "make Titi eat."

"Bucky gladly obeys my command," said Fay, "and he gets Titi to eat by barking, whining, and generally making a pest of himself while she is near her food bowl. Titi becomes so angry with Bucky that she eats all her food just to keep him from having it."

One of the many remarkable things about Bucky is his sense of humor and love of pranks. As soon as he was bigger than Maggie, the Boston bull terrier, he would drag her by her sweater and slide her on the hardwood floor, which he thought was the funniest thing in the world. In spite of Bucky's little game, he and Maggie were bosom buddies, going with Dave and Robin on long walks and camping trips until Maggie died in 2012.

By far, Bucky's favorite prank to this day is the "water trick." One evening when Bucky was about a year old, Robin was down on her hands and knees fixing something in her mother's house when the big dog walked by and, for some unknown reason, dropped a mouthful of water on Robin's back. Robin screamed! Apparently, Bucky decided it was such a good trick that Robin has to be careful whenever she is on her hands and knees. Bucky has caught her several times with the water trick. Considering the love he bestows on her mother, Robin does not begrudge the big dog his little prank.

Although Bucky lives with Fay, Dave and Robin are responsible for his exercise routine. Dave and Bucky have enjoyed long daily hikes in the mountains around Butte as well as frequent camping trips into the mountains with Robin. In 2011, Dave had to restrict Bucky's exercise to the backyard because the gentle dog developed arthritis related to his birth defect. "It broke my heart not to be able to take him out for his walks," said Dave. Bucky's condition improved, and their veterinarian recommended that Dave and Bucky resume their daily walks in the woods but for much shorter distances. Dave is very happy to get his walking buddy back. Bucky continues to be a faithful service dog to Fay in spite of his own pain and disability. Each day he brings unconditional love, joy, and laughter to Fay, Robin, and Dave.

Update: Bucky had extensive surgery on his legs in 2014, followed by physical therapy and at-home therapy sessions from Dave. The puppy that Dave saved is doing just fine and is in great form. In an article about our heavy snowfall during the winter of 2015, Robin described how at age seven, Bucky is very active and still enjoys the snow and the cold, unlike many of us humans. "I wish I loved winter as much as our dog Bucky does. Bucky, the 130-pound husky–German shepherd, thinks snow is the best thing in the world. He loves nothing better than to run full-tilt in the deep snow we have been getting. He lies in it, grinning from doggy ear-to-ear without feeling the cold through his thick fur. He even loves eating it in big mouthfuls" (*Butte Weekly*, December 30, 2015).

Shadow's Love Helps a Grieving Family and a Grandmother Recovering from Cancer

Shadow was only five weeks old when he went to live with the Barry family of Butte. Adopted by their second son, sixteen-year-old Tanner, the puppy soon became an integral part of the life of Christine and Daniel and their four sons. Christine described Shadow as being highly intelligent and very sensitive and supportive to family members. When he was first adopted, the Barry family had an aging Great Pyrenees, and Shadow became very attached to her. By the time Shadow was one year old, his canine companion was very sick, spending most of her time lying on a blanket. Shadow would gather his stuffed toys and place them next to her in a loving gesture of concern.

Shadow grew into a very tall and lanky adult with beautiful green eyes. His long fur with fawn, gray, and black coloring suggests that he is a Belgian Tervuren, German shepherd, and husky mix. He is also a very vocal dog. Shadow's most notable characteristics are his devotion to his family and his desire to protect them from both physical and emotional harm.

In 2011, the Barry family was devastated by the sudden and unexpected death of their third son, Cullen, then seventeen years old. Shadow was with the young man when he died, and the dog grieved along with the family. For the longest time, Shadow would not go into the bedroom where Cullen died, and he tried to prevent other members of the family from entering the room as well.

Christine Barry, an elementary school counselor, told me how Shadow seemed to understand what the entire family was going through and did everything he could to comfort the grieving parents and their three surviving sons. "Whenever I was at home, thinking of our son and so overwhelmed with grief that I had to sit down, Shadow was suddenly there beside me. When I couldn't stop the tears, he came over to me and put his head in my lap to comfort me." Christine credits this wonderful family dog with helping her to endure every parent's worst nightmare. "There are times when our grief has been so profound that words don't reach us, and all we crave is a loving touch. Shadow understands this and is a natural healer."

Unfortunately, several of the Barry's neighbors objected to Shadow, perhaps because he looks, as do many of our long-haired shepherds, like a wolf. On more than one occasion the Barrys had to stop neighborhood children from throwing rocks at Shadow when he was in his backyard kennel. Whatever the reason for this dislike of Shadow, this amazingly loving dog was in real danger.

Although Shadow had never attacked a person or animal, in the spring of 2012, the neighbors pressured animal services to seize Shadow and take him to the Chelsea Bailey Animal Shelter. The problem was that Shadow was very intelligent and an escape artist who doesn't like to be alone and knows how to turn a doorknob with his mouth. Neighbors complained when they saw Shadow walking around the neighborhood. If the family locked him in his kennel, the neighborhood children might hurt him, and if they left him in the house, he might get outside.

The prospect of Shadow being seized and taken to the shelter was especially frightening to the Barry family because they knew the shelter director was hostile toward the Camp Husky dogs. Fearing Shadow would be killed if taken to the shelter, Camp Husky volunteer Cindy McIlveen encouraged Christine to get Shadow out of town to a safe place as soon as possible, and the Barry family took Cindy's advice.

In 2012, Shadow moved to the country with Christine's parents, Jodie and Ray Tilman, who lived on twenty acres. Christine reported that Shadow was being "spoiled rotten" by her parents. Shadow became good buddies with the couple's black Lab, and the two dogs had lots of fun playing together. Christine's dad no longer had to throw a ball for the Lab, because Shadow took on that job. "Shadow throws a tennis ball for the Lab, the Lab brings it back, and Shadow throws it again until both dogs are exhausted," said Christine.

Christine's parents soon came under the loving spell of Shadow. Then in 2013, Christine's father died of kidney and liver cancer, adding to the grief that Shadow's family had to endure. Once again, Shadow used his gift of healing love, this time to encompass Christine's mom, a cancer survivor herself, and help her cope with the loss of her husband. "Since my dad's death, Shadow has taken over as my mom's protector, and he is constantly by her side," wrote Christine. "Although he has a nice new doggie bed, Shadow likes to climb in bed and cuddle next to my mom. And in turn, Mom's cat actually cuddles up with Shadow and licks his ears, so Shadow thinks he is in dog heaven." Love is the most powerful healing force in the universe, and dogs like Shadow are the masters at giving unconditional love. "Shadow is just a big love bug," said Christine.

When Shadow moved to the country, it was especially hard on ten-year-old Carson to be separated from the loving dog when the boy needed him most. Carson missed the way Shadow would walk beside him, always pushing the boy as far away as possible from the street to protect him from cars. Luckily, the Barry family visits their grandmother frequently, and Carson gets to play with Shadow, even giving him baths when needed. When Jodie goes out of town, Shadow boards with Samantha Collier at All about the Dawg, a special treat for both Shadow and Sam.

Mia (#53) Comforts a Widow

While Denise Fett of Bozeman was grieving the deaths of her husband and the companion dog they both loved, the story of the school bus with 125 dogs first appeared on the nightly news in southwestern Montana. As she watched that broadcast, Denise's attention focused on the face of a white dog looking through a window of the bus. There was an uncanny resemblance between the dog looking out the window and the recently deceased wolf-malamute dog that had comforted Denise after the loss of her husband. Denise just knew she had to have that dog on the bus. "I am going to adopt that white dog," she said to herself.

Denise knew the Camp Husky dogs would need good homes, and she needed a dog to fill the double void in her life. Denise kept phoning to find out when the dogs would be available for adoption, and in November she made the ninety-mile trip to Butte to adopt her white dog. When she walked into the Camp Husky building, she looked around and saw the many mother dogs with their puppies. While she was scanning the room, she was drawn to one quiet, calm, pure-white German shepherd mother dog named Mia (#53) with her puppies. At the sight of that one dog, her heart melted. "That is my girl," Denise told herself. Denise filled out the adoption papers, but since Mia was still nursing her puppies, she had to wait a few weeks to take Mia home.

While Mia bonded quickly with Denise, the dog had problems with separation anxiety. When Denise left for work, Mia did some damage to the furniture and a door. Surprisingly, the problem was solved when Denise put her in a room where she could look out a large window. Additionally, Denise adopted a husky from the Bozeman shelter to keep Mia company. With a playmate and a loving owner, she is now one happy dog.

Denise told me when we first spoke about the adoption that "Mia is such a sweetheart, and I love her to pieces. She came into my life at the perfect time. She is my baby." I was curious to know if Denise actually adopted the dog in the window, so I looked through the photographs taken of dogs looking out the window and of Mia. Sure enough it is the very same dog. Denise did end up adopting—out of the over one hundred dogs on the bus—the very one looking out of the window!

Mia's Pup (#53c) Brings Joy to a Retired Man

Unknown to Denise, Glen Gordon, also of the Bozeman area, had adopted one of Mia's ten puppies just a week before Mia herself was adopted. Glen had just lost his very special canine companion, a border collie, and was missing that dog, when he saw the television news story about "the Husky Case." Like Denise, Glen was persuaded by the news story to drive into Butte and adopt one of our dogs. Glen and the puppy he named Orphan Annie were featured in the Belgrade, Montana, newspaper.

Annie now weighs ninety pounds and is white like her mother but with some red tones. Glen sees both Siberian husky and white German shepherd characteristics in his dog. Fearing Annie might be missing animal companionship, Glen adopted Buddy, an older husky–border collie mix from the Heart of the Valley Animal Shelter in Bozeman. Now the two dogs have a fantastic relationship. "Buddy taught Annie to be a dog and play. I am Annie's dad," said Glen, "and Buddy is her playmate."

Tipper of Anaconda Helps the Franks Adjust to Retirement

While Glen and Denise watched the husky rescue on the news, the Franks of Anaconda were reading about it in the *Montana Standard*. Due to a work injury, Loveta Frank had to give up her job, and she felt that a companion dog would help her cope with the loss of a job and colleagues she enjoyed, and the prospect of being home alone with just her two cats. And that is how a puppy named Tipper came to live with Loveta and Leslie.

The Franks say Tipper has been an easy dog to own. Although just a little eight-week-old puppy when they brought him home, Tipper was house trained in only two days. He is also well behaved at home and when visiting. The Franks' two cats readily accepted the puppy, and now the big dog and the cats are good friends.

Tipper is another vocal dog and loves to talk. When the Franks are driving around Anaconda, one can see the 115-pound cream-colored German shepherd sticking his head out the back window and talking (not barking) to the people in passing cars until they take notice of him. "Whenever there are people around, Tipper will start up a conversation, really talking to them, not barking at them, until the people pay attention to him. In fact, he can actually say the word *mama* so distinctly that we all understand what he is saying."

You only have to talk to this couple for a short time to understand how remarkable Tipper is and how much happiness he has brought them in their retirement years. The Franks are gregarious folks who enjoy socializing and traveling, and Tipper usually goes with them and seems to enjoy visiting with people as much as they do. "Tipper even goes to weddings with us," said Loveta. "People know that Tipper is part of our family, and if they invite us, they need to invite Tipper as well."

Tipper of Butte Keeps His Owner Fit

Numerous studies show that owning a dog can improve your mental and physical health, and this seems as true for retired people as it is for active young adults who spend their leisure time backpacking in the mountains with their dogs. This is evident with the adoption of another Tipper to Staci and Tom Davis of Butte.

Since retiring from his job at the city jail, Tom has taken on the major responsibility for Tipper's care, and the dog is doing his best to keep Tom healthy. "He is a great dog, and because I am trying to give him the care he deserves, we take a one-mile walk every morning." Tipper's task is to keep Tom walking! For many folks like Tom, the healthful habit of a daily walk did not develop until they adopted a dog.

When Staci and Tom decided to adopt a Camp Husky dog, they asked volunteer Barb LeProwse to select a pup for them from the large number available. She selected the smallest dog in his litter, and he turned out to be a perfect match. Named Tipper because of the white tip of his tail, this Siberian husky–German shepherd mix grew into a 120-pound adult. This strikingly handsome canine with husky markings on his face is now just another member of the Davis family.

Like Huck, Bella, and Tipper of Anaconda, this Tipper also loves to talk. "Tipper always starts talking when our grandchildren come to visit. It is as if he is saying to us, 'Isn't it wonderful that someone important is coming to visit us?' Tipper is so good natured and especially gentle and playful with our three grandchildren, who live next door."

The Davis family almost lost Tipper when he was about one year old. He jumped the fence and was hit by a car. Fortunately, Tipper survived with only a broken leg. His leg was in a cast for six weeks, and although he still walks with a limp, he is a mature but healthy adult with "a great disposition."

Luci Finds a Job and a Loving Home in Three Forks and Is Reunited with Her Puppy

As a public-health nurse in Alaska, Glenda Barnes depended on her sled dogs to take her from one Eskimo village to the next, sometimes in deadly winter conditions. On more than one occasion, she owed her life to her loyal and intelligent huskies. In Alaska and now on Indian reservations in Montana, Glenda has been distressed by encountering many neglected dogs. "I spent many a sleepless night worrying about some of the dogs. At times, there were late-night rescue efforts to find safe and healthy homes for some street-bound pups."

Before training as a registered nurse, Glenda earned a degree in animal science, and she is very knowledgeable about dogs, having owned and trained as many as twenty-three sled dogs over a nine-year span. Her gratitude toward the sled dogs, as well as her concern for any abused or neglected dog, led Glenda to drive the 112-mile round trip from Three Forks to Butte on Saturdays to volunteer at Camp Husky.

While her motive in volunteering may have been to help "huskies," it did not stop her from volunteering or adopting when she discovered that the dogs were primarily German shepherds. "Being so familiar with husky breed characteristics, it was obvious to me immediately that the dogs at Camp Husky were not huskies but shepherd-type dogs," said Glenda. (Glenda was correct, of course. Genetic testing revealed that many of our dogs were Siberian husky–German shepherd mix, but even more were white German shepherd or Belgian shepherds.)

Glenda wanted to adopt a dog, and when she was assigned to work in the "maternity ward," she developed an attachment to a mother dog named Luci, who was approximately six years of age and had an exceptionally sweet nature. Glenda believes that the right dog "just comes to you," and that seems to be the case with Luci. She is a beautiful black-and-tan dog with long fur, most likely a Belgian Tervuren–white German shepherd mix. Glenda remembers that Luci's puppies were all cream colored except one that resembled his mother. Obviously, the father was one of the white German shepherds.

Following the adoption, it was Glenda's husband, Richard Seiler, who spent the most time with Luci. Richard, who owns the local hardware store, took Luci to work with him six days a week. Luci doesn't just "chill out" at Seiler's Hardware; she has a job. Luci greets customers and entertains children while their parents are shopping. "She is very good with children. If they bug her too much, she just walks away from them. Sometimes little kids curl up with her on one of her three dog beds in the hardware store. Frequently, a child, teen, or adult will come into the store just to visit Luci, usually giving her a treat."

When she is not working with Richard at the hardware store, Luci is content just to be in the company of Richard and Glenda. She enjoys riding in a car and is well behaved on auto trips. She is also "an excellent camping dog. She sets herself in a position to 'watch the herd' (us), and one would hardly know she is there," say Glenda and Richard. She is also a great companion on horse pack trips as well as long hikes. (Luci is the dog featured on the top of the back cover, looking down from a mountaintop into Lake Plateau far below while on a backpacking trip with Glenda and Richard in the Beartooth Wilderness of southwestern Montana.)

Like most adult dogs at Camp Husky, Luci has some emotional problems as a result of the horrible conditions in which she grew up. Her first problem has been severe separation anxiety. For the first few days after Glenda brought her home to Three Forks, Richard tethered Luci to his belt as he worked all day at his store until she "imprinted" on him. As a result, Luci became extremely bonded to Richard. While she is well behaved in the store and when she is with Richard, Glenda, or a pet sitter, she can be destructive if left alone for several hours.

Another emotional trait that many adult Camp Husky dogs developed is a fear of strange dogs that invade their territories. Richard and Glenda approached this problem by taking Luci to an obedience class shortly after her adoption. Luci learned the basic commands easily and learned to be more comfortable around strange dogs. As for fear aggression, Luci is kept on leash when out in public and not allowed to run loose in dog parks.

While she still has fear of large dogs she doesn't know, Luci loves small dogs and puppies. "We think she is a true mama dog," said Glenda. "She kept sneaking out the back door of the hardware store when she discovered two new Lab pups in a nearby yard. She would plant herself near them and not want to leave their area. She also developed a close bond with two other neighbor dogs that she 'raised' from pups. When those dogs moved away with their family, she watched for them to return for weeks with a sad look in her eyes."

Luci has two communication behaviors that are common among Camp Husky dogs and that are identical with the dog Huck that was introduced earlier. Glenda said, "Luci 'smiles' with her teeth showing when she greets me or others she knows well. She 'talks' when she is happily greeting me, when she wants me to get out of bed, or when she needs to go outside." Luci is also very affectionate and loves playing chase in the house with Glenda and Richard and bringing her toys to them.

In 2014, Glenda reported that Luci had been reunited with one of her pups, one of the dogs this author was not aware of and did not include in this book. "We have had the pleasure of meeting one of Luci's pups around the Bozeman–Three Forks area. He is a *big* Luci look-alike. His owner loves this dog and can find nothing negative to say about him. Luci is most sweet to her son when he visits the hardware store. He was adopted from Heart of the Valley Animal Shelter in Bozeman sometime after I took Luci home at weaning time." This is obviously the one dark-colored pup referred to earlier. One of Luci's cream-colored pups, named Laz, is introduced next.

As for her volunteer work at Camp Husky, Glenda would gladly do it again. "I would jump in again in a minute if Butte—God forbid!—ever had to take on a dog-rescue operation again. I was proud—and honored—to have been a part of such a selfless operation of dedicated humanitarians."

Update: Luci now has a gray muzzle at age eleven, and although she still enjoys a good walk, she no longer wants to go on the very long hikes she previously enjoyed with Glenda and Richard. Luci and Richard are semiretired now, working only three and a half days a week at the hardware store. Glenda is retired from nursing but is volunteering her skills with the Montana Spay-Neuter Task Force.

Luci's Pup, the Dog That Plays with Horses

One of Luci's puppies, Lazarus, a strawberry-blond German shepherd with beautiful brown eyes, lives outside of Anaconda, Montana, with Jeffrey Johnson and Lorrie Stiffler. Lorrie began fostering the pup when he was about three months old and suffering from digestive problems. The problem cleared up with a special diet, and Laz now weighs about ninety pounds, although he is still skinny. The couple kept the pup, and they are glad they did so.

Jeffrey described his dog as a little headstrong with a happy disposition. Like his mother, Laz is very affectionate. He lives with two cats, who are aggressive toward him, and an older border collie–heeler mix named Chron, who ignores him. When he could not bond with the other pets in his household, Laz developed a friendship with the next-door neighbor's two horses. "Laz chases the horses, and they chase him. The horses wait by their fence in the morning for Laz to come out and play."

Animals of all types are capable of forming close bonds. When visiting my cousin and his partner in their rural home of Orange, Australia, I watched their delightful border collie go outdoors first thing every morning to greet the neighbor's horse and goat that were standing by the fence waiting for her. It was obvious that the three animals had formed a close bond.

Before he was fully grown, Laz learned some manners from a sixteen-hundred-pound horse that Jeffrey and Lorrie owned. One day Jeffrey observed Laz eating the horse's feed. The good-natured horse tried to warn Laz off with snorting and stomping; however, Laz did not take the hint. Finally, the frustrated and hungry horse grabbed hold of Laz with his mouth, lifting him up in the air and tossing him about eight feet! Jeffrey ran over thinking his big pup might be dead; luckily, Laz just had the wind knocked out of him, and there were no bite marks on him. Apparently, the horse did not injure him, but from that day on, Laz respected the horse's food and minded his manners.

Jeffrey and Lorrie enjoy sharing their leisure hours with Laz. "He is fun to take anywhere, whether it is a road trip, river rafting, swimming, hiking, or visiting with friends in a pub. He is friendly toward people and dogs, and loves to play until he drops from exhaustion."

One only has to talk to Jeffrey to know how much Laz has enriched his life. Laz is "a jewel with a nice personality," said Jeffrey. "You can't help but love him. We started off wanting to help a dog that needed a home. The irony is that Laz has done much more for me than I have done for him. Sharing my life with this dog is a tremendous blessing. He has done so much for me."

Mylie Coyote Protects Her Family from a Mountain Lion

Ask the Hoxworths about their Camp Husky dog, and this couple who live "in the middle of nowhere" near Ovando, Montana, will tell you that their eighty-pound female is their heroine. The couple already had three little dogs and a cat. They didn't need another pet, but when they heard on the radio about the dogs in Butte that needed homes, they decided to make the long drive to Butte. That would prove to be one of the best decisions they ever made.

They chose one of Gypsy's puppies and named her Mylie when they brought the sweet little puppy home from Camp Husky. (Gypsy is featured in the next chapter.) As expressed by the Hoxworths, "Mylie is a beautiful, protective part of our family. She is great with little children, and she is always gentle with our cat and our little Pomeranians as well as our new addition to the household, a miniature Australian shepherd. Mylie will occasionally step on one of our small dogs, but never intentionally. She mothers all the little dogs, licking their faces, and never picks a fight with any of them."

This "supersweet" German shepherd puppy with a yellow tint to her fur reminded the couple of the "goofy but lovable cartoon character Wile E. Coyote"; however, there was nothing looney tunes about Mylie. When she was only nine months old, she saved her new family from disaster.

Jewelie and Duane will never forget what happened one evening about six months after adopting Mylie. They were in their living room watching television with Mylie, their three little Pomeranians, and their cat. Their television program was almost over, and in a few minutes, they would open the front door and go outside with all their pets before the whole household retired for the night. This was their usual evening ritual, and everything seemed normal about that night except Mylie's behavior. The typically calm and quiet nine-month-old started growling and "threw a fit," warning the Hoxworths of danger that none of the other dogs seemed to recognize. When Duane opened the door to see what was bothering Mylie, she demonstrated the courage and intelligence of her German shepherd heritage. She rushed past Duane, ran outside, and started growling with all the ferocity she could summon as she stared into the eyes of a mountain lion more than twice her size. Even a full-grown male German shepherd is no match for a mountain lion, but young Mylie stood her ground, showing no fear in her fierce determination to protect her family. Miraculously, the hungry mountain lion decided to retreat. Duane and Jewelie shudder to think what would have happened that night in Ovando if Mylie had not been there to protect them. Mylie is most definitely a dog with a mission to protect her human and animal family, and the Hoxworths will always be grateful to the city of Butte and the volunteers of Camp Husky.

Puff, the Pup That Was Mentored by a Wolf

Puff was a malnourished and frightened four-month-old puppy when volunteers took him off the bus. A few months later, he was one of seven dogs driven by volunteers to Help for Homeless Pets, the shelter in Billings that offered to help us place some of the Camp Husky dogs. Unfortunately, Puff was so severely injured while at that shelter that his right hind leg had to be amputated, making adoption of this sweet and beautiful Belgian Tervuren–husky mix quite problematic. Puff stayed at the shelter until ten-year-old Devina Menard of Lake Tahoe saw "this cute and just adorable tripod dog on the Petfinder website." Before Devina was born, her mother, Jana, had adopted a little wolf puppy she named Islay, and that amazing wolf gave so much love to her family that Jana was inspired to adopt and foster wolf- and coyote-mix dogs as well as special-needs dogs. That is why she had to agree when Devina said, "We have to adopt Puff."

Through her connections with a great organization called Pilots and Paws, Jana was able to arrange for Puff's transportation to Lake Tahoe. One volunteer pilot flew Puff from Billings to Twin Falls, Idaho, where a second pilot was waiting to fly him to Lake Tahoe. "Puff liked the first flight so much he was ready to jump right up on the second plane and go." Jana remembers watching that plane circle over the airport, with Puff looking out the passenger window, but strong winds prevented the small plane from landing until the next day, September 28, 2009, just one week short of a year after the Camp Husky rescue began.

Puff greeted his new family affectionately and needed no encouragement to jump in the car, but when he entered a house for the first time, he was terrified. He ran into a closet, refused to come out, and did not eat, drink, or relieve himself for three days! In addition to the three humans, his new family included an old wolf, an adolescent coyote-husky mix, a black wolf dog, horses, and a good-natured cat. On the fourth day, Puff came out of the closet, and, as Jana described it, "bonded with us like Velcro." About that time, Devina changed Puff's name to Monsieur Marcel Marshmallow to reflect his "demure, delicate, and gentle nature."

When Puff (now Marcel) had arrived from Billings, he had been underweight with badly matted fur, especially around his stump. He was so weak he could barely walk, and Jana could tell he was suffering from phantom pain, which is, of course, real pain that amputees experience. Jana resisted the impulse to groom Marcel or touch his stump for fear of inflicting more pain. Instead, she concentrated on gaining his trust and building up his strength and stamina with a very nutritious diet, supplements, and frequent but easy walks. She also got in touch with the veterinarian who had operated on Marcel to learn what she could about his special needs and how she could help him.

Jana has developed a very nutritious diet for her dogs that surely helped the malnourished Marcel gain strength. Jana uses high-nutrition dog food, adding flaxseed oil or salmon oil or salmon heads when available. She adds sweet potatoes or pumpkin for extra nutrition but avoids white potatoes. Her dogs also like raw carrots and broccoli. She adds blueberries in the fall. She adds bone meal and glucosamine to protect from arthritis. Jana warns that raisins, grapes, and onions should be kept away from dogs.

Not only did Marcel form a close bond with his new human family, but he also bonded with Islay, the wolf. By the time the family adopted Marcel, Islay was an old wolf with degenerative arthritis, requiring a special wheelchair so he could walk with Jana. Islay and Marcel started bonding as soon as Marcel came out of that closet. Jana described this friendship in a journal entry dated October 7, 2009, only nine days after Marcel arrived: "Marcel has formed an unlikely friendship with my old wolf. We took a forty-five-minute walk at dusk, Islay in his wheelchair and Marcel hopping along. Periodically, they would stop and Marcel would snuggle up to Islay, and then Islay would groom Marcel. This is something I did not expect, but it made my heart melt to see it."

Islay was what one might call a "once-in-a-lifetime dog," only he was pure wolf, not a mix. Jana rescued him as a pup and soon discovered that he had an amazing ability to help her control her type 1 diabetes. Jana is among a relatively small percentage of diabetics who cannot control fluctuations in glucose levels even when they follow a careful diet, exercise regularly, and do everything right. Consequently, life-threatening drops in blood sugar can occur without warning, even when they are sleeping. Some folks who suffer from brittle diabetes, as it is called, are fortunate enough to receive diabetic service dogs that have been carefully selected for aptitude and temperament and subjected to thorough and intensive training. Unlike these other "service dogs," the remarkable Islay was able to sense the chemical changes in Jana's blood and warn her, even before he had any formal training. This gentle wolf became a first-rate certified therapy dog, traveling on planes and trains with Jana and even following her up escalators, even though he was terrified of them. Since Jana is the owner of the Fragrance Vault in South Lake Tahoe, Islay, by necessity, had to be a greeter as well.

Not only was Islay a lifesaver for Jana, but he also once saved Devina and two of her friends from a bear that was clambering onto the deck where the young children were playing. Before the adults were even aware of the large intruder, Islay had jumped through a window in order to protect the children. With the good sense of a wolf, he was able to persuade the curious bear to leave without a violent confrontation.

While Marcel was gaining strength, putting on weight, and even growing in height by one inch, Islay was slowly deteriorating. Sensing that Islay was fading, Marcel stayed right beside the old wolf for the last twenty-four hours of his life, licking the wolf's face. When the family placed Islay in a grave on the property, Marcel jumped in and frantically tried to retrieve his friend. While Islay's death was devastating for both Jana and Marcel, the old wolf had lived long enough to mentor Marcel, helping him develop the confidence he would need to fit into the pack and help Jana. Perhaps Islay knew that Marcel would need to take his place as Jana's special companion. (Marcel is the dog with snow on his face on the top of the cover.) After Islay's death, Jana and Marcel became absolutely bonded, and the young dog took over some of Islay's duties, including working at the shop with Jana. His temperament makes him ideal for a greeter in the store. In spite of the bad start he had in life, "Marcel's emotional understanding and intelligence are unparalleled," said Jana. When Marcel first started accompanying Jana to her store, two regular customers came into the store, a woman in her early twenties and her mother. This young woman was born without limbs but with a bright spirit and keen intelligence to compensate. While Marcel has a sweet disposition and is friendly with customers, Jana had never seen him react as positively to anyone outside his own family as he had toward that young woman in the wheelchair. The special aura of this woman pulled him in, and he also realized that she had wounds like his own. He gently licked the places where her arms should have been. Currently, Jana is working on a canine good-citizen certificate from the American Kennel Club, and then they will start on therapy training for Marcel. Jana and Marcel have also been invited to visit the veterans' hospital in a nearby city.

With the confidence he gained from his association with Islay, Marcel soon became comfortable with his pack, and now he especially enjoys playing with the young coyote-malamute mix when he is not with Jana. At first Marcel was at the bottom of the pecking order, but he is now in the middle. It was an exciting time for Jana when Marcel was strong enough to actually run with the pack. Worrying about his safety, she encouraged Marcel to walk beside her when the other dogs went running and exploring in the woods. She need not have worried, because the other dogs understood how Marcel's handicap made him vulnerable, and one of the bigger dogs would always stay beside him as a protector. Once a coyote tried to attack Marcel, but his pack came to his rescue and scared it away. With his daily runs, Marcel is now physically fit with very strong front legs to compensate for his compromised rear end. The formerly malnourished dog now weighs eighty-five pounds. Jana is confident he will live a long and happy life.

Jana and Devina are grateful to Angie and the staff of Help for Homeless Pets in Billings, and the volunteers of Camp Husky, for making it possible for Marcel to bless their family. Marcel's "lovely attitude and expressive countenance make him a star" wherever he and Jana go. This sweet dog is doing his very best to fill the large tracks that Islay left behind.

Frightened Dogs Come Off the Bus—October 6, 2008

1. Beauty #68 (left) and Dolly #67 (right)—these cage mates and best
friends from this first day of the rescue were adopted by Connie and
Bob Landis (ch. 7). Beauty is typical of our white shepherd-husky
mixes, and Dolly is typical of the white German shepherds. Nellie #24
(bottom), one of our young mother dogs, was adopted by April Rogers.
Photos from Camp Husky archives, photographer Adrienne Herren.

2. Six dirty, hungry, and frightened dogs right after they came off the bus on the first day of the rescue. Rhett #38 (top left) was adopted by Jay Walden of New Mexico (ch. 7). Snowball #61 (lower left) and Frosty #34 (top right) are typical of the many large white shepherds coming off the bus. Christy #27 (a.k.a. Nippy) was adopted by volunteer Christy Stack (ch. 10). Ginger #20 came off the bus with her adult son, and both were adopted by the Schwartz family (ch. 10). Mia #53 was adopted by Denise Fett (ch.5). Photos from Camp Husky archives, photographer Adrienne Herren.

Routines at Camp Husky

3. Five young friends in their kennel at our heated Arizona street location, spring of 2009. Notice the checklist on the kennel door for medications, feedings, fresh water, walks, and so on. Volunteers worked hard to keep the kennels clean and give the dogs adequte exercise. Photos from Camp Husky archives, photographer unknown.

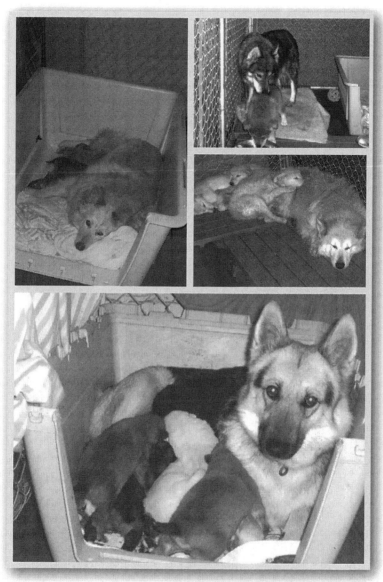

4. Camp Husky nursery in winter 2008. On the left are Cinnamon
and her litter (ch. 8). Upper right is Ethel, a husky, and her puppy,
Ollie (ch. 9). Middle right is Sasha (ch.7) with her three puppies, Disco,
Glitter, and Sparkle (ch. 8). At the bottom is Star with her puppies
(ch. 6). Photos from Camp Husky archives, photographer unknown.

5. Camp Husky dogs playing in the yard at our Arizona Street location in March 2009. Susie #72 (upper left) was adopted by Bob and Alice Davies (ch. 6). Luna #80 (upper right) was adopted by Deirdre Fitzgerald of Spokane, Washington (ch. 7). Mufasa #85 (lower left) was adopted by John and Mary Lawrence (ch. 6). Pinkie #71 (lower right) was adopted by volunteer Cathy Decker (ch. 10). Photos from Camp Husky archives, photographer unknown.

Dogs and Families

6. Monte and Merlena Moore, Camp Husky volunteers extraordinaire, with Zeva and their two Chihuahuas in their home in Butte, summer 2012. Zeva (ch. 10) is the daughter of Mufasa and Luci, the dog on the back cover. Photo courtesy of John Ray.

7. Shadow (ch. 5) with the Barrys, happy and exhausted after a day-
long hike exploring a ghost town and not encountering another
human. From left: Tanner with Shadow, Cullen with Buddy,
Christine, and Carson. Photos by Dan Barry, courtesy of owners.

8. Cree (age twelve) described his dog, Sasha, as "98 percent sweetheart and 2 percent husky and wolf" (ch. 7). Adopted by Maer and Paul Seibert. Photo courtesy of Deni Elliott and Pam Hogle.

9. Casey Clark, helicopter pilot, and Lucy, his devoted companion,
live in Houston, Texas (ch. 8). Photo courtesy of owner.

10. Patrick and his puppy, Finn (a.k.a. Rocky Raccoon). Finn was adopted by Patrick and Shelly Merkt (ch. 8). Photo courtesy of owners.

11. Heather McMilin and Cooper enjoy a beautiful spring day in 2014 (ch. 8).
Photo by Kim Wishcamper, courtesy of Heather McMilin and Jennifer Clary.

Dogs with a Job

12. Top: Marcel, the greeter dog at the Perfume Vault in South Lake Tahoe, with his wolfdog friend, Shelby. Bottom: Marcel walks in front of his mentor, Islay, the old wolf. Adopted by Jana Menard (ch. 5). Photos courtesy of owner.

13. Nap time in the Brodheads' Colorado home. Fiver is nose to nose with baby Henry, while Honey naps after an exhausting day of babysitting. Adopted by Wendy and David Brodhead (ch. 6). Photo courtesy of owners.

14. Sergeant Huck (a.k.a. Rocky), the Marine Corps dog of North Carolina, typical of our beautiful long-haired white German shepherds. Adopted by Marine Staff Sergeant Josh Macer and Erin Lanrigan Macer (ch. 5). Photo courtesy of owners.

15. Mia #53 (top) was adopted by Denise Fett (ch. 5). Mia can be seen on the back cover, looking out of the back window of the bus. Jasmine #53a (bottom) is one of Mia's pups, adopted by Judy Bardouche (ch. 7). Photos courtesy of owners.

Puppies

16. Camp Husky puppies from upper left and down: Sophie (ch. 8), Jasmine right before she was lost in the wilderness (ch. 7), Kia and her mom (ch. 6), and Apollo (ch. 9). Upper right and down: Huck (ch. 5), Boons (ch. 8), Trixie (left) and Hunter (ch. 7), and Christine with Ollie (ch. 9). Photos courtesy of owners.

Active Dogs

17. Max (a.k.a. Mr. Mustard) enjoying a day outdoors with his family.
Adopted by Brian and Jena White (ch. 8). Photo courtesy of owners.

18. Rudy and friends snowshoeing in Montana. Rudy was approximately six months old when he came off the bus. He was very friendly toward volunteers and other dogs at Camp Husky. Adopted by Mary Ann and David Lopez (ch. 7). Photos courtesy of owners.

19. Ollie and Christine Handler skijoring near their home in
northern Michigan, winter 2014. Adopted by Christine and
Stephen Handler (ch. 9). Photo courtesy of owners.

20. Jake (above) adopted by Sarah Martin (ch. 6). Luci (below)
adopted by volunteer Glenda Barnes and her husband,
Richard Seiler (ch. 5). Photos courtesy of owners.

21. Winston (a.k.a. Walrus) on the river watching Kevin fly-fishing (ch. 8). Photo courtesy of Kevin Pierce.

22. Top: Casey Drummond and Japhy (a.k.a. Sparkle) hiking the high country of Montana (ch. 8). Bottom: Japhy with Santiago behind her on an outing with Casey in Washington in winter 2016. Photos courtesy of owner.

23. Sasha #45 (a.k.a. Lady), one of the adult dogs on the bus.
Adopted by Tom Susanj (ch. 9). Photo courtesy of owner.

24. Hazel #41 (a.k.a. Gypsy), one of our mother dogs, resting after a summer hike with owner Sarah Sadowski (ch. 6). Photos courtesy of owner.

25. Rusty, adopted by Janet and Bill Foster (ch. 9). Rusty is
typical of the many long-haired white German shepherds
at Camp Husky. Photo courtesy of owners.

26. Sir Lancelot (a.k.a. Mr. Jones) out for a wilderness walk
(ch. 6). Adopted by Jenavieve. Photo courtesy of owner.

27. Bucky, the largest dog from Camp Husky at 130 pounds, enjoying a hike with Robin Taylor Jordan, 2015 (ch. 5). Adopted by Fay Taylor. Photo courtesy of Dave Jordan.

28. Lizzy (one of Mufasa's daughters) napping on the rocks after an active day on the river (ch. 10). Adopted by volunteer Dana Cotton. Photo courtesy of owner.

Best Friends

29. Top: Lisa Reimer and her daughter, Allison, with
Olive (lower right) and her daughter Pepper in December
2010. Bottom: Olive on the left and Pepper on the right
at home with Lisa 2015. Photos courtesy of owner.

30. Top: Gus #59 on the left with one of his husky friends. Bottom: Basil #62, on the right, with his best friend and brother, Gus (ch. 9). Photos courtesy of Auguste and Suraya Lockwood.

31. Django (a.k.a. Nova) with his mentor, Hogan, an Australian shepherd, in 2014 (ch. 8). Adopted by Christy and Alan Bradley. Photo courtesy of owners.

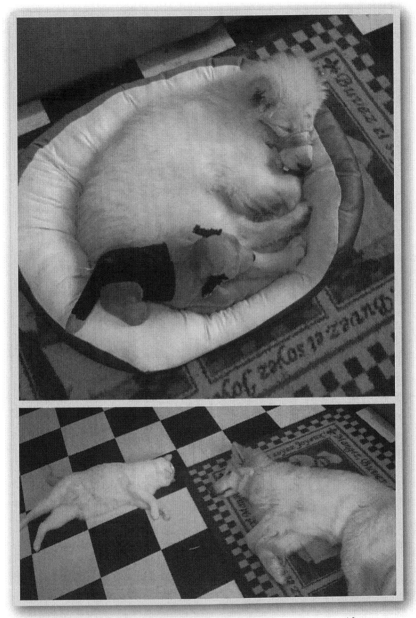

32. Top: Flippy as a small puppy with a broken jaw. Bottom: About four years later, Flippy with her best friend, Tazo, taking a break after wrestling together (ch. 10). Adopted by volunteer Sarah DeMoney and her husband, Paul Blumenthal. Photos courtesy of owners.

33. Missy the cat and her protector, Pearl #60c, born at Camp Husky (ch. 9). Adopted by Becky Johnson. Photo courtesy of owner.

34. Gwenie (born at Camp Husky) and playmate, Tigger, napping on the bed (ch. 9). Adopted by Janet and Jay Cornish. Photo courtesy of owners.

35. Momma #26, lying in the kitchen and napping after playing outdoors with her best friend, Skya, a husky-whippet cross. Adopted by Larry and Louette Jaeger (ch. 6). Photos courtesy of owners.

Photogenic Dogs

36. Juno, the incredible talking dog, was born at Camp Husky. Adopted by Cory and Sonja Foster (ch. 6). Photo courtesy of owners.

37. Clockwise from top right: Kai, adopted by Megan Maes (ch. 10); Wiley, adopted by Kelsey Estabrook (ch. 10); Toki, adopted by Jonathan Williams (ch. 7); and Tipper, adopted by Staci and Tom Davis (ch. 5). Photos courtesy of owners.

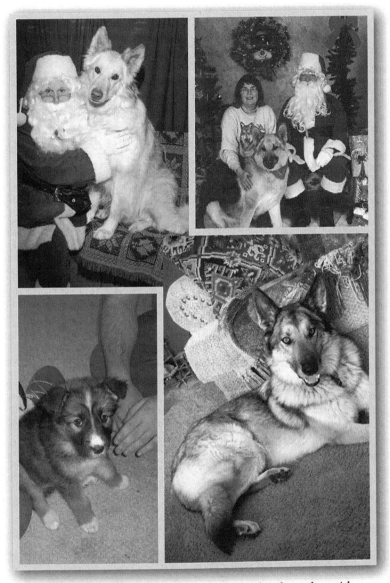

38. Top left: Lazarus 2012 (ch.5) and (top right) the author with her wolfdog, Duke, in 2000. Both photos by Gregg Edelen at the Santa Paws Fundraiser for Butte Spay-Neuter Task Force. Bottom left: Bella, a therapy dog, on Christmas morning 2008 with David (ch. 5). Lower right: Lucy in Houston (ch. 8). Bella and Lucy are sisters. Photos courtesy of owners.

39. The author with her two Camp Husky dogs, November 2015. On the left is Sunshine, a white German shepherd born at Camp Husky, and on the right is Hector (a.k.a. Ace #33), a Belgian sheepdog–husky mix (ch. 10). Photo by Robert Noble, MD.

"You think those dogs will not be in heaven!
I tell you they will be there long before any of us."
--Robert Louis Stevenson

40. Winston (ch. 8) and his golden retriever friend looking
out over the city of Missoula. Photo by owner.

**More photos can be viewed on our Facebook page, "Camp Husky
2008 Butte Montana."**

CHAPTER 6
Second-Chance Dogs

Many of the Camp Husky dogs could have been classified as "hard to adopt" because they were sick, old, or afraid of people. What inspired me most about Camp Husky were the volunteers who worked with these special-needs dogs to make them more adoptable, and the wonderful people who came to adopt, many of whom chose one of these hard-to-adopt dogs. In this chapter are fifteen dogs that could not have been adopted if not for the dedication of the volunteers who worked with them and the compassion of the people who chose to adopt them.

Two of these dogs had narrow escapes from animal shelters whose directors had a strong dislike for the Camp Husky dogs, believing them to be part wolf or coyote. In fact, the only people I interviewed who had anything negative to say about our Camp Husky dogs were the directors of these two shelters and folks associated with them. In a separate instance, two other dogs were first adopted by people who neglected them, but fortunately, they ended up in loving homes.

Dogs with Physical Challenges
Juno, the Puppy with a Weak Heart, Finds a Loving Home and Learns to Talk

Born to a Siberian husky–shepherd mother and fathered by Mufasa, a husky-shepherd mix, Juno was the runt of the litter and was diagnosed with a level-four heart murmur. When Sonja Foster of Butte and her seventeen-year-old son, Cory, went to Camp Husky to adopt a puppy, volunteers steered them away from little Juno. Sonja explains that the volunteers did not want to see her and her son form an attachment to a puppy that could die at any time. One sick puppy had already died after being adopted, as volunteer Sue Madison recalled, and volunteers did not want it to happen again. "While we understood that the volunteers were trying to be very honest with us and save us from the pain of a premature death of a pet, Cory and I saw it differently. We wanted this little puppy to know the joy of belonging to a family no matter how short her life might be."

Cory and Juno formed a special bond, and the teenager taught the puppy some special tricks, such as how to give a high five while standing on her hind legs. Juno is one of our most talkative dogs, and Cory taught her to say "I love you." She is one of three Camp Husky dogs who are reported to say actual understandable words.

In 2012, Sonja informed me that Juno had added to her vocabulary. When I had follow-up questions about Juno's speech, this is what Sonja reported: "Yes, our neighbors and everyone who knows Juno can understand her when she says, 'I want out; I want to go,' and 'I want Cory.' Juno says, 'I want out' and 'I want to go' whenever I am leaving the house. After she says those words, she makes short barks and grumblings that sound like she is chewing me out. Juno has her own language when she is 'talking' to the cats. It is the only time I hear those particular sounds." (I had no trouble believing that Juno says actual words because my sister Penny's mother-in-law had a dog that could talk, and in the 1960s that dog appeared on the Art Linkletter show. But that dog was not nearly as verbal as Juno—or Kia, in the next story.)

Juno never suffered separation anxiety or loneliness when Sonja was at work and Cory was in school because the puppy bonded instantly with Sonja's two-year-old black Lab named Shadow. "Shadow took care of Juno as if Juno was her own pup, and Juno loves her best friend and foster mom. While Shadow is very mellow, Juno is hyperactive. Juno also bonded with our family cats, even appointing herself their guardian and following them from room to room."

In addition to the animals in her own household, Juno formed attachments to two other dogs, as Sonja explains: "Juno made friends with a female Chesapeake who has since passed away—Juno was depressed afterward—and a male yellow Lab. These dogs belonged to Cory's friends." Like some other Camp Husky dogs, Juno is fearful of dogs she does not know. "She is terrified of other dogs, especially little ones. I do not allow her around any small dog. She was like this from the get-go," said Sonja.

Juno is definitely a people-oriented dog: "Juno loves, loves, loves people, all people." She developed a very close attachment to Sonja's two grandsons, who were only two and three when Juno came to live with the Fosters. Sonja notes that "Juno is always happy to welcome visitors to the house, but she especially enjoys the grandsons."

Currently, at nearly seven years of age, Juno is healthy and does not take any medications. Sonja described her as "friendly and rambunctious." Both traits were no doubt fostered by growing up around a teenage boy and his friends, as well as having two energetic little boys as frequent visitors to the house. Cory is an adult, living on his own now, so mother and son have joint custody of Juno. The happy dog divides her time between the two residences.

Kia, Another Amazing Talking Dog

Kia was a seven-week-old puppy suffering from *Giardia* when Brenda and Mick Sullivan decided to adopt her rather than one of the many puppies in good health. Volunteers sent medicine home with the Sullivans, and with their good care, the puppy quickly recovered. She has had no health problems since. Kia's mother was Mia (chapter 5, "Dogs with a Mission"), and her father was White Cloud. Like her parents and the majority of Camp Husky dogs, Kia has a pure-white coat and a pale-pink nose. Although she is primarily German shepherd, the Sullivans believe that Kia has some husky in her.

Brenda described Kia as "long, lanky, and quite tall. She can rest her head on the kitchen table, and she weighs about seventy-five pounds. She is very beautiful, with a playful and affectionate nature." As an example of her playful nature, "Kia will get on our sofa and try to hide under a pillow. Kia is overly affectionate and likes to give kisses, so we have to tell her 'no kisses.' Kia is a good dog but hard to walk because she gets so excited. She doesn't like being brushed, and after she has tolerated all she can take of brushing, she will turn and take a little of my hair in her mouth as if to say, 'See, how do you like it?'"

As a puppy, Kia especially enjoyed the little nieces and nephews who frequently came to the house to visit. When she got older, she would pick the little ones up by their shirts and carry them around like puppies. She also likes other dogs. Before adopting Kia, Brenda's brother found a pregnant Lab cross (about one and a half years old) wandering the streets of Butte. The Sullivans took this dog into their home and named her Dora. Dora soon gave birth to seven pups. The Sullivans found homes for all of them and receive frequent updates from the owners. Dora was a mature dog when Kia arrived, and the Sullivans describe her as "getting snippy when Kia wants to play." However, Kia found a special friend in another Camp Husky dog named Rudy (chapter 7, "Adventure Dogs"). Rudy lives nearby and used to jump his fence and come down to visit Kia. After his owners made the fence higher, Rudy has not been able to visit, but Kia still howls to him.

By far the most amazing thing about Kia is that she talks, and some of her talking can be understood. "Kia actually says 'hello' when we come home from work," reports Brenda. "Also, when she is exasperated with something our older dog does, she will turn her head toward her and say, 'Dora.' Kia also says 'Mom' if she wants to go out in the middle of the night. She comes to the bed and says 'Mom,' and if I don't respond, she taps me on the back and says a louder 'Mom.'"

Kia and Dora are both pampered house dogs. They get a cup of vanilla ice cream every night and lots of attention. Mick and Brenda are very glad they adopted their very special talking dog.

Nikki (Puppy #36c) and Allen Hanson of Butte

Allen Hanson was another of those kind folks who came to Camp Husky willing to adopt a special-needs puppy or adult. Number 36c was one of the pups born to Luci #36, the dog at the top of the back cover. We believe her father was one of our white German shepherds. In chapter 5, I introduced Luci and her blond puppy, Laz. Also, Luci's owner told of visits she has had with another of Luci's puppies, a male who looks just like Luci. Nikki has the large stature and long hair of her mother and two brothers. I checked my records, and Nikki is indeed one of Luci's puppies, but I am not sure if she comes from an earlier litter. Some of the mothers with young puppies on the bus were pregnant as well. Glenda Barnes, Luci's owner, was a volunteer caring for Luci and her puppies, and she recalls just one dark puppy, a male. The rest were blond like Laz. Nikki has darker coloring.

Nikki is an exceptionally attractive dog. When Allen sent me a picture of Nikki cuddling with his daughter, Emily, I saw this dog's resemblance to her mother, Luci. When Allen saw a picture of Luci, he agreed that they are very close in appearance, with the same long fur and black, tan, and white coloring. When Allen walks Nikki, people frequently comment on her beauty.

Nikki was a sick and malnourished puppy when Allen adopted her on December 31, 2008. Volunteers provided Allen with a special formula that they were using to nourish the skinny puppy. In addition, Allen prepared Nikki a special diet of rice, yogurt, and beef. Nikki grew into a healthy, strong, and good-natured adult dog, but she still needs encouragement to eat. To make eating more fun for this pup with a poor appetite, Allen purchased a large hollow bone. When Nikki is hungry, she will bring the bone to Allen, and he will stuff it with canned dog food (she won't eat dry). When Allen eats an apple, carrot, or some other healthful snack, he will say, "Share?" Nikki understands and will sit and wait for Allen to cut her a piece. On the other hand, if Allen is eating something that would not be good for Nikki and she begs a bite, all he has to do is say no, and Nikki will walk away.

Allen, who is semiretired, keeps busy training his dog and teaching part time at Highlands College in Butte, where he was recently nominated for an outstanding-teacher award. Allen said that Nikki has a very large vocabulary and seems to understand most of what he tells her. "Our communication has improved through the years we have been together, and now she is able to let me know what she wants from her actions and her verbalization. Nikki is fun to live with because she is so smart."

As a puppy, Nikki was fond of chewing on envelopes or other paper she found on the desk or in a wastebasket. Allen was concerned that eating the paper would hurt her. When he asked her to release the paper, she thought it was a game. He then tried giving her a biscuit in exchange for the paper. The very smart dog now has a fun way to get a biscuit: she keeps an eye out for any slip of paper she can grab and exchange for a biscuit.

Nikki seems to understand whether Allen is simply dressing on a Saturday or dressing to go to work on a weekday morning. If he is preparing to go to work, Nikki will lie on his shoes as if to say, "I don't want you to leave." When Allen comes home from teaching in the evening, Nikki greets him with a "crying sound" as if to say, "I really missed you." Then the two sit in their recliners for fifteen minutes while Nikki proceeds to talk to Allen. "I fear that if someone saw me through the window talking with my dog, they would think I am crazy. I don't understand her, but I know she needs this communication time." Nikki likes people and enjoys visitors, but she is very protective of her home and Allen. She will stand at the door, blocking a stranger from entering the house, until Allen says, "It's OK." It is obvious from our conversations that Nikki and Allen share a special bond. Nikki receives devoted care and lots of attention, and, in turn, she enriches Allen's life.

One of the strange things about Nikki is that she likes to have her fur vacuumed. Whenever Allen vacuums his carpet, Nikki demands to be vacuumed as well—a blessing because she has a very heavy coat and sheds frequently.

Update November 2015: Allen tells me that the skinny pup that didn't like to eat now has a very healthy appetite. Following the advice of his veterinarian, Allen put Nikki on a diet, switched to dry kibble, and got her weight down from 130 to 120. Nikki still insists on an apple following her two daily meals of dry food. Allen continues to enjoy life with his beautiful, playful, and intelligent companion.

The Sickly Mr. Jones Now Sings a Happy Tune

In May 2008, a beautiful and gentle malamute-husky-wolf hybrid named Stetson died from cancer in the arms of Jenavieve, leaving her despondent for six months. She did not think that any dog could ever fill the void left by the death of Stetson, her beloved and faithful companion of thirteen years since she had adopted him as a puppy. When she read about Camp Husky on the Internet and decided to help by adopting one of the dogs, her intention was to choose a dog that did not resemble Stetson in any way. "My only criteria were that the dog must be large, have lots of soft, fluffy fur, preferably in a dark color, and that he interact well with me.

"When I arrived at Camp Husky in February 2009, I came with a list of dogs I thought might be a good fit based on the website. I intended to take one of the larger, older, and harder-to-place dogs, since my house was all set up for a very large dog. The volunteers introduced me to everyone on my list one by one, but none of those dogs seemed to pay any attention to me at all. They were just happy to be out of their cages wandering around.

"Finally there was only one left on my list, a white German shepherd named Mr. Jones. When the volunteer opened his cage, that dog raced over to me, stood up on his hind legs, and greeted me enthusiastically, as if to say, 'It's me; I'm the one you came for!' From that moment on, Mr. Jones watched every move I made, and he even came to me when I called him by his name. It was as if he'd always been my dog."

And, just like the first time she met Stetson, the moment Mr. Jones looked into her eyes, Jenavieve knew he was her dog, even though he was the last dog she expected to take home. In the end, "You get the dog you need," said Jenavieve. "Ironically, Mr. Jones looks almost exactly like my beloved Stetson, without the wolf traits. When people see photographs of my two dogs side by side, they can't tell the difference.

"When the adoption process was complete, Mr. Jones hopped right into the back of my SUV and curled up in a ball as if he'd done it his whole life. He was quiet, calm, and happy as we made the long drive to my home. I believe he knew he'd finally found his forever home. In fact, I believe Mr. Jones had been waiting patiently for me all along. Suddenly, those four long months at Camp Husky, being passed over time and time again, were worth the wait. As I drove, I decided to change my dog's name to Sir Lancelot. It was the first name that came to me, and it fit; he has been my white knight and loyal companion since that first day we met.

"My home is located on twenty-four acres in the mountains, and once Lancelot was accustomed to my house and his kennel, I took him for a walk to explore the property. It was then that an event occurred that further convinced me that Lancelot was the dog I was meant to have. I let him go off leash to explore, and Lancelot immediately climbed up a hill and sat on the very spot where Stetson is buried! It was as if he was letting his predecessor know that he'd arrived to take over the job."

This author remembers Mr. Jones and his brother, Mr. Smith, as sweet and gentle dogs that were well behaved and easy to walk. Mr. Jones, however, had some serious health problems and was much too skinny, even though volunteers had fed him well and walked him regularly; he was simply failing to thrive, and he suffered from frequent diarrhea. Also, he did not have the beautiful fur so characteristic of most Camp Husky dogs. As Jenavieve later discovered, this sweet-natured dog had a very thin, dull coat because of poor digestion and the resulting malnutrition. For this reason, folks looking to adopt passed him by in favor of the many fit and healthy-looking dogs.

After adopting Lancelot and realizing the extent of his illness, Jenavieve conducted extensive research on the Internet and consulted with several veterinarians. She was determined to discover the cause of his health problems. "His body was in such distress that his tail was yellow as if jaundiced, while the rest of him was white. After consulting several veterinarians and investigating various types of dog food to no avail, I cooked all his meals from scratch for three months, trying to help him gain weight and improve his digestion. Finally, after numerous incorrect diagnoses from several veterinarians, his problem turned out to be a severe allergy to all grains. Ironically, Lancelot has better health insurance than I do, so he's always received the best medical care. With the right diet, special vitamins, and lots of love and affection, my wonderful dog started thriving in his new home and grew into a beautiful 125-pound adult with a long, thick, and silky coat that is perfectly suited to his new moniker, Sir Lancelot."

Jenavieve estimates that Lancelot was about nine months old when she adopted him because he not only put on weight but also grew three inches taller within their first year together. When she took him home, he was longer than he was tall, but he filled out nicely and grew to his true height once he received the proper nutrition.

It is unlikely that Lancelot had ever been inside of a house before he went home with Jenavieve. "I slept on the living room floor with Lancelot for two weeks before he learned to navigate a flight of stairs so he wouldn't be alone at night. At first, he wouldn't approach the furniture; however, that changed quickly. First, he took over the sleeping mat I had used, and then a club chair, eventually commandeering a loveseat and a large portion of a king-size pillow-top bed, where he can now be found whenever he isn't outside surveying his mountain domain from the top of his dog house.

"While he was gaining health and vitality, Lancelot was also slowly learning to feel comfortable and confident in a house with a family. Initially, he would not let me out of his sight without becoming very distressed, so

I stayed with him for the first six weeks. It was very much like watching a child discover the world and grow up. Slowly, he became curious and would explore rooms in the house on his own. Eventually, he started getting used to my parents and relaxed enough around them to discover the joy of tummy rubs…they turned out to be his very favorite thing!

"Once he settled into his forever home and got over his fears, Lancelot seemed to be starved for love and affection. After discovering tummy rubs, for over a year Lancelot would quickly lie down on the floor at the feet of anyone walking through a room to get a tummy rub. I dubbed it 'the tummy-rub toll' as he wouldn't let you walk anywhere near him without requiring a tummy rub dozens of times a day. The tummy rubs are hard to resist because Lancelot is an exceedingly sweet and loving dog with a beautiful smile and angelic disposition."

If there was ever a rags-to-riches story from Camp Husky, it is the story of how sickly Mr. Jones found a great home and became the robust and healthy Sir Lancelot. Apart from the blessing of a devoted owner and her parents to look after him, Lancelot enjoys exploring the heavily forested mountainside where they live. He has a twenty-by-eighty-foot kennel with a large dog house and ramps, a custom-made doggie door, a huge array of toys, and his own chairs.

"Originally, Lancelot didn't seem to know what a toy was, and his teeth were so tender that he would chew the thread on the seams of the squeaker toys and take them apart with surgical precision since it was too painful for him to chew through the fabric. These days his teeth are much better, and he chews on dental bones and other hard dog treats with no trouble. In the early days following his adoption, he also had problems with his feet and couldn't bear to walk even a few steps in snow when it was very cold, as his pads were just raw red patches of skin. Over time, he grew new nice black pads, but the texture was never as rough as most dogs' pads. So on smooth floors he could be quite the comedian, slip-sliding around with wild abandon while chasing his toys."

Surprising for a dog that never saw a toy while a puppy, "Lancelot, as a mature dog, seems to really appreciate his toys and still plays with each and every one. He loves to lie in the center of his toys, surrounded on all sides, and play with each of them one at a time. Although Lancelot is the only pet in the house, he is never lonely." Since his mistress works at home, he gets plenty of attention, and when Jenavieve goes out of town, her parents enjoy staying with the playful and affectionate dog, who is considered their "grand dog," and he certainly lives up to that description with his regal and beautiful bearing.

Jenavieve said, "Lancelot is truly a teddy bear of a dog! He just loves to be cuddled and be near his people. Whenever he's in the house, he always likes to be very close by and have at least one paw touching you whenever possible. He's so tall you don't have to bend down to pet his back when you're both standing. And he loves to lean against you. Lancelot loves to lie down right next to any occupied chair so he can be petted and cuddled while you read or watch television. Hour-long cuddles and ear rubs are normal, expected, and part of his routine. He can never get enough TLC, and yet he always gives you more than you can ever give him in return. He's just an amazing angel of a dog!

"As time passed, Lancelot realized he was well loved and secure in his home, so now he doesn't require quite so many tummy rubs per hour these days, but he still expects to be cuddled whenever you come into a room he's in, and he will lift up his head in expectation. If he wants attention and you're distracted, he will shove his head under your elbow to make sure you have to pet him. When I am reading a good book, he will rest his head on my shoulder or lap and cuddle up with me, falling asleep, snoring softly."

Jenavieve is an accomplished musician, singer, and songwriter, and by happy coincidence, she adopted one of the most verbal dogs at Camp Husky. Lancelot is exceptionally talkative with a "lovely deep voice," and with her keen ear for subtle pitch changes, Jenavieve has learned to understand what Lancelot is communicating with his various vocal changes. For example, when she asks him a question, Jenavieve can tell when her dog wants to play with his toys by the tone of his voice. When Lancelot thinks she's been gone too long, he gives her a good talking-to when she gets home, as if to say, "I missed you; you were gone too long!"

Lancelot truly seems to appreciate his forever home with Jenavieve. "He is the most patient dog you could ever meet. I have to check on him frequently as he is so quiet and polite that he won't make noise or disturb my work to let me know that he wants to eat or go for a walk. If he is outside and wants in, or inside and wants out, he doesn't scratch on the door or bark; he just waits patiently like a perfect gentleman until I have time and notice he's waiting. Lancelot's perfect manners are even more apparent inside the house. He only plays with his toys, no matter what else is within his reach, which is pretty much everything when you're six foot tall on your hind legs.

"Amazingly, once Lancelot knows it's his walk time, he's off like a rocket. If anyone touches his walking leash he can go from sound asleep in his chair, to wagging his tail at the back door in mere seconds, bounding across the entire length of the house to get there and be raring to go. Lancelot is a bundle of pure love, joy, and enthusiasm with the refined manners of a true gentleman, while being a cuddly teddy bear to boot. He's the best dog anyone could ever hope to have the pleasure of living with and loving!

"Lancelot matured so beautifully. He was so very shy and insecure at first that he'd bark at a blade of grass moving and every sound; he was very afraid of people and even refused to go near any houses other than his own. Now, several years later, he's very relaxed, enjoys meeting new friends, and loves to have company over to visit. He especially loves children."

The love and companionship of two special dogs has sustained Jenavieve through the difficult times and made the good times even better. "Adopting my wolf dog, Stetson, and later Lancelot, were two of the highlights of my life. If I had to list the five greatest blessings of my life, Stetson and Lancelot would be there. My parents and I feel very blessed in so many ways to have him in our lives! This quotation by an unknown author, truly applies to my Lancelot: 'Anyone who says diamonds are a girl's best friend *never* had a dog!'"

Tess (a.k.a. Tres #70) Finds Her Forever Home with Linda Johnson, MD

Number 70 was a good-natured, noble-looking German shepherd with a golden-brown coat and a dark face. The veterinarian who examined her at Camp Husky estimated that she was at least seven years of age and had borne many litters of pups. Because an old injury had left her with only three toes on one foot, volunteers named her Tres. Her teeth were worn down like those of many of the older Camp Husky dogs. Volunteers acknowledged that Tres would be difficult to place due to her age. However, she was destined to experience human love and a good home thanks to Dr. Linda Johnson of Joliet, Montana.

Linda heard about Camp Husky through an animal-rescue group in her community. In addition to running a busy medical practice, she enjoyed training and showing black Labradors in field competitions around the country, but Dr. Johnson had always wanted a German shepherd companion dog. Around the time she heard about the Camp Husky rescue, Linda had two reasons to adopt: she wanted a companion dog for herself and she wanted one for her oldest male Labrador, who was lonely because he was no longer able to travel with the other dogs to the field competitions.

Linda drove about 220 miles, nearly four hours, to adopt one of our dogs. When she arrived, she told volunteers she wanted "a hard-to-adopt female dog." Volunteers matched Linda with Tres, a very calm and sweet-natured dog that got along well with all the other dogs. "It was love at first sight. Tres was the German shepherd I had always wanted, so I put her in the car, and we headed home to Joliet." Those of us who volunteered at Camp Husky have a special place in our hearts for compassionate people like Linda.

When they stopped for lunch on the long drive home, Tres almost escaped. "I could tell that she missed the big pack of dogs she had lived with for so many years," said Linda. Tres was depressed for the first two weeks, missing her pack. Linda also gave her a new name, Tess, and by the third week, Tess understood that she had a home with Linda and the Labs. "All of a sudden, I could tell that Tess was very happy, content, and had a sense that she now had a real home where she was needed."

Tess enjoyed the company of the older Labrador, and all was well until Linda took the old dog away for the day, leaving Tess alone in the house. This is when Linda discovered that Tess had an anxiety disorder and became destructive in the house when alone. (Dogs are pack animals. They hate being alone and crave companionship. This was especially true for the Camp Husky dogs.) That was the one and only time that Tess was ever destructive because from then on Linda would leave one of her Labs as a companion for her.

Linda described Tess as "just wonderful, loving, and nurturing toward me and the other dogs in the household. Tess was a calm and serene dog. She loved to be petted, but she was never pushy or in your face." While the Labs were busy retrieving and training for competition, Tess saw her job as guarding and watching over her new pack. Although never aggressive, she watched with suspicion any stranger who came to the house, most especially men. Linda described how Tess was "very leery" of men she did not know who came to work on the property or make a delivery. "She would lie down and watch them from a distance, and when they got close she let them know from her nonverbal behavior that she did not trust them and that they had better behave themselves around her family."

Tess especially enjoyed the times when Linda's grandkids would come to the house to visit. "She was great with kids. I had always wanted a German shepherd, and I got a great one. Tess was everything we admire in German shepherds: a faithful and dependable guardian with a calm and affectionate nature." In the summer of 2012, while Linda was out of town with the Labs at a field competition, Tess developed a distended stomach, and she died before the pet sitter realized how sick she was. Until those last painful hours, Tess was "supremely happy in her home in Joliet." She died knowing she had a home and was loved.

Bear (a.k.a. Wooley #19), Our Oldest Male, Finds a Loving Home

Wooley was the oldest male and one of the largest dogs at Camp Husky, and for that reason, we volunteers worried that no one would adopt him. Our veterinarian estimated that he was ten years of age or older in 2008. Ironically, Wooley would be the first dog adopted. John and Mary Lawrence of Butte were volunteering at the spay-and-neuter event held for Camp Husky dogs, when they were assigned to take care of "a very sweet but huge dog." Mary and John were so impressed with Wooley that they adopted him and took him home that day, changing his name to Bear. Bear looked more like a German shepherd than a husky, and he had a lot of scars on his face from fights. Volunteers believed that Bear was the father or grandfather of many of our black-and-tan shepherds.

Bear was one of the adults taken off the trailer (along with his mate and young puppies) at the Chelsea Bailey Animal Shelter the night before the big "unloading" of the bus at the Anselmo mine. Samantha Collier said the older dog appeared confused but also relieved to be out of the trailer. He was given food and water and a bed for the night inside the shelter. He was soon transferred to the Anselmo. A few days after his rescue, volunteers groomed Bear by combing him and giving him a bath. It took three volunteers working together for four hours to finish grooming him, thus his Camp Husky name, Wooley. Volunteers recalled that Wooley enjoyed the attention they lavished on him, and he was relaxed and smiling during the grooming. Everyone commented that Wooley had such a good temperament.

Wooley, now Bear, lived contentedly with the Lawrences for one year until he developed cancer and had to be euthanized. The family missed Bear so much that they wanted another Camp Husky dog.

The Lovable Mufasa (#85) Takes Bear's Place

In the year that Bear lived with the Lawrence family, another great dog, Mufasa, was adopted by a resident of Anaconda. While living there, Mufasa was found wandering around town and was taken to the Anaconda Animal Shelter. The Anaconda owners did not claim Mufasa from the shelter, and his story might have ended there had it not been for two of the most generous and dedicated volunteers at Camp Husky, Merlena and Monte Moore. They were following up to find out how Mufasa was doing, when they discovered he was in the shelter. They bailed him out and took him to Cindy McIlveen, who fostered several Camp Husky dogs.

Cindy described Mufasa as "a real sweetheart. A kind of gentle giant, who was easy to walk and always well behaved." This author was familiar with the good-natured Mufasa. He was a favorite among many of us who volunteered at Camp Husky. The last time I saw him, he was at Cindy's home in Butte and as easygoing and friendly as ever. Mufasa was a very large dog with definite husky markings and characteristics, but he was likely part white German shepherd as well.

When the Lawrences met Mufasa after losing their Bear, they asked Cindy if they might adopt him. Cindy was very attached to Mufasa by this time, but since she already had one Camp Husky dog, she reluctantly parted with Mufasa. She loved the dog, but she also knew the good life he would have with the Lawrences.

Mufasa, along with many of the Camp Husky dogs, took a while to warm up to and trust men. John knew this and allowed Mufasa to develop trust at his own speed. He was well behaved at Camp Husky and when he lived with Cindy, and he continued to be well mannered and easy to have around the house when he moved in with the Lawrences. John said of Mufasa, "He is a little jealous of the attention our minipinscher gets, but mostly he is chilled and relaxed at home. Mufasa is a house dog and apparently thinks he is the size of our mini, because he will jump on our bed at night just like the mini, although he weighs one hundred and twenty pounds!" I understand that the couple had to get a king-size bed to accommodate the giant dog.

Both Wooley (Bear) and Mufasa were very popular with volunteers at Camp Husky because of their sweet and loveable dispositions; however, they were very different looking. While Wooley was a brown German shepherd in appearance, Mufasa had the markings of a Siberian husky, although he was much larger than the typical husky. Both Wooley and Mufasa had very thick fur, and John shaved them in the summer to keep them comfortable. And like his daughter, Juno, and his son, Simba, Mufasa was a talker and had a "real outgoing personality."

Cindy McIlveen sent the following e-mail to a number of volunteers on August 8, 2012: "Hi Everyone. Some terrible news, I'm afraid. I just got off the phone with Mary Lawrence. Mary and John had to put Mufasa down about an hour ago. He developed liver troubles a few days ago and went into full liver failure today. Dr. Cornelius did everything he could... even consulted with other vets...but nothing worked. Our big gentle giant...patriarch of Camp Husky is gone. But I can say for sure...on behalf of all 120+ volunteers...that he will never be forgotten. He was lucky to have such a nice life with such wonderful people...John and Mary...they just adored him. Cindy."

As I was finishing this book, I received this e-mail from the Lawrences: "Thank you so much for your diligence in getting this love story written. We miss our babies Bear and Mufasa every day, but they will remain forever a part of us."

Simba (#86), a Belgian Malinois, Knows When His Owner Is Coming Home

Simba, a fawn-colored puppy about three months of age, was the eighty-sixth dog to be photographed and named that first day at the Anselmo mine-shaft building. Volunteer Samantha Collier recalls finding little Simba with Mufasa together in one of the many wire cages on the large trailer Brode pulled behind the bus. We have no idea who Simba's mother was, but Mufasa was definitely Simba's protector and probably his father as well, and that is why volunteers named the two dogs after the father and son in *The Lion King*.

Those familiar with the breed noticed that Simba looked like a Belgian Malinois, a herding breed often used for military and police work because of their alertness, intelligence, fearlessness, and strong protective instincts. While his father, Mufasa, was a husky-shepherd mix, Simba's mother was probably a Belgian Malinois. Most people will associate the Belgian Malinois breed with Cairo, the canine member of the Navy SEALs team that took down the world's most notorious terrorist, Osama bin Laden. Simba may not be a highly trained military hero, but he is highly intelligent and very special member of his human family, and from the photos I have seen of both dogs, they have similar markings and coloring. While Simba has the appearance of a Belgian Malinois, he also has some characteristics of a husky—most notably, talking.

Simba's early adoption history isn't very clear. I understand he was adopted by a young family from Missoula with a little girl. Apparently, all was well and this was a good home for Simba until the husband and wife both lost their jobs and had to move out of their home. Through no one's fault, Simba lost his first human family because of the recession. Simba again went up for adoption and was placed on the Montana Companion Animal Network website. He was adopted a second time by individuals who kept him for only three weeks. Apparently, Simba suffered from separation anxiety, so when the couple went to work, he destroyed their curtains. Unfortunately, many people who adopt have very little understanding of dogs and the severe grief, anxiety, and fear they feel when separated from people with whom they have bonded. For the third time, Simba went on the adoption website. Only this time, luck was with him!

In the city of Port Orchard, Washington, outside of Seattle, Walt Harvey, who grew up in Butte, was searching online for a dog to adopt when he saw Simba. He knew this was the right dog for him and his wife, Susie. For the previous thirteen years they had shared their home with Angel and Angel's daughter, both Belgian Malinois and wonderful companion dogs. Like German shepherds, Belgian Malinois require training and owners who understand and appreciate the breed. They are high-energy, very sensitive dogs that will do anything for an owner they respect. They are very loyal and prone to forming deep attachments to their families.

Walt first noticed Simba on the website when the couple had just lost Angel. Simba caught Walt's attention because he looked like Angel. Time passed; Simba went through two adoptions and was back on the website. By then, the Harveys had lost Angel's daughter to cancer. Susie was devastated from losing both dogs in a short period of time, and like so many of us after the death of a beloved pet, she told herself, "I can't go through this grief again." Many people who have these emotions following the loss of a pet eventually decide that the best way to heal from grief and to honor the faithful companion they have lost is to rescue and provide a good home to another pet. And so, after seven months of living without a dog, Walt and Susie made the decision to drive to Missoula and adopt Simba.

Walt knew that this was the dog for him from the first time he saw the picture on the website. Susie wasn't entirely convinced until she actually met Simba. "Once I looked into those soft brown eyes, I was a goner," she said. Simba seemed to know that this was his forever home because he bonded very quickly with Susie, Walt, and their three cats. Susie described how her oldest cat plays with Simba by using his paws to box with the eighty-four-pound dog.

Simba had some serious health problems when the Harveys adopted him. Their veterinarian diagnosed him with low thyroid and mange brought on by a grain allergy and the stress of losing three homes in his brief life. Now, thanks to a healthful diet, good medical care, and a secure and low-stress life with good people who love him, Simba is a healthy, normal-weight dog with a beautiful coat.

Walt and Susie described Simba as "a mindful, easygoing, well-behaved, and devoted companion. He follows me around the house all day," said Susie, who is retired. Simba is also a very curious and intelligent dog. "When we are working on a project around the house, Simba is very curious and sticks his nose right in there as if he is managing the job," said

Walt. Simba is also a talker, especially in the morning when he thinks it is time for Walt to wake up and start the day.

Perhaps the most interesting thing about Simba is that he always knows exactly when Walt is on his way home from work. This is all the more remarkable because Walt's work takes him out of town to different locations, so even Susie cannot predict when he will be home on any given evening. Not long after they adopted him, Susie started noticing that exactly twenty minutes before Walt's car would pull into their driveway, Simba would leave Susie's side and stand at the living room window, looking out on the front of the house, waiting for Walt.

After about four years with the Harveys, Simba got a special surprise. Walt and Susie adopted a golden retriever puppy named Annie. Following in Mufasa's footsteps, Simba was nurturing, loving, and protective toward the little puppy. Now the two are best friends and inseparable.

Jake (#46) Meets Sarah Martin of Missoula

Jake was one of many older puppies on the bus, and from the black tip on his tail and other features, volunteers determined that he was probably the son of Mufasa and brother to Simba. I have compared their photos, and Jake does resemble Simba. Jake was off to a good start when he was adopted by a mature woman living alone in Butte; however, in 2009, when loss of jobs and economic distress were displacing many families, pets were often the first casualties. That was the case with Jake in Butte, as it was with his brother, Simba. Jake did well for several months with his first owner until her adult daughter, grandchildren, and their dogs all moved into the home. Although Jake was reported to be good with the grandchildren, there was conflict between the dogs, and Jake found himself homeless. By this time, Camp Husky had closed, but there was still a core of volunteers looking out for the dogs and trying to make certain they did not end up in the Chelsea Bailey Animal Shelter, a dangerous place for Camp Husky dogs. First among these volunteers was Cindy, who stepped in to rescue Jake and provide a temporary home at her house. Cindy was working on an oil rig off Saudi Arabia at the time, but her house sitter and pet sitter, Carl, a college student and former Camp Husky volunteer, set about finding a home for Jake. Carl was employed part time with a corporation that had offices in Butte and Missoula. Carl e-mailed employees about Jake's plight, and Sarah Martin of Missoula read the e-mail and saw the photo of Jake.

Sarah had enjoyed the companionship of a large female Lab for nearly fourteen years. Now without a dog in December of 2009, she wasn't sure whether she wanted another dog. Cindy and Carl offered to drive Jake to Missoula, and Sarah decided to see if this beautiful dog could be happy with her. At first Jake showed obvious signs of separation anxiety, not surprising since this was his third home after Camp Husky. Many folks adopting don't stop to think how traumatic it is for dogs to change homes, but Sarah was well prepared.

When she decided to give Jake a try, Sarah did something very smart: she used a three-day weekend so that she could give total attention to Jake. "While Jake was afraid at first, we were very bonded by the end of the three days. I knew he would be my dog when he jumped up on my bed that first night and fell asleep with his head resting on my feet!" From the very start, Sarah found Jake to be a "well-behaved dog who always wants to please me. He is quiet, sweet, and affectionate. My Lab was so active that she often knocked things on the floor with her tail, but Jake is just calm and never disturbs anything in the house, although he does enjoy playing with the many toys I bought for him, especially his football." Sarah's description of Jake reminds me of his father, Mufasa, who was always easygoing and affectionate with volunteers.

When Sarah is working at the computer or doing paperwork of some kind, Jake will bring a toy, as if to say, "Let's play." If she says, "Not now, Jake," the dog will go back to his toy box and pick out another toy to see if this one interests Sarah. This goes on until Sarah gives in and takes a break to play with her dog. In addition to playing indoors, they both enjoy their regular walks.

Sarah said that Jake always wants to please her. She suffers from migraines, and when she has a headache Jake seems to understand, and he plays quietly with his toys, letting her rest. Otherwise, he shows his happiness by tossing his toy in the air and prancing around the house like a prince in his domain. This woman and her dog are attuned to each other. Jake seems to be able to understand what Sarah is saying from the tone of her voice, and Sarah can tell Jake's moods by his very expressive ears.

Jake stands out as one of the smaller Camp Husky dogs, weighing only about sixty pounds. He is also unusual in that he is quiet and does not talk like his brother, Simba. Sarah is grateful that Cindy and Carl helped her adopt this great dog. Since adopting Jake, Sarah has a new job she loves in a kennel, boarding, and training facility where she can work with dogs.

In a 2015 update, Sarah said that Jake "has matured but is still a wonderful boy. He is playful and affectionate with me and with some of our close people and dog friends. Otherwise, he is calm and gentle but content to observe when around most other people and dogs. Jake is definitely a more confident dog now, but he does get anxious when we are apart. He loves his daily walks, whining in anticipation and prancing as we take off."

Louette and Larry Jaeger Adopt Momma (a.k.a. Phyllis)

Momma, a beautiful white German shepherd and an exceptionally sweet-natured dog, would encounter a lot of human meanness and abuse before she found her forever home. Phyllis was one of the fourteen dogs that Phyllis Ruana took to the Dillon shelter in November 2008. The stay in Dillon must have been a traumatic experience for this poor dog, but at least she escaped being killed like the other thirteen wonderful dogs. Phyllis the dog went back to Camp Husky, where volunteers discovered that she was pregnant. When her delivery time came, she trusted volunteers Mary Ann and Tim to stay and help her. They renamed her Momma to honor the fact she was the last Camp Husky dog to give birth.

After her puppies were weaned, Momma was adopted by a family from Helena who had a cat, although volunteers warned them against adopting her if they had a cat. When the new owners discovered that their cat and Momma were not compatible, the dog once again found herself at Camp Husky. Next, Momma was adopted by a man in Anaconda with many dogs, who kept Momma in his backyard and was slowly starving her to death. Luckily, Tim was conscientious and drove out to check on Momma. He found her in a very malnourished state, having lost nearly half her body weight! Tim brought Momma back to Camp Husky; it was then that her luck started to change.

The Jaegers had two wonderfully playful golden retrievers, and shortly after one of them died, Louette learned from volunteers about Momma's ordeals. Louette remembers seeing Momma with her puppies in the enclosed yard at Camp Husky before she was adopted for the first time. After she was returned to Camp Husky for the third time, volunteer Jocelyn Dodge stepped in to foster Momma. Jocelyn is skilled in working with fearful dogs and helped Momma to trust again after her distressing experiences, starting with the Dillon shelter. In the meantime, the Jaegers determined to adopt Momma and give this hard-luck dog "a family and not just a home." However, when they phoned Tim to say they wanted Momma, he said he was at that moment driving Momma and another dog to a husky rescue in Hamilton. Apparently, it took two phone calls and firm insistence to get Phyllis Ruana to allow the Jaegers to adopt the dog.

When the Jaegers and Momma met for the first time, it was love at first sight. Momma eagerly jumped in their car. Finally, Momma had the loving forever home she so deserved.

Before the Jaegers adopted her, Momma had formed a strong attachment to Jocelyn's dog, Tucker. While she was happy at the Jaeger home, she missed Tucker, and so, shortly after her adoption by the Jaegers, Momma jumped off their eight-foot-high deck and ran away to visit Jocelyn and Tucker. The Jaegers were frantic when Momma disappeared, so they took action to "Momma proof" the deck. "To keep Momma from escaping to visit Tucker while we were at work, we had to turn that deck into a Fort Knox with wire," said Louette.

Momma quickly formed a close bond with Maggie, the family's golden retriever. Maggie taught Momma to toss a ball back and forth to her, a game Maggie had played with the golden retriever who passed away before Momma was adopted. After a little time passed, it became evident to Louette that Momma had too much energy for the aging Maggie, so she set out to find a third dog. Louette and Momma went to a no-kill shelter, Pintler Pets, in Anaconda, where they found a fourteen-week-old husky-whippet cross named Skya. Momma lavishes affection on the puppy, and Skya ensures that Momma gets lots of exercise running around the one-acre property.

When I had a follow-up interview with her in October 2015, Louette said that Momma, then about ten years of age, is doing very well and still plays with Skya. Maggie, the golden retriever, has passed away and is missed by the whole family. Skya is so devoted to Momma that she howls in sorrow when the older dog is at the groomers for a few hours. The two dogs are inseparable, and Momma stays active playing and running with Skya and the neighbor dog as well. I have a photo of the three dogs sleeping by the Jaegers' fireplace after a hard morning of play last winter 2015.

Louette described her beautiful shepherd-husky mix as a sweetheart. Although they are dog people, having owned a great German shepherd and very loveable golden retrievers, they say they have "never known a dog with as much personality as Momma has." Like several other owners I interviewed, the Jaegers say that their Camp Husky dog "smiles when she is happy. She lifts up her top gum and shows her teeth and smiles when we greet her." Momma is also quite verbal and among the most talkative of the Camp Husky dogs.

Many dog people will say that while they loved all of their dogs, they had an extraordinary bond with one special dog. For Louette, Momma is that once-in-a-lifetime dog. "Momma is my dog," said Louette. "Momma is very affectionate and has many lovable traits. When I am sitting in the living room, she will come up and nudge my arm to get me to pet her." Momma shows affection with "gentle love nibbles" on Louette's arm, or she will tease Louette in the wintertime by pulling off her throw blanket. These playful behaviors might not seem unusual for most dogs, but they represent extraordinary improvement for our Camp Husky dogs, which were so afraid of people that many cowered in corners and did not want to leave their kennels in the early weeks of the camp.

The Jaegers admit to spoiling Momma. She spends lots of quality time with them and sleeps in their bedroom at night. With affectionate owners and great canine companions, Momma now has everything a dog needs. She will be able to handle one more challenge, a disease called pannus that is causing her to go blind. Incidentally, three other dogs mentioned in this book have the disease as well. Louette was told that this is a common condition in both Siberian huskies and German shepherds, and it seems to be more common in dogs living in high altitudes.

Even though Momma is an affectionate dog, she still had some fear of strangers when first adopted by the Jaegers. Now that fear is gone, and she enjoys meeting new people. She likes children—especially the grandkids and little nieces and nephews who frequently come to the house—but gets agitated when the children run around her, perhaps because of her failing eyesight. The Jaegers are examples of wise owners who use a little forethought to avoid potential problems. The children know that Momma is losing her sight and that they should not upset her, and when there are simply too many children for Momma to cope with, she is allowed quiet time away from the children.

Louette has a long history of helping animals in our community. I first met her some years ago when we were both part of a very large group of concerned citizens lobbying the Butte-Silver Bow City Council because of our anger at the way dogs and cats were treated at the Chelsea Bailey Animal Shelter. This group wanted Butte Animal Services to take dogs seized in Butte to the volunteer-run Pintler Pets shelter in the neighboring town of Anaconda rather than the Butte shelter. Consequently, Louette and I joined others from Butte in volunteering at Pintler Pets during the time in which Butte animals were taken there. Louette has also been very active with the Butte Spay-Neuter Task Force, the volunteer organization that spayed and neutered the Camp Husky dogs and puppies at no cost.

Louette and Larry are especially remarkable because they have reached out time and time again to help animals in spite of their own personal tragedy. One year before the bus full of dogs arrived in Butte, this couple lost their son to ALS (amyotrophic lateral sclerosis). As tragic and devastating as this loss was for them, they have continued to selflessly volunteer for animals. Louette spoke of how much comfort her two affectionate and playful golden retrievers gave her in the difficult time of her son's illness. Later, Momma would also help soothe the pain. "Without a doubt, my dog family consoled me with their unconditional love whenever I was crying and overcome with sadness." Louette is so glad she adopted Momma. When asked if she has any regrets, she answered, "That I could not adopt more of those poor dogs!"

Fiver (a.k.a. Comet) and Honey, Neglected Puppies, Find a Loving Family

In February 2009, a young woman named Wendy Schwab, a native of Kansas City, Missouri, who had recently moved to Butte, went to the Chelsea Bailey Animal Shelter, where one Camp Husky mother dog and her pups were being housed. (It's unclear why they were there, given the shelter operator's dislike of Camp Husky dogs.) Wendy was determined to adopt one of the pups, Comet, although the shelter director discouraged her from doing so, saying that the Camp Husky dogs were part wolf or coyote and could be dangerous to have around cats or children. Fiver today at age seven is living proof of how very wrong that woman was.

After adopting Comet, Wendy tried to find out from the shelter staff what had happened to Comet's mother and her other pups, but they would not tell her. Because of the hostile way the shelter director talked about the mother and her pups, Wendy feared that the shelter director might have had them all killed. This author also tried in vain to find out what happened to that mother dog and her puppies.

Comet was three months old when Wendy adopted him, and Wendy believes that he had never been taken outside or socialized by the shelter staff. It appears that Comet had a narrow escape and would have been euthanized if Wendy had not chosen to trust her own judgment and intuition rather than the opinion of the shelter director. Wendy changed the puppy's name to Fiver, and he grew into a very gentle and affectionate dog. "He is the sweetest dog you ever met," said Wendy.

While Fiver was thriving in a secure and loving home, another Camp Husky puppy was not so fortunate. The first owner to adopt little Honey wasn't ready for an active puppy. Honey ended up with a second owner who was no improvement over the first. Wendy first encountered Honey when she and her fiancé, David Brodhead, were remodeling a house next door to where Honey lived. According to Wendy "the dog was frequently left without food, water, or shelter from the cold. He would jump the fence and roam the neighborhood looking for food in garbage cans." In the fall of 2010, when the owner had gone to Missoula for a week, leaving the dog in the backyard without food or water, he once again jumped the fence looking for food and was hit by a car. That would have been the end of poor Honey had David not been there working on his house. He saw the accident and immediately took the injured dog to a veterinarian.

The newlyweds took Honey home with them after his injuries were treated. Not only was poor Honey badly injured by the accident, he was also sick from eating garbage. As one might expect, the young dog had a lot of insecurity, fear, and abandonment issues as well. It took patience and persistence to help Honey adjust to the first loving home he had known. Now, Honey and Fiver are brothers and are very devoted to each other and their human family.

Fiver, another son of Mufasa, looks like a husky, while Honey looks like a German shepherd; both have turned out to be great family dogs. Had it not been for Wendy and David, both dogs would have died without ever knowing human kindness. About a year after Honey was rescued, Wendy gave birth to a beautiful baby boy. Fiver and Honey lavished love and devotion on baby Henry. With her baby strapped to her chest, Wendy enjoyed taking both dogs for long walks while the family lived in Butte. Later, this young family and their two dogs moved to Colorado, where a second baby boy, Wren, arrived for Fiver and Honey to love.

After Wren was born, the family moved back to Butte so that David could earn his nursing degree at Montana Tech. In November 2015, when graduation was only a month away for David, I visited the Brodheads' home in Butte, meeting David and Wendy, their two delightful little boys, and their great dogs. In 2016 the Brodhead family returned to northwestern Colorado.

Fiver and Honey have both grown into very large, friendly, calm, and mature dogs. Honey still has some problems related to his days of surviving on garbage, but otherwise both dogs appear to be in good health. The dogs have benefitted from regular walks and good care.

David and Wendy showed me a video of the day they brought baby Henry home from the hospital. In the video you see the young couple gently placing their infant on their bed, and then the two dogs starting to sniff and circle the bed with a combination of intense curiosity and wonder. Suddenly, the two dogs seem to realize that they have a wonderful new addition to their pack, and their nonverbal behavior expresses what I can only describe as joy. Fiver and Honey have been part of the family for both Henry and Wren since each boy was born. Because of the compassionate actions of their parents nearly seven years before, these boys are fortunate to have two good-natured dogs to look after them.

Camp Husky Dogs with Extreme Fear of People

There were two beautiful black-and-tan German shepherd mother dogs at Camp Husky, Star and Susie, who were extremely fearful of people. Both dogs are now in good homes thanks to special volunteers who worked with them before they were adopted. A third mother dog, Gypsy, stood out because she was a more exotic-looking German shepherd and also very fearful of people. This author fondly remembers all three dogs and their puppies at Camp Husky.

Siri (a.k.a. Star #40)

Star was one of our mother dogs, a classic black-and-tan German shepherd with a very sweet face. I remember watching a young man, Russ Wagoner, work with Star to help her overcome her fear of people. It was obvious that Russ felt a deep attachment to this young mother dog, and he deserves credit for teaching her to trust people and preparing her for a successful adoption. I believe Russ wanted to adopt Star but was unable to do so at that time. Volunteer Jocelyn Dodge also counted Star among her favorite Camp Husky dogs. Star was "a real sweetheart," recalled Jocelyn.

While Russ socialized Star, volunteer Barb LeProwse was instrumental in getting Star adopted. Jerry McCalloch wanted to adopt a German shepherd, and he was under the impression that the Camp Husky dogs were all Siberian huskies. As fate would have it, Jerry went shopping at the Kmart store where Barb and her team of volunteers were holding a Camp Husky fundraising event and had puppies present. She also had a display with several pictures of the adult dogs available for adoption. Having owned German shepherds since he was twelve years of age, Jerry's eye went immediately to a photo of Star. That photo was enough to motivate Jerry to drive to Camp Husky and adopt her.

As Jerry tells it, "Star was very timid at first, and she just wanted to stay in her kennel. After a few days, she came out of the kennel and approached me." They changed her name to Siri, and she soon evolved into a wonderful and affectionate family dog. "Now, she loves everyone, and she especially enjoys playing with our little granddaughter." Siri is also best buddies with the couple's miniature schnauzer.

Her veterinarian estimated that Siri was only one year old when the McCallochs adopted her. Jerry reports that Star has been quite healthy since she was adopted, and she has a heavy coat of fur to keep her warm in the cold Butte winters.

Susie (#72)

Susie, a beautiful black-and-tan German shepherd with a sweet face, was another of our young mother dogs that was extremely frightened of people. I remember what a good mother Susie was, but no one could put a leash on her or take her for a walk. I don't think she would have survived and found a good home if not for two dedicated volunteers, Cindy McIlveen and Tim.

I was working at Camp Husky on the day of the spay-neuter clinic in December 2008. All the volunteers and dogs had gone to the mall where the spay-neuter clinic was being held. Only Tim and one dog, Susie, remained at Camp Husky as I started cleaning the empty kennels. Volunteers had not been able to coax Susie out of her kennel and into a crate for transport. As I worked nearby, I watched the patient way that Tim talked to Susie, calming her down and eventually getting her into a crate and on her way to the mall.

Susie ended up at Cindy's house with two other "unadoptable" dogs. One Saturday soon after Camp Husky closed, several volunteers met at the home of volunteer Katie Donovan for a day-long seminar based on *The Dog Listener*, by Jan Fennell. We were trying to learn how to help Susie and some of the other dogs that volunteers were still fostering. Later, Cindy arranged for a trainer to come from Helena to work with Susie and Jack, two of the dogs most frightened of people. I witnessed Cindy's patient devotion to helping Susie and the other dogs.

Cindy found a good home for Susie with Bob and Alice Davies. These dog lovers had owned German shepherds in the past and were willing to take Susie with all her problems. They tried to bring Susie inside their home, but "she freaked out and hid under the bed." Instead, they fixed up a place for her on their upper-level deck, overlooking the city of Butte. She also has a warm bed on the ground floor where she can hang out when the temperature drops. Susie enjoys accompanying Bob and Alice on walks. Although off leash, she stays close to the couple, who are in a rural area. When not walking with Bob and Alice, Susie likes to stay on the deck. She is still extremely timid and does not like being petted. However, recently that has changed a little. When Bob and Susie are walking they sometimes meet up with a neighbor and his dog. When the neighbor dog comes up to Bob to be petted, Susie follows that dog's example, allowing Bob to pet her. Susie is in good health at about eight years of age with the exception of a recent development of cataracts.

Without the devotion of Tim, Cindy, and Bob and Alice Davies, this extremely timid dog would not have had a chance of finding a safe and secure home.

Hazel (a.k.a. Gypsy #41)

As I write this nearly seven years later, I can still clearly see a very young German shepherd–husky mix with her three pups. She was quite thin but still beautiful, with a touch of the exotic about her, and I suspect that is why volunteers named her Gypsy. What I remember most about Gypsy was how afraid she was of people. Unlike the other dogs, she would not walk outside on a leash, so volunteers would carry her to an outdoor kennel each day to enjoy fresh air and sunshine or snow. I also remember the day an attractive young woman from Helena, Sarah Sadowski, came to Camp Husky and expressed an interest in Gypsy. I then observed Sarah coming on several Saturdays to work with Gypsy, and her devotion to that fearful dog inspired me. The following is Sarah's story of how she transformed our Gypsy into her Hazel.

"It was the week of my birthday when news broke of the arrest of a man outside of Butte who had been driving a school bus and trailer crammed with over one hundred dogs. The news reports of Camp Husky had a special appeal for me, because less than five months before, I had lost the beloved husky mutt I had raised up from a pup to an old age of thirteen and a half. I phoned Camp Husky in October to inquire about adoption. I was told that volunteers were caring for the dogs and that they could not be adopted until the court case was settled.

"On a very cold Thanksgiving Day, while I was enjoying a delicious dinner and good conversation with friends, I made up my mind to pursue adoption of one of the dogs from the school bus. The next day, a friend agreed to accompany me on the sixty-five-mile drive to Butte, so we headed down to see the dogs at Camp Husky. As we drove up to the bright orange Arizona Street building, the sound of dogs filled the air. When we walked through what had formerly been an auto-repair shop, our senses were overwhelmed by the deafening sound of more than one hundred adult dogs barking, a pungent odor, and the sight of dog kennels everywhere. We observed several volunteers scooping poop and moving it to a huge pile out back. While one group of volunteers were mopping out kennels, a second group was walking the dogs from those kennels in one of two yards, while a third group was putting clean water in the kennels as well as clean bowls with food. One volunteer was washing the stainless steel bowls, and another was outside washing the plastic pallets on which the dogs slept. All the volunteers were busy, and I understood then why it had taken so long for someone to pick up the phone when I had phoned.

"As we entered the building, the first thing we saw was the 'maternity ward'—a series of chain-link kennels each with a mother dog and her pups. Each kennel contained two plastic pallets covered with warm blankets to keep the little families warm and cozy. At the far end of this maternity ward was a young mother dog with a litter of only three pups, all asleep on their blanket. When I looked at dog #41, she stared right at me with amazing yellow eyes. I asked a volunteer about her, and she said 'Gypsy is a tough one—really shy and fearful but a devoted mother.' On her kennel was a warning: 'Don't turn your back on this dog.'

"Heading home, I felt a deep sadness for the abuse these dogs had suffered. In early December, I decided to go back to Butte and see that yellow-eyed-big-eared-bag-of-bones dog again. On the next two Saturday visits to Camp Husky, I simply sat in the kennel with Gypsy and her pups. By January, the pups were weaned, and the volunteers determined that I could start trying to train and socialize this fearful dog.

"At that time, Gypsy was one of only three dogs that could not be walked on a leash by volunteers. Since she was not leash trained, volunteers had to carry her to the outside kennel area so she could get fresh air and sunshine. A volunteer carried her outside and put her in a kennel. There was snow on the ground and the temperature was well below zero as we sat on opposite sides of the kennel fence, chilling out.

"While volunteers were walking dogs on the other side of the kennels away from us, I decided to start the training and took hold of the leash that the volunteer had attached to Gypsy. This simple action seemed to terrify her; she freaked out, thrashed, and rolled around on the ground in a complete state of fear. I pinned her down in an effort to calm her, and Tim came running out after watching us from the window. Tim scooped her up and carried her back to her inside kennel, and now I was clear about what I needed to do for this animal. I looked at Gypsy and said, 'I will be back in a week for you.'

"Before I left, another volunteer told me that some of the more adoptable dogs were being sent to animal shelters across the state for adoption, but 'this one will be here for a while.' Volunteers told me they were hopeful I would take Gypsy and that I might be her last chance.

"Returning to Helena, I purchased a thirteen-foot-by-eight-foot chain-link kennel with six-foot walls, a hard plastic crate, ropes, and a cozy dog bed, and that week a friend helped me set up the kennel in my yard. When I returned the next Saturday, the volunteers and I agreed on a thirty-day foster. Tim put Gypsy in the crate and carried the crate out to my truck. My experience with my husky pup convinced me that I could do this. The need for people to adopt was great, and this dog in particular needed me and I needed a dog to accompany me on my mountain hikes. During our first month together I managed to accustom Gypsy to taking baths, walking on a leash, getting in and out of cars, and going in and out of her crate. Although I provided toys for Gypsy and observed her playing with the toys in her kennel, when I approached, she would always stop playing.

"The most serious problem with Gypsy in those early weeks was the extreme fear that made her want to run away. One evening when we returned home after some errands and before I could get out of the car to get to the back door, Gypsy launched herself out of the back window and ran off down my street with her short leash still attached to her collar. As I waited in the front yard, I kept thinking how much I actually liked that little dog and I dreaded calling the volunteers at Camp Husky and telling them I had lost their dog. Finally, eight hours later, at around ten, I looked out the window; I saw Gypsy standing in the yard near her kennel with an expression on her face that looked like a smile. So I told her to 'get in here,' and into the house she came. That's when I knew she had figured out that she belonged with me. I decided to fill out the paperwork and make her mine.

"I thought that Gypsy was a horrible name for a dog that wanted to run away. I mulled over names and arrived at Hazel. Not only does it match her coloring but also this dog and I would work together to draw her out of her hazelnut. Under what I refer to as 'the Fear,' Hazel is a sweet girl. Over time, Hazel put on weight, gained confidence, and became my mountain dog. As we hike alone carrying our backpacks through forests or climbing to mountaintops, Hazel prances with her tail held up high with a sense of purpose and belonging. Here and there she has even exhibited protective behavior, reflecting confidence, not fear.

"With each passing month, Hazel is slowly but surely emerging out of that fearful place where she learned to survive on that bus. She is still unpredictable with new dogs but loves the doggie friends she has made. She is also leery of new people and prefers to be in her kennel outside when the house is full of people. Generally it's just the two of us at the house; however, we host friends and family for overnight visits and longer. Hazel takes a while to get used to a new person being in the house; she used to hide in the bedroom but over time is more apt to join the group, especially if there is another dog around! I find that it works best for Hazel if people who are new to her just ignore her at first until she is comfortable with them rather than trying to talk to her or pet her when first introduced.

"I have had great support with Hazel's training. An eight-week puppy kindergarten with a woman named Rita Munson was very helpful. It takes a community to rehabilitate and teach a traumatized animal, and Jim at Dogwood Kennel in Helena has been great. When I am away, Hazel gets very anxious, so I leave her at Dogwood Kennel, and Jim takes her for walks and helps her develop confidence.

"Like most of the dogs on the bus, Hazel never had a chance to play in a safe and nurturing environment, so I had to teach her to play. It took months of effort, but I can still remember the first time she wagged her tail and the first time she actually played with me. It took an enormous amount of work, but going from several leashes on her to a long rope to off leash on verbal command is totally awesome. Now we have adventures; we swim, canoe, cross rivers, climb onto snowy mountaintops in the summertime, and go on road trips. She still needs to gain more confidence in town and in busy settings with lots of people, and that's OK; we have time. I have discovered that my fearful dog is also very brave. She is healing, and we have learned to trust each other. I have found that behaviors she developed to protect herself on the bus are the most challenging to change, but we are making significant progress. For example, when we are on the walking path on Mount Helena, and we pass unfamiliar people and their dogs, I try to stay upbeat as Hazel is wild on the leash. Fortunately, most people understand, and several folks we have seen over the last three years while on our walks have commented on how Hazel has improved in her physical appearance as well as her behavior. It's special to reflect back on how far we've come, and it's special to have a doggie companion in the backcountry."

Tips from Sarah on How to Train a Fearful Dog

"Roberta asked for some tips to share with folks who may adopt a dog that was not socialized as a puppy, or any dog with lots of fear. For a dog that has not been socialized, learning to fit in takes time. Be prepared to deliver commands in a clear and calm voice with an even tone. Be consistent and persistent; it may take many months to teach some of the essentials. Family and friends who interact with the dog need to be patient and understanding as well. Work in a variety of diverse situations. A trained dog is a versatile dog. I have taught Hazel to interact appropriately with cats, horses, and some other livestock. Each interaction needs to be seen as an opportunity to teach the dog and develop positive habits. To train your dog, first train yourself. Take puppy classes and obedience classes, consult with trainers, read books, and find a vet you trust. A puppy class is a good place to start even if the dog is a young adult. First and foremost be patient and aware of what vibes you are sending to your dog.

"The leash is a direct line in training. A common mistake is to take the dog off the leash too soon. Spend lots of time training on leash; then transition off and on the leash frequently. Be careful with off-leash work for the fearful dog. I used a fifteen-foot rope to begin off-leash training; it allowed Hazel to practice recalls and learn the command 'stop.' My goal for Hazel is 100 percent off-leash obedience.

"Set your dog up to succeed in training and overcome her fears by gradually desensitizing her to fearful situations and giving her lots of praise when she performs correctly during training so that she gains confidence. Above all, protect her from situations which are highly stressful and might set her up to fail and develop undesirable habits. When new dogs or children are visiting my home, and things get a little too intense for Hazel, I put her in a crate in the room so that she can observe people and animals while chilling out in her safe space until she is ready to come out and join the fun once again.

"Consulting with my vet, I learned that Hazel will probably never grow as large as she was meant to be due to malnutrition as a puppy. However, with lots of exercise Hazel has filled out and gained significant muscle tone. Keep your pet healthy with lots of exercise! A tired dog is a good dog.

"Hazel has taught me that it takes real commitment, consistent effort, and time to train a fearful dog, but the progress we have made together is highly rewarding. The dog that would not leave her kennel at Camp Husky will now take treats from my friends and even give them a high five with her paw. Having a dog like Hazel is a journey filled with surprises; it requires me to be humble, patient, and willing to adapt. Hazel continues to steadily improve her ability to function in town. She is a brave, playful, and obedient dog that has taught me serenity and mindfulness. Truth is, I'm her best friend, and we have many more mountains to climb."

CHAPTER 7
Adventure Dogs

O ne of the most common problems that owners of Camp Husky dogs reported to me is the tendency of the dogs to be timid and afraid of people or dogs they don't know. This was most true of dogs that were adults or older puppies on the bus. As a result of timidity and lack of socialization when they were young, some dogs ran off when first adopted and gave their owners quite a chase. In some cases, the dogs may have been trying to return to their pack.

Rhett (#38) of New Mexico Runs like the Wind
Rhett, a Belgian Tervuren, was a sweet but timid adult when volunteers took him off the bus in October 2008, and he was one of seven Camp Husky dogs taken to Help for Homeless Pets in Billings, Montana, when the manager offered to help us find homes for our dogs.

While Rhett was at the Billings shelter, Jay Walden, caretaker for a large ranch in Durango, Colorado, was grieving the loss of his beloved Belgian Tervuren, Julius, a faithful companion for fifteen years. Jay, whose avocations are fly-fishing and writing poetry and short stories, explained how he came to adopt Rhett: "One night I was really missing Julius and decided I would browse the Internet for pictures of Belgian Tervurens, just to bring back some fond memories of my dog. I came across the Help for Homeless Pets website and saw Rhett. The resemblance to Julius was uncanny. They could have been brothers, except for the age difference. The next day, I contacted HHP, found out as much as I could about Rhett, and officially adopted him on November 7, 2009." More than a year after he came off the bus in Butte, Rhett would finally have a forever home, but he would not make the transition easy for those who wanted to help him.

Jay waited a month while volunteers were found to drive Rhett to Colorado. Among the unsung heroes of animal rescues are the many good people who drive dogs from shelters to their new homes. One volunteer drove Rhett to Cheyenne, Wyoming, where Rhett spent the night and was to leave the next morning with another driver; however, things did not go as planned. Rhett jumped the fence of a corral where he was boarded that night. Although he stayed by the corral, no one could catch him. After three days of futile efforts, a Billings shelter employee who had won Rhett's trust drove down to Cheyenne and was able to persuade the dog to come to him. Finally, with the help of three generous folks, Rhett was on his way to Jay.

It would take a full month for Jay to earn Rhett's trust. Jay described what happened their first night together near Durango: "The first night I brought Rhett home, we spent about two hours together in the living room of my house, and I felt Rhett was really warming up to me. When it came time for me to go to bed, and I turned out the light, he started letting out some sad, mournful howls. Fearing that he might be trying to tell me that he needed to go outside to relieve himself, I turned on the light and went into the living room where I had left him. I stood near the door with his leash in hand and called to him, but he refused to budge. As soon as I cracked open the door, Rhett bolted over me, knocking me onto the porch, and then he was gone. I spent half the night searching and calling him, but he was nowhere to be found. At that time, I was living on a ranch with hundreds and hundreds of acres, and Rhett had lots of places to hide. I spent the next two weeks trying to catch him, but he would never come within two hundred yards of the house, and there were days when I didn't see him at all. When I did see him, he was usually in a field far off and would disappear like a wild animal when I called him. I was heartbroken and very worried. I was on the phone a lot with HHP in Billings, and they offered many ideas to get him back, but nothing worked. The only thing that gave me any hope was that he would come during the night and eat the food I left for him on the porch.

"Finally, at my wits' end, I called the local animal shelter for help, and they suggested I come by and rent a live trap. I was skeptical to say the least; Rhett seemed too wild and wily to fall for that. But that afternoon I drove to the shelter and got the trap along with a little instruction on how to set it up. When I came back to the house, Rhett was lying about two hundred yards away, across the pond from my house. I set up the trap next to the front porch where he had been coming for food, filled his bowl, and placed it inside the trap. I went inside and closed the front door and began to make dinner. As I worked, I looked out the window, watching him circling and sniffing the trap. Just as I thought—he was too smart to fall for this ruse. The next time I looked out, he was inside the trap eating his food, but his front feet were a few inches from the trigger mechanism. At this point, I was thinking, 'He's going to eat all that food and just back out of the trap; he's too smart.' About that time, he inched forward and triggered the door, which closed behind him. I expected to see him start to freak out, but he continued eating nonchalantly as I approached. Now I had another issue—how would I get him out? I decided the safest way was to take the trap and dog both inside the house before attempting his release. For the next month, my door was never opened without Rhett on the leash and the leash wrapped tightly around my hand. Over time, we bonded, and he was then able to roam the ranch on his own, always returning when he was tired out from a good run and ready to eat and spend the rest of the day hanging out with me at home."

Jay described his eighty-five-pound dog as "a big furry teddy bear" with "the classic markings of a Belgian Tervuren sheepdog." Rhett's face and muzzle are black, but his belly and legs are blond. Like most Camp Husky dogs, Rhett has a long and thick coat. Fortunately, he has had no health problems since Jay adopted him.

Jay said that although Rhett is "a very strong and powerful animal, he is also extremely loveable, gentle, and loyal. When I am around, he's always at my side and will follow me from room to room in the house; yet he can be independent and disappear to his little cave area between the couch and wall if he wants to take a nap and is sure I am not going anywhere." Unlike most Camp Husky dogs, Rhett isn't verbal. Other than whining when separated from Jay, he is normally quiet. Although he rarely barks, Rhett is a good watchdog. Unlike most dogs, Rhett will bark only once or twice to let Jay know that someone is approaching the house.

Now thoroughly bonded with Jay, "Rhett is still very timid around strangers, but never aggressive. When I have company, he'll hang out just out of reach, and it takes him quite a while to warm up enough to other people to allow them to pet him. On the other hand, Rhett is friendly with other dogs and never exhibits any aggressive tendencies."

In 2011, Jay and Rhett moved to the small town of Navajo Dam, New Mexico, a beautiful place in the San Juan River Valley, surrounded by towering sandstone buttes with pinyon pines and juniper. Jay, an avid fly-fisher, enjoys living near one of the top trout streams in the country, managing Abe's Motel and Fly Shop, and writing about fly-fishing on the business website or in short stories. Whether he is fly-fishing or writing, Jay always appreciates his quiet and loyal companion. "I am so glad I adopted this dog. He has filled a void left by the passing of Julius. His companionship has been invaluable, and he is my best pal. I am grateful to all the volunteers at Camp Husky, the town of Butte, and the folks at Help for Homeless Pets who make it possible for me to have this great dog in my life."

Since Jay and Rhett now live on the edge of the Navajo Dam State Park and BLM land, Rhett can still enjoy good, long runs on his frequent outings with Jay. "I have never known a dog that likes to run as much as Rhett, just for the sheer sake of running," said Jay. "His favorite times are when I take him out and let him off leash to run wide open until he's had his fill of exploring. That's another area where he's highly independent. He will do anything I tell him, except come back to me until he is ready. I have decided to let him have that degree of independence." Although he "runs like the wind," Rhett's days of running off are over—this special dog knows where he belongs, and he is not about to leave his best friend.

Bucky (a.k.a. Beauty #68) and Agate (a.k.a. Dolly #67) Live on the Edge of Yellowstone Park

Volunteers made every effort to put two, and sometimes as many as five, compatible dogs together in the enclosures at Camp Husky. Often these dogs developed very close bonds. Such was the case with Beauty, one of our mother dogs, and her cage mate, Dolly, a young adult unrelated to Beauty. Dolly is typical of the large white German shepherds at Camp

Husky, while Beauty is typical of the many white shepherd-husky mixes. Beauty is large and white like Dolly but with husky markings on her face.

Connie Landis, an artist and professor of art at Montana State University in Billings, and her husband, Robert Landis, an Emmy Award–winning wildlife filmmaker, heard about Camp Husky and decided to adopt one of our dogs. On February 25, 2009, Landis made the long drive to Butte from his home in Gardiner, Montana, on the border of Yellowstone National Park. At Camp Husky, volunteers introduced Landis to Beauty, the sixty-eighth dog to come off the bus, and described her as "shy but good on a leash." Since he spends long hours filming in Yellowstone most days, Landis decided to adopt Beauty's cage mate, Dolly, as well so that the two dogs could keep each other company.

As it turned out, Dolly would be an ideal companion dog for Landis, while Beauty would be quite a challenge because of her very shy and fearful nature. On their second day with Landis, Beauty broke through the fence surrounding the yard. It seems two neighbor dogs frightened her into the escape. Landis watched as his dog headed into Yellowstone Park. Beauty spent one day in Yellowstone before heading north, swimming the Yellowstone River, and then taking up residence in the national forest above Gardiner, Montana. A search-and-rescue team was organized consisting of the best wolf spotters, an expert trapper, and a woman who had trapped feral dogs in New Orleans after Katrina. For twelve days, Landis and others searched for Beauty. Fresh snow helped the tracking. Often they found Beauty's tracks crossed by wolf and coyote tracks. After several failed attempts to trap Beauty, new traps were brought in courtesy of the Humane Society. On the thirteenth day, Beauty walked into one of these traps.

It is difficult to imagine a more dangerous place for a dog than Yellowstone National Park and surrounding lands. No one could be more familiar with those dangers than Landis, who has been filming wildlife in Yellowstone for more than thirty years. For a dog to have survived nearly two weeks in the area is remarkable when one considers the dangers. While the grizzly bears would have been in hibernation when Beauty had her adventure, a lone dog could have been prey to mountain lions, wolves, or even coyotes. The geothermal dangers in the park were even more threatening. There are many places where a human or animal can take a step onto what looks like solid ground but is in fact only a thin crust over a boiling mud pot. Also, I marvel at how she managed to swim in freezing river water. How she did not die of hypothermia after that swim, when temperatures on land would have ranged from about a high of twenty-five degrees to a low somewhere near negative five, is rather remarkable. Beauty has to be a highly intelligent and strong dog to have survived as long as she did. Both dogs were exceptionally lucky to be adopted by a man who developed patience and persistence first as a high-school math teacher and chair of a math department, and later as a filmmaker.

In the summer of 2014, Robert told me that Beauty was still challenging his patience and compassion. Unlike Dolly, Beauty would not allow Robert to put a leash on her or brush her. "Now, after five years of hand-feeding her, Beauty still has not overcome her fear of being touched. Meanwhile, Dolly has become the best dog I have owned. She follows right behind me on walks in the forest; she always comes when I call her, and she is waiting at the gate to greet me when I come home from a long day of filming."

The dogs have a large fenced backyard to run and play in and a doggie door so they can go inside on cold days. Since her Yellowstone adventure, Beauty has stayed in her yard. Both dogs were skinny when adopted but achieved normal weight after two years with Robert. When I interviewed him, he reported that both dogs were "really healthy." I later received an e-mail from Robert telling me that he renamed both dogs. "I changed Beauty's name to Bucky after she spent the twelve days with wolves, and I changed Dolly's name to Agate, after the Agate Creek wolf pack that I filmed in 2002."

Luna (a.k.a. Luca #50) of Spokane Adventures in Riverside State Park

Deirdre Fitzgerald resides in Spokane, Washington, but she is a native of Butte, so when she was visiting her mother in March of 2009 and heard about Camp Husky, she decided to help us by adopting one of our dogs. We were down to about forty dogs by then, but even so, Deirdre found it hard to decide which dog to adopt. Finally, she chose Luca, a long-haired, black-and-tan German shepherd–Belgian Tervuren mix about one year old. Luca was one of few adult females who never had puppies.

Luca proved to be well behaved and easy to have around the house. The family Luca joined consisted of Deirdre's son, twelve-year-old Liam, and their cat, Scarface. It did not take Scarface long to figure out that he could easily dominate the seventy-pound dog.

Deirdre and Liam decided to change their dog's name to Luna. While Luna is an easy dog in most ways, heeling well on a leash and never jumping on people, she suffers from a fear of both new people and strange dogs. "Luna is highly fearful but never aggressive. When a strange person or dog comes to visit, Luna will run and hide in her crate. If we are walking Luna and she sees a dog she doesn't know, she wants to turn around and go in the opposite direction."

Only a few months after Luna's adoption, Deirdre and a friend decided to take their dogs walking at nearby Riverside State Park. The women took their dogs off leash so they could play together. Apparently, Luna became afraid of the other dog. One minute she was walking beside Deirdre, and the next minute she had disappeared. Deirdre and her friend searched for two hours with no luck. Then Deirdre informed the park rangers about her missing dog. Every evening after work, Deirdre biked to the park and searched for her dog. After two weeks of searching, Deirdre gave up hope of ever seeing Luna again. Then Deirdre got a phone call from a woman who found Luna. The woman had been driving in the park near where Luna had disappeared, when her two little girls saw Luna and insisted that their mother stop and pick up the lost dog. Luckily, Luna had her collar and tags with a phone number. After two weeks of wandering in the park, Luna was back with her family thanks to two little girls and their mom.

Luna was fortunate to be adopted by Deirdre, who is "in it for the long haul" and has read numerous books on dog behavior, trying to help Luna overcome her fear of strangers and the inclination to run away when frightened. When I interviewed Deirdre, she reported that Luna was in excellent physical health. Although she is by nature a gentle and sweet dog, Luna may always struggle with fear of new people and other dogs.

Toki (a.k.a. Whisper), the Smallest Camp Husky Dog, Finds a Home in Bozeman

In late March 2009, Jonathan Williams of Bozeman, Montana, adopted Whisper, an adult female about four or five years old. Like Luna in the previous story, Whisper was very timid, with a tendency to run away when frightened. Whisper ran away on several occasions when she was first taken to her new home, but she did not go far and always returned to Jonathan's house at night. Jonathan changed his dog's name to Toki and began training her to heel on and off leash. Jonathan's patient dedication to training paid off. Soon Toki was trained to walk on and off leash. Then Jonathan adopted a second dog to keep Toki company. With training and a dog companion, Toki is contented to stay at home and has gained considerable self-confidence.

While Toki has the beautiful physical appearance of a typical Camp Husky dog, with both German shepherd and Siberian husky characteristics, she is unique in that she weighs only thirty-five pounds, less than half of what the typical Camp Husky adult female weighs. Jonathan described Toki much like Deirdre described Luna, and said that Toki is "timid but very gentle, and has never shown aggressive tendencies toward animals or people."

About two years after he adopted Whisper, Jonathan updated Camp Husky volunteer Cathy Decker on his dog's progress:

"I haven't heard from you in a while, and I haven't sent updates in a long time. Just wanted to let you know that Toki (Whisper) is doing great. I have her trained off the leash now, so we can walk around town without a leash and she does a fantastic job of not running away. We take her and our other dog to the dog park whenever we can and they love it; Toki is even starting to explore rivers and streams. She seems to like the water but is still a bit scared of going in too deep. She doesn't recoil from traffic or strangers when we go for walks, and all around she really seems to be warming up. She is a great dog and I thank you all for your hard work and patient help over the past couple of years. It's great what you did for all these dogs, and I hope some of the others are doing as well as Toki."

The Amazing Sasha (#26) and Her Dance of Gratitude

Maer Seibert started reading the *Missoulian*, looking at job ads, when she saw "The Dog of the Week" story about the last Camp Husky dog waiting to be adopted at the local shelter. Maer needed a job; she did not need another pet. Maer, her husband, Paul, and their two boys had three dogs and three cats at that time. "Yet, when I looked at that photo of Sasha, it was as if she was calling to me from the newspaper ad. The ad described Sasha as a very shy dog requiring an owner with special training skills. My husband and I did not have any special training skills, yet I was obsessed with adopting that dog from the moment I saw the photo. I could not take my mind off of her. I knew I had to rescue her. I went to the shelter ASAP and was told visiting hours were at 4:30 p.m. A member of the staff told me that if I stood in the parking lot, I could watch the dogs walk to their outside kennels. Sasha was the only dog that stopped, turned around, and stared at me. It was another connection and a direct line of communication from her. I was convinced that she wanted to go home with me, and I wanted her. I had learned from my mother, a member of the Lakota tribe, to appreciate the strong spiritual bond that can exist between people and animals. I cannot explain it, but I always felt that bond with Sasha, something I never felt with any animal before she came into my life."

When the visiting hour arrived, Maer was led in to meet Sasha. The volunteer told her that one reason Sasha had not been adopted was that she hid in her igloo and would not come out to meet folks who were looking to adopt a dog. The volunteer was surprised when this exceptionally shy dog came out of her igloo and jumped on top of it to look at Maer as she approached. Maer adopted Sasha, and she proved to be "one amazing dog."

Shortly after her adoption, Sasha, Paul, and Maer were in the car listening to the radio when the song "Just a Small Town Girl" by Journey came on. Although Paul and Maer don't like the song, Sasha started howling with delight while the song played, and every time she heard the song she would howl along for some strange reason. It was her song.

The Seiberts prepared a special bed for Sasha in the living room, and the dog seemed to think that she had to stay on the bed except when going outside. It took three months before she realized that she was free to explore the house and follow family members into other rooms. After five or more years of living on Brode's land, where she likely never entered a building, and then being confined on the bus and in a kennel at Camp Husky, it is not surprising that it took a while for Sasha to learn that she was free to roam the house and yard.

About three months after Sasha moved into the Seibert home, Maer took a trip to Hood River, Oregon, to attend a training session for yoga instructors. Maer thought the trip would be a great opportunity to bond with Sasha, since they would be staying in a campground. Maer had not calculated how stressful it would be for Sasha to leave the safety of her bed in the house in Missoula and be in a strange place. Maer was walking Sasha off leash down by the river to let her get some exercise when a man suddenly stepped out from behind a bush. The stranger meant no harm, but he startled and frightened Sasha, and she ran off! That happened in August, and Sasha would be running loose in Hood River for the next three months!

Maer did everything she could think of to find Sasha, posting flyers with Sasha's picture all around Hood River, talking to people and searching on foot and in her van. It is fortunate that Sasha was lost in a "dog friendly" town where animal control and the local shelter proved most willing to help. There were lots of Sasha sightings, but no one could catch her. One day the sheriff called the Hood River Animal Control, saying folks had sighted a wolf and he might have to shoot it. "No way," said the animal-control officer. "That is a family dog, and her owners are frantic to find her." Finally, in October, Paul set off with his younger son, Cree, and their older husky, Luna. In Hood River, Paul met Marge, a dog lover who agreed to help with the search. Early one morning, while Cree was still sleeping, Paul drove out with Marge and Luna to where people had reported seeing Sasha near a restaurant. They waited awhile, and suddenly, Sasha appeared but kept her distance. Paul parked the car and let Luna out. Luna ran to Sasha, and the two dogs exchanged enthusiastic greetings. Paul called for Sasha to come to him, but the now very timid dog would not move toward him. She hung back, afraid and uncertain. Suddenly, Paul got a crazy idea. He sat down on the ground by the restaurant and started singing "Just a Small Town Girl" with as much gusto as possible. The ploy worked; Sasha came up to Paul, and he was able to grab her harness.

For the entire five-and-a-half-hour drive back to Missoula, Sasha never stopped talking. "It was as if she was telling Cree, Luna, and me all about her adventure," said Paul. When they took her to their veterinarian, they were relieved to find that Sasha had lost only seven pounds during those three months. Apparently, the food in the restaurant Dumpster was pretty tasty. Paul and Maer will be forever grateful to Marge and the other good people of Hood River for the return of their dog.

In time, Sasha developed a deep affection for and comfort with Maer, Paul, and their twelve- and sixteen-year-old sons. "Sasha was the most gentle, loving, and grateful dog I have ever met," said Maer. "She was very intelligent and intuitive. Sasha and I were very, very close by the end of that first year. I have never experienced that kind of bond with an animal before. She became bonded with me first, but after Paul found her in Oregon, he took her for runs every day, and he accepted her and let her be who she was, and they became equally bonded. My youngest son, Cree, snuggled with Sasha every day. She enjoyed his pets and kisses, but she never felt secure to go on outings with him or his brother. If the boys tried to take her outside for a walk, she would drop to the floor and go limp and not budge."

After her return from Oregon, Paul and Maer trained Sasha to walk on a leash and obey basic commands off leash by starting with long ropes. Maer and Paul tried to be relaxed but consistent in training Sasha, letting her learn at her own pace. Sasha made steady progress and soon got to the point where she could walk off leash. Maer, who once worked as a special-education teacher, believes that "both dogs and children need sensible boundaries to feel safe, but they also need as much freedom as they can safely handle, a stimulating environment, and lots of love."

Maer said that "Sasha was not the kind of dog that wanted to do tricks like 'roll over,' and that was fine with us. We just wanted her to be the smart, loving, unique creature she was." Within a year after her adoption, Sasha was running off leash with Paul every morning and accompanying Maer on her bike rides. She never again tried to run off, although it would take another year before Sasha would overcome her fear of strangers.

At first, when anyone came to the house, "Sasha would hide in her bed, move as close to the wall as possible, shiver, and shake. It was a sign of progress for Sasha when she started barking at strangers who knocked on the door rather than quaking with fear in her bed. Finally, she would move toward the door and bark. She was never aggressive, but she let people know that she was the protector of the household. As shy as she was around people, if she didn't trust someone, she would place herself between me and that person. At first, Sasha was afraid of children as well as adults, but she gradually overcame her fear of children and would stand still and let children pet her, rather than backing away in fear.

"On hikes Sasha would stay away from the people but would love to visit with other dogs and give 'lovings' to any puppies she encountered on the trail. She enjoyed playing with and snuggling with Luna. Sasha was especially attached to our cat, Inky, who would sleep beside Sasha whenever the dog was on her bed. We used to wonder if Sasha had a pet kitty or Inky had a pet husky."

Sasha was six years of age or older when the Seiberts adopted her, and those first six had been years of inadequate nutrition, no veterinarian care, abuse, neglect, and more litters of puppies than any dog should have. Amazingly, Sasha had only two health problems their veterinarian could find: food allergies requiring a special diet and damaged teeth requiring $500 in dental work. Apart from the teeth and allergies, Sasha enjoyed good health until a week before her death in the fall of 2012.

The happy part of her story is that Sasha found a good and loving home with Maer and Paul, their boys, and her animal companions. After nearly four happy years with the Seibert family, Sasha developed a lung disorder, and one day she died peacefully in the home she loved while Maer was holding her. One and a half weeks before that, the Seiberts had adopted a little husky puppy. Sasha was delighted with the pup and spent the week lavishing motherly attention on it. Then she developed the sudden lung problem. The veterinarian said it was most unusual that the bronchial tubes would shut down so suddenly without previous signs of shortness of breath or wheezing, even in an older dog like Sasha. He had never seen a dog become so ill so quickly.

As Sasha died in her arms, Maer had another deep spiritual experience. "It was as if gentle Sasha was telling me that I need not fear her death because all living creatures, man as well as animals, are connected. I realized then that Sasha was a part of us, so even death could not separate her spirit from us." When I first phoned the Seiberts about a year after Sasha died, Paul was still too upset to talk about the dog he loved so much, but later he revealed to me that one of the things he missed most about Sasha was her dance of gratitude. "Sasha always showed gratitude for her food and for her walks. When her bowl of food was placed beside her, she would dance in a circle as if to say 'thank you, thank you.' She would do the same when Maer or I would take her for a walk," explained Paul. "Sasha was the most gentle, loving, grateful dog we have ever met."

The Story of Hunter (a.k.a. Jude #24g), Trixie (a.k.a. Zena), and Sipher

Before Christmas 2008, Dicie and Fred Jangula adopted a male Camp Husky puppy named Jude from the Humane Society of Western Montana in Missoula. Jude was one of several puppies born to a tricolored mother named Nellie and named after Beatles songs. The couple had wanted to adopt two puppies, but they were allowed to adopt only one, since there was a waiting list for Camp Husky puppies in Missoula. About five weeks later, the couple drove to Butte and adopted two more Camp Husky dogs, Sipher, an adult female, and Zena, a young puppy. Sipher was skittish and fearful like some of the other dogs, and she escaped within a week of arriving in the rural area near Clinton. Tragically, she was never found. I suspect that she may have been trying to return to her pack at Camp Husky.

The Jangulas changed Jude's name to Hunter and Zena's name to Trixie. The two puppies formed a close bond as they grew up. Hunter grew to be a very playful dog with "a supersweet personality, never threatening to anyone. The docile Hunter let Trixie dominate him, and the two loved to play together. Often they would play at stalking each other as well as chase. It was the first time we had two puppies and we enjoyed seeing the dogs playing so well together. Both dogs were easy to train and a joy to have as part of our family. Hunter and Trixie especially liked to ride with us on nearby mountain roads either on our four-wheelers or in our truck." All was well until November 2010.

When they were about two years of age, Hunter and Trixie dug out of the fenced backyard and disappeared. Later, Trixie came home and led her owners to where Hunter lay dead. Some sadistic person with a gun had killed the gentle dog. That cruel act left Trixie, Dicie, and Fred devastated. Trixie would grieve for many months. A few days after she returned home, Trixie started limping, and the veterinarian found a pellet in her leg that could not be removed. The Clinton area proved a dangerous place for dogs.

In spite of the heartbreak caused by human cruelty, Dicie and Fred do not regret adopting their Camp Husky dogs. They continue to enjoy Trixie's companionship and are grateful that she survived. Trixie is healthy except for the pellet in her leg that causes her discomfort. Trixie spends her days with Dicie, who now works from home. Trixie stays very close to home, having learned how dangerous the countryside can be. Like Hunter, Trixie is a gentle and very affectionate dog. "Trixie enjoys being the center of attention. She likes to give us kisses and nibbles gently on our arms to show affection, and, in turn, she loves having her belly scratched."

Trixie is typical of the talking Camp Husky dogs. "For example, when she looks out the window and sees wild turkeys walking by, Trixie just talks up a storm. When we ask Trixie if she wants to go for a walk, she almost mimics us."

Update: Dicie wrote recently of how smart Trixie is, as she can tell as they leave the house whether Dicie is just walking to the mailbox or taking one of their two-mile fitness walks. Although both routes are in the same direction initially, Trixie will run out ahead only if Dicie is heading for the mailbox. "Trixie will beat me to the mailbox and climb up to the row of seven mailboxes and nose our very box. If I am taking her for a real walk she stays right beside me until we are three-quarters down the driveway, and then she will stop so I can put on her leash." About four years after being shot, "her wounded leg does not bother her much anymore." Dicie writes that "all remains well with Trixie. She continues to be the center of our attention and very special to us."

Jasmine (#53a) Survives in the Wilderness against Incredible Odds

Of all the Camp Husky dogs, puppy #53a has the most remarkable survival story. Judy Bardouche was watching the nightly news when she saw the first report about Brode and the bus and trailer full of dogs. She called Camp Husky the next day and let the volunteers know that she wanted to be on a list to adopt a dog. "I kept phoning and the volunteers returned my calls, but it was a long process waiting for the city to get legal possession of the dogs."

About a week before Christmas 2008, Judy visited Camp Husky to pick out a dog. She saw Mia, the pure-white German shepherd featured in chapter 5, nursing her ten puppies. As Judy looked on, she saw one little pup leaving the others and managing to crawl up a five-gallon water bucket to get a drink. Judy was "so impressed by this smart, determined, and agile little puppy" that she stopped looking for her special dog—the puppy named Jasmine went home to live with Judy and her husband, Joe.

Joe was less than enthusiastic about adopting a dog, but it did not take long for the puppy to endear herself to him and become part of the family. Joe liked Jasmine so much that he suggested they adopt her mother as well; however, when they inquired, they found that Mia had already been adopted. The couple gave their puppy the nickname Jazzy "due to her spirited jumping and dancing around."

Judy and Joe live on twenty acres in a remote mountain area outside of Drummond, Montana, fourteen miles off the highway on a logging road. To get to the highway in winter, they have to travel seven miles by snowmobile to reach a plowed road where they park their vehicles.

When she was less than three months old, Jazzy disappeared one winter day. Judy knew no one had taken the puppy because of the remote location of their home and the fact that there were no tracks in the deep snow. Judy was frantic, searching the area on snowmobile, phoning neighbors, and posting missing-dog signs in the small towns nearby. As the weeks passed, Judy lost hope that her puppy could have survived in the mountain wilderness with the bitter-cold temperatures, hungry mountain lions, and so many other dangers. In the meantime, Judy's work as a caregiver for the elderly took her to the town of Philipsburg, Montana, where she encountered Lila, a beautiful and well-behaved adult husky needing a good home.

Seven weeks had now passed since Jazzy disappeared; Lila had settled into her new home, and Judy was mourning the loss of her special puppy. Then at two o'clock one morning, Lila started growling at something outside. As Judy walked toward the front door to investigate, she suddenly recognized the talking sound so characteristic of most Camp Husky dogs. Jazzy had returned! Judy said her puppy was "very skinny but otherwise in remarkably good shape." Why she disappeared and how she survived remain mysteries. Perhaps Jazzy ran off chasing a rabbit or some other critter and became lost and disoriented in the deep snow. It may be that the puppy was found and protected by a wolf pack. By observing Jazzy's scat, Judy discovered that she had survived by catching and eating mice. At any rate, the adventure taught Jazzy a lesson, and she is content to stay at home with Judy, Joe, and her sweet-natured playmate, Lila. As this book goes to publication, both Jazzy and Lila are healthy, and Jazzy has gone from being an adorable puppy to a stunningly beautiful seven-year-old. (Photo 16 shows Jazzy as a puppy shortly before she disappeared on her wilderness ordeal.)

Rudy of Butte, the Friendly Stowaway Dog

Among the dogs I most enjoyed walking at Camp Husky every Saturday and Sunday were two older puppies named Rudy and Ace. Ace was a well-behaved, quiet, and shy Belgian sheepdog. His cage mate was a tricolored, long-haired German shepherd–husky mix, twice the size of Ace. These two buddies played constantly. It did not surprise me at all that Rudy was adopted first. He was not only a strikingly handsome dog, but he was very friendly toward other dogs as well as people.

Mary Ann and Dave Lopez of Butte were empty-nesters when Dave decided that he would like to adopt a Camp Husky dog. "Our children were grown up, and we had not had dogs for seven years since our German shepherd and poodle-terrier mix both died of old age." It is little wonder that Dave chose Rudy, a very large dog with a winning personality to match his good looks. While it was Dave's idea to adopt him, Rudy has become Mary Ann's dog.

Mary Ann described Rudy as "a really good dog and a charmer." His veterinarian refers to him as the "gentle giant." Rudy loves people, and Mary Ann's friends love Rudy. The Lopezes are active and gregarious folks, and Rudy is the perfect dog for their lifestyle. They enjoy camping and hiking in the summer and cross-country skiing and snowshoeing in the winter with a large group of friends. Rudy thoroughly enjoys this active outdoor life with his human companions. He enjoys cooling off in a mountain stream in the summer and rolling in the snow in winter. His heavy coat is well suited to the cold Montana winters.

Rudy's gregarious nature created some challenges for Mary Ann and Dave during their first year with the big puppy. He proved to be a Houdini, always looking for a way to escape so he could visit neighborhood dogs, especially other Camp Husky dogs living nearby. After several such escapes, Mary Ann and Dave had to raise their fence a few feet and keep Rudy confined to the house when they were at work.

From the start, Rudy was everyone's friend, and he always enjoyed going for a ride in the car. Before Christmas 2009, when their daughter came over to the house with a trunkful of Christmas presents, Rudy disappeared and did not respond when called. When their daughter was leaving, she went to close her car trunk and discovered Rudy inside. "Rudy was so friendly and fond of riding in cars (perhaps from his adventure on the bus) that we feared he would go off with anyone who invited him." His owners' fears were justified. As it turned out, Rudy did go off with someone, but he was uninvited. The first summer in his new home, Rudy was in the front yard with Mary Ann as she planted flowers. Mary Ann remembered the mail carrier giving her the mail and then heading across the street. Intent on her gardening, she did not notice Rudy climbing into the mail truck when the carrier left the door open and walked across the street with mail. Rudy hid in the back of the truck with the mail, where he could not be seen by the driver. The mail carrier was driving along when all of a sudden the big dog jumped up and gave him a friendly greeting. No doubt Rudy had broken some federal law, but the mail carrier returned Rudy to Mary Ann, and all was well.

With time, Rudy grew into adulthood and stopped trying to stow away in cars. Now he is content to stay close to home unless he is traveling with his owners. Rudy is still friendly but much more protective. As a young dog, he never barked, and he welcomed anyone to the house. Now, he will bark at strangers. Although Rudy is huge, he seems to think he is a lap dog. Mary Ann shared a couple of photos Dave took of Rudy snuggled up with Mary Ann on the sofa, and another of Rudy cuddled up with the couple's cute little granddaughter. Contentment and bliss show in the dog's face. This adventure dog now has everything he needs at home.

CHAPTER 8
Moms and Pups

More than half the adult dogs Brode had on the bus and in the trailer were females with young puppies, pregnant females, or both. In fact, during the first week at Camp Husky, one of the moms with young puppies gave birth to another litter. I have fond memories of helping to care for moms and puppies, as do many of the volunteers. Most of the puppies were adopted directly from Camp Husky, but many puppies and adults went to other shelters in the state. The Humane Society of Western Montana in Missoula took the most adults and puppies, and the busy director, Lora O'Connor, helped me to locate individuals who had adopted Camp Husky dogs. This chapter tells the story of one of the mother dogs and many of the puppies that were adopted out of Missoula.

Nellie and Her Puppies
Nellie, a young tricolored German shepherd, gave birth to a large litter on December 19, 2008, while she was being fostered at the home of volunteer Samantha Collier. After her puppies were weaned, Nellie was fostered and then adopted by April Rogers of Anaconda. April was divorced at that time, but she and her former husband, Joe, chose to live next door to each other for the sake of their children, a twelve-year-old son and an eight-year-old daughter. This arrangement proved to be beneficial when April took Nellie home with her. "One of the few faults Nellie has is that she gets destructive when left alone," said April. "Shortly after Nellie moved into my house, Joe and I decided that it would be best for Nellie and my furniture if Nellie

stayed with Joe during the daytime when I am working and then returned to my house for the evening when Joe is working the night shift."

Both April and Joe describe Nellie as "loving toward both people and animals." In April's words, "Nellie is a very good dog, but she thinks she is a person." When Nellie first moved to Anaconda, Joe had a twelve-year-old German shepherd named Roxie. Nellie developed a deep attachment to the older dog, licking her and giving her lots of attention. Joe said, "Nellie made the last two years of Roxie's life much happier." Now Nellie enjoys the company of Joe's two cats. "The trouble," he added, "is that Nellie acts like she is a cat that can sit in your lap instead of a giant dog."

Nellie still shows a few symptoms of the abuse on the bus and her early life with Brode. For example, Joe said that if he makes a sudden unexpected movement, or if he drops something and makes a loud noise, Nellie will "duck down and squeal as if she is afraid of being hurt."

Joe and April almost lost Nellie the summer following her adoption. In Montana, people are allowed to set off firecrackers in residential neighborhoods, often terrifying pets. Nellie became so frightened of the firecrackers that she jumped the fence and ran until she was far outside the city. Nellie could easily have been hit by a car as she ran down the highway out of town trying to escape the terrifying noise. Luckily, a compassionate couple found her on the highway and took her home with them. When they saw one of the "lost dog" flyers that April had posted around town, they phoned April to say that they had Nellie. When April entered their house, she found Nellie happy and quite at home with these kind people who had given refuge to a frightened dog. Currently, Nellie is a happy and well-adjusted dog with two adults to care for her, two teenagers to play with, and two cats as companions.

I have two photos taken of Nellie as she was taken off the bus on the first day of the rescue. She is a large and long white German shepherd, but, unlike our other white German shepherds at Camp Husky, Nellie has the most unusual dark patches on the right side of her face, her side, and the top rear of her body. No other dog at Camp Husky had Nellie's coloring, and she passed on her unique but beautiful appearance to her puppies. The second thing to stand out in the photos is how pathetically thin the young pregnant dog was on that day of the rescue. Finally, Nellie's facial expression, especially the eyes, reveals a sweet and gentle disposition, as well as confusion and apprehension at entering a building for the first time and encountering so many people. It must have been terrifying, but I like to think that these sensitive dogs knew that the people they encountered that day wanted to help them. April sent me a recent picture of Nellie, and I am happy to report that she is as lovely as ever but now reflects the fact that she is well fed and loved. As you will read in this chapter, her puppies have brought a lot of joy to their families.

Nellie's litter was among the many puppies and older dogs that were transported to Missoula and put up for adoption at the Humane Society of Western Montana, where Camp Husky puppies were in great demand. Nellie's puppies, only about six weeks old when they arrived in Missoula, were all named after Beatles songs. One of them, Bella (a.k.a. Eleanor Rigby), was introduced in chapter 5, "Dogs with a Mission," and Hunter (a.k.a. Jude) was introduced in chapter 7, "Adventure Dogs." I was able to interview several individuals and families who adopted Nellie's puppies. These are some of their stories.

The Stewart Family Adopts Boons (a.k.a. Prudence)

Allen and Sheryll Stewart adopted a Norwegian elkhound in early 2008 and decided to adopt another dog so he would not be lonely. Sheryll went online to see what dogs were available at the Humane Society of Western Montana. She was impressed by the beauty of two Camp Husky mother dogs (Cinnamon and Sasha) and their litters, but when she inquired about them, she was told that they had all been adopted; however, she learned that the very next day, another litter of Camp Husky puppies (Nellie's pups) would be arriving from Butte. Arriving early that day, Sheryll got first pick of the litter. Sheryll explains why she chose Prudence: "I was attracted to the quiet runt—4.4 pounds at birth—and the only white dog in the litter." (Actually, Boons, as they named her, is tricolored but primarily white like her mother, with the long hair so common among Camp Husky dogs.)

Shortly after they adopted her, the Stewarts noticed that Boons had a problem with her eyes; they were clouded over, and the little puppy could not see. The veterinarian said that it was either something serious or something she would grow out of in a few weeks. Luckily, it was the latter. Boons is now a healthy and very active adult. She grew to be very tall like her littermates, but at seventy-one pounds, she is still the skinny runt of the litter. Boons and her elkhound companion are "inseparable and get lots of exercise playing together." Boons is protective of her friend, alerting everyone with her "panic bark" when the elkhound escapes from the fenced yard.

The Stewarts are very glad they adopted their Camp Husky puppy. Boons is "a gentle and calm dog." The Stewarts had three children, ages four, five, and twelve, when Boons came to live with them. The puppy soon formed a very close bond with "her kids." The Stewarts sent me a photo of Boons at about one year of age sitting on a large bed and playing with their two youngest children. The bond of love between the big dog and the little girl and boy is evident in that photo. "Boons loves our children and is very protective of them," said Sheryll. While her role as guardian of the household is quite natural for a German shepherd, Boons also has some personality traits not usually associated with the breed. "She is funny and even silly at times. She keeps us laughing with her quirky behavior." It is interesting to observe that the only one of Nellie's puppies that did not go to Missoula, Bucky (chapter 5), shares this unusual personality trait with Boons, and Bucky is the giant of Nellie's litter at 130-plus pounds.

Three years after adopting Boons, Sheryll wrote to me about the fact that she can easily recognize Camp Husky dogs when she sees them in the Missoula area. "I saw another Camp Husky dog with his owner out at Fort Missoula when I was at a soccer game. It is amazing how you can tell right away where they come from. This dog had the same build as Boons but very different coloring—almost a strawberry blond." The dog Sheryll saw may have been one of Cinnamon's many puppies or a dog adopted in Butte, but from her description it is not one of the dogs in this book. Those of us who volunteered at Camp Husky or adopted one of the dogs would agree with Sheryll that there is something unique about these Camp Husky dogs that enables us to identify them, even though the dogs are quite varied in appearance.

Kevin Pierce Adopts Winston (a.k.a. Walrus)

Kevin Pierce was probably the second person to adopt one of the Beatles pups. Kevin had a fifteen-year-old Siberian husky named Kayla and wanted to adopt a puppy, when a friend told him about the Camp Husky puppies available at the shelter. Kevin described how he chose Walrus over his many littermates: "This one puppy in the litter, with the lightest coloring, came running toward me unafraid and confident. He was very interested in what was going on. I knew he was the puppy I wanted."

Kevin is an avid fly-fisher, and he renamed his new puppy Winston after the Montana-made Winston fly rods he uses. The puppy grew to be "gigantic, weighing about 105 pounds with a very long and lanky frame." Winston has his mother's German shepherd shape and tricolored coat. He is primarily gray, with Siberian husky markings on his head. Like a few other Camp Husky dogs, Winston had some skin-allergy issues that improved when wheat was taken out of his diet.

Winston is Kevin's "best buddy and a great companion because he learns quickly and strives to obey." Kevin is keen on catch-and-release fly-fishing, and Winston is his assistant. They like to fish the upper Big Hole near Jackson, Montana. Winston stands by Kevin and watches the fly intensely until there is a nibble. When Kevin wheels in a fish, "Winston has to examine it and give a good sniff." Once he has given his approval, Kevin throws the fish back into the river. On his first fly-fishing trip, Winston thought that the fish might be his dinner, but a quick no from Kevin was all it took for the smart dog to understand that he was not supposed to injure the fish. Winston has learned from Kevin that fly-fishing is serious business!

Besides fishing with Kevin, Winston enjoys swimming in rivers and lakes. If they see folks floating on tubes, Winston will swim out just to give a friendly greeting. Winston just loves people and enjoys greeting them. However, when company comes to the house, Winston is so excited and happy to have folks visiting that he does not listen as well to Kevin as he normally does. He is especially fond of kids, "wagging his tail with enthusiasm and wanting to lick them."

Kevin described Winston as "the most amazing creature of any kind I have been around. He is a happy and playful dog who likes cats and other dogs as well as people. He can be quite silly at times, but he can also act like the alpha dog if another dog gets aggressive. If another dog starts to pick on him, it will end up with Winston holding the other dog down but never hurting him. Later, Winston acts upset that a conflict took place. It is clear that he does not want conflict with another dog." Kevin believes that dogs respond best to kindness and patience. "No one should ever hit a dog," he insists.

Kevin does much of his work from home, so he and Winston get to spend a lot of time together. When Kevin's job requires driving around Missoula and Hamilton, Winston often accompanies him. For a few years, Kevin had a roommate with a golden retriever, and the two dogs were good friends. Like many of the Camp Husky dogs, Winston likes to sleep on the bed with his owner. He has a sweet and gentle nature, but he has a fierce "German shepherd bark" when he is protecting Kevin.

Patrick and Shelly Merkt Adopt Finn (a.k.a. Rocky Raccoon)

Shelly and Patrick Merkt were grieving the death of a twelve-and-a-half-year-old Siberian husky with whom they had "a very special bond," and debating whether to get another dog, when Nellie's puppies arrived at the Missoula shelter. There were five puppies left when they picked out Rocky Raccoon, a seven-pound pup with a curly tail. They renamed him Finn.

It was January when they adopted Finn, and with the bitter Montana cold, they needed a way to confine the pup indoors while they were away at work. The solution was to buy a child's play yard, something like a playpen with plastic lining and paper on top of that. This set-up worked well for potty training. Finn went only on the paper, making clean-up easy. This good puppy never had accidents in any part of the house. Finn was never a destructive puppy, but he did develop the habit of stealing little things to play with, like a hair curler or plastic coat hangers.

The Merkts thought they were taking home a husky, but they soon discovered that they had a dog that was primarily German shepherd but with some husky from his father. While their previous husky had weighed fifty-five pounds, Finn reached an adult weight of ninety-five pounds, and after a couple of growth spurts, grew to be much taller than a husky. Shelly described Finn as "big and beautiful with white, brown, black, and gold coloring. His neck is white and he has some light gold spots. He is short haired, but the fur is thick with a fine downy undercoat." In other words, he looks a lot like his mother.

Like Nellie's other pups, Finn has a sweet and playful nature. Shelly described him as "high energy but not hyper." The Merkts' house borders some undeveloped acreage on one side, and deer and other wild creatures occasionally visit their neighborhood. One day as she looked out the window, Shelly saw "Finn and a young deer playing together. Finn was running up and down our chain-link fence, and the deer was running beside him on the other side of the fence. They were just playing and having a good time together, and Finn was not barking. Finn also enjoys playing with a neighbor dog with a bordering fence line. Sometimes, Finn will take a toy and run along the fence to show off his toy to the other dog the way young children like to show off their toys to other kids. Luckily, Finn is not inclined to jump his fence."

As a young dog, Finn was shy when folks came to the house, but now he enjoys having visitors—he is just a friendly guy. He likes people, other dogs, and even cats. However, he is a little leery of children because some neighbor kids teased him when he was a small puppy. One habit Finn has is to take the hand of someone he likes gently in his mouth in an effort to lead the person, not to bite. Shelly and Patrick took Finn to a trainer but could not break him of the habit. (A few other Camp Husky dog owners also described this trait in their dogs.) Finn has had obedience training, and the Merkts were considering more when I interviewed them. A recent photo I received showed Finn on a sofa with a young boy. It would seem that the dog has overcome his fear of children.

Patrick and Shelly have been impressed by how intelligent Finn is. "He reads us quite well. When I ask Finn if he wants to go outside, I can tell by his facial expression that he is thinking about my question. He understands me when I ask him if he wants to play with the neighbor dog; he looks over toward our neighbor's yard. He also lets us know if something isn't right in the environment."

Shelly said that "Finn enjoys his toys and likes to play. In fact, he tends to be in your face about playing." He has one toy shaped like a large bone, and he will actually toss it to Shelly or Patrick when he wants to play fetch, or he will get a plastic bottle and shove it into their hands so they will throw it. "Finn has a playful growl during game time."

Finn and Patrick get regular exercise walking in Blue Mountain Recreation Area, a fifty-five-hundred-acre park just two miles southwest of Missoula. Patrick walks the dog on leash but allows him to run loose on the Blue Mountain trail, where dogs are allowed off leash and where Finn is well behaved with other dogs. At home, he has a fenced yard and an outdoor kennel, but he sleeps in a wire crate in the house at night. Although he is not allowed on their bed because of his size, Finn will put his paws on the bed, and he has been known to get on the sofa to look out the window. When the Merkts go to Minnesota to visit their daughter, son-in-law, and little grandchildren, Finn boards at Dog Works in Clinton, Montana.

Finn has enjoyed excellent health, and the Merkts have been careful to feed him a healthful diet and keep him safe. They consulted with the owner of the Go-Fetch Pet Store and Training Center in Missoula about the best diet for their dog. They feed him good-quality dog food without grain (Canidae), as well as the occasional dog biscuit or knuckle bone for a treat. Raw eggs are also added to the diet to keep his coat healthy.

When I interviewed her, Shelly said that Finn was a very good and loving dog, but her biggest concern was that he might accidently knock her or Patrick over since he is so large and enthusiastic. When Finn was two years of age, Shelly fell and broke some bones. Since then, she has been extra careful about avoiding falls. In a 2015 follow-up interview, Shelly informed me that she and Patrick are well and enjoying retirement, and their wonderful companion dog is doing well at age seven.

Brian and Jena White Adopt Maximum (a.k.a. Mr. Mustard)

Like the Merkts, the White family of Missoula found themselves without a dog and looking to adopt when Nellie's puppies arrived in Missoula. In 1993, before their two children were born, Brian and Jena White found a lost puppy, and it was part of their family for the next fourteen years. On January 2, 2009, the Whites, along with their sixteen-year-old son and twelve-year-old daughter, chose Mr. Mustard to be their next family dog, changing his name to Maximum (Max).

Max is now a healthy adult dog, but the six-week-old puppy was not well when the Whites took him home. While adopting him, they noticed that the puppy was shivering and attributed it to the January cold. However, when they brought him into their warm house, he got worse. When he started dragging his legs and whimpering, the Whites took little Max to their veterinarian, who was quick to attribute the problem to "poor breeding" and to suggest euthanizing the pup. Luckily, the Whites saw a second veterinarian, who suggested a "wait-and-see" approach. Within one week, the pup was much improved. The second veterinarian diagnosed the problem as a head injury, possibly sustained when the puppies were transferred to Missoula. The cooler temperature in the shelter had possibly kept Max's head from swelling until he entered the Whites' warm home, and then the swelling caused pain and affected his ability to walk. The lesson here is to be careful with a vet who attributes a puppy's health issues to poor breeding. Having interviewed seven individuals or families who adopted Nellie's puppies, I can say that her offspring are exceptionally healthy, sound, and affectionate dogs.

Brian White described Max as a "beautiful German shepherd with the low slanting rear of a German shepherd and the very heavy and thick fur of a husky. His heavy fur is ideal for the cold winter days when he enjoys being outdoors in the snow. Although we keep him as a house pet, Max loves to play in the snow." Max is very tall and weighs ninety-seven pounds.

His family described Max as "the best dog ever." Like Winston, Max is affectionate and especially good with children and babies. The family agrees that Max is daughter Julianna's dog. "She is crazy about him," her father said. Julianna has posted some great pictures of Max on the Camp Husky Facebook page. My favorite is a photo of Julianna and Max on the sofa just hanging out together. It is obvious that the dog adores the teen, and I am sure the feeling is mutual.

Like his brothers Winston and Finn, Max is good natured and tolerant with other dogs, although he does not want to be dominated. Max has had the opportunity to play with littermates Boons and Winston at the local dog park. According to Brian, "Max enjoys playing with dogs, cats, and other animals but not with the intention of hurting them. If the cat stops, he will stop. Sometimes cats chase him." Julianna, now a college student, said, "I was out in the forest with Max, and he saw two deer and started to chase them. When the deer stopped running and froze in fear, Max stopped and made no effort to hurt them." Like Finn in the earlier story, Max just enjoyed playing with the deer.

College Student Casey Clark Adopts Lucy

Lucy was a Camp Husky puppy that got off to a poor start with a failed adoption. Unfortunately, she was crated a lot and not socialized during the two and a half months she spent in her first home. She was returned to the Humane Society of Western Montana and put up for adoption once again when she was four months old. In the meantime, a young man named Casey Clark found out about the puppy from a friend. "My friend worked with differently abled children at that time and took them to the shelter on a field trip. While there, she saw Lucy and thought the puppy would be ideal for me because of my fondness for German shepherds and wolves. I knew nothing about the Camp Husky rescue at that time."

Because she was not properly socialized in her first home, Lucy was rather afraid of people and other dogs when Casey adopted her. While she was generally more comfortable with women, she bonded very quickly with Casey. Lucy is also very fond of Casey's parents and their German shepherd, Koda; however, Lucy has been known to show signs of jealousy when Casey plays with Koda. Casey says that "Lucy has only two faults: She can get aggressive with other dogs and often acts the alpha. She has also been known to give in to temptation and steal a steak off the barbecue."

Like her littermates, Lucy is a large dog with a long and tall frame and a weight of eighty-five pounds. Lucy also has her mother's tricolored coat of beige, dark tan, and white, and she is long haired. Casey reports that "Lucy's health has been good, but around the time she turned three she developed spay incontinence, causing her to urinate when asleep without knowing it. Her veterinarian seemed to think it was caused by being spayed too early. We put her on a medication called Proin, which she takes once a day, and it seems to help with the problem." (Unfortunately, many of our puppies were spayed too early because we had only one weekend to spay-neuter every one for free. Merlena Moore reports that her Camp Husky dog, Zeva, developed the same problem as Lucy from being spayed at too young an age.)

Casey was a college student at the University of Montana majoring in business administration with a minor in computer science when he adopted Lucy in 2009. When I first interviewed Casey in 2011, I could tell from his voice just how much this young man loved his dog. Casey said he was extremely glad he adopted Lucy. "I love this dog so much. She goes everywhere with me, and we especially enjoy hiking together."

In 2012, Casey moved to Houston, Texas, to continue his education and train as a pilot, and sadly, that meant that he had to be away from his Lucy for a while. "Lucy is with my parents and Koda, and they split their time, spending winters in Arizona and summers in Great Falls, Montana." Casey was looking forward to having Lucy with him in Houston when he found suitable housing.

By Christmas 2014, Casey was working as a commercial helicopter pilot patrolling pipelines for oil companies, and he was finally able to have his dog living with him once again. In his last e-mail, Casey reported that "Lucy now weighs one hundred pounds, and at age six is still in very good shape and condition." Lucy has not adjusted well to the heat and humidity of Houston summers, but Casey keeps her active with games of Frisbee, her favorite. Casey wrote from Houston that the spay incontinence was not improving and the Proin made Lucy restless and unable to sleep well, so Casey took her off the medication. He chose a house with tile floors and no carpets so it isn't much of a problem.

Casey concluded his last e-mail by saying, "I am still extremely glad that I was able to adopt Lucy. After six years she is still my best friend and continues to go everywhere with me." This author is also grateful that Lucy has had such a wonderful life, with Casey (and his parents) taking such good care of her. I only wish that all dogs and cats waiting in shelters around the country could find as devoted an owner as this young man. Casey sent me several photos of Lucy. I included my personal favorite in this book.

Cinnamon's and Sasha's Christmas Puppies

Two beautiful apricot-and-white, long-haired German shepherd mother dogs, Cinnamon and Sasha, were transported to the Humane Society of Western Montana in Missoula, along with their puppies, in December for adoption as Christmas puppies. Sasha (chapter 7, "Adventure Dogs") was one of the older mother dogs, with only three puppies in the litter born at Camp Husky. I believe she was also one of the dogs that had puppies with her on the trailer. One of those older puppies, Rusty, is featured in chapter

9. Cinnamon had a much larger litter than Sasha, and Cinnamon's puppies were all named for classic cars. Rhett ("Adventure Dogs") was probably the father of Cinnamon's litter because folks describe the puppies as looking like Belgian Tervurens. Cinnamon was adopted, but I have not been able to locate her owners. Sasha's pups appeared to be pure German shepherd, and their father was probably one of our beautiful white German shepherds.

Randy and Jodi Haddick Adopt Sophie (a.k.a. Porsche)

Ironically, Randy and Jodi Haddick were looking to adopt a Welsh corgi when they saw Cinnamon's litter. The couple chose one of the females named Porsche and renamed her Sophie. Sophie was an adorable puppy with beautiful blue eyes and would grow to be very large, magnificent, and sleek, with long fur.

Sophie is very playful and, like her father, loves to run. "She has the husky need to run for exercise," but that is no problem since the young couple has a large fenced yard, about three-quarters of an acre. With her heavy coat, Sophie enjoys being outside in the snow. When the snow is really heavy, Randy will plow trails for her.

Sophie likes cats, other dogs, and children. The Haddicks have three rescue cats, and Sophie loves them. She also enjoys visiting with the neighbor dogs on each side of her fenced yard. Randy's parents have a Siberian husky–Rottweiler mix that is best friends with Sophie. Randy said that about the only dogs Sophie doesn't like are black Labs because one once attacked and hurt her.

Sophie is especially fond of children. Neighbor children like to walk by and talk to her. Most of all, she loves the Haddicks' baby boy. When they were expecting their first child, the Haddicks gave thought to how they should introduce Sophie to their baby, as Randy explains: "When we brought our baby home from the hospital, we placed him on the living room floor in his car seat. Sophie looked at this strange new creature as if asking herself, 'What is this?' Then she sniffed him. Finally, she licked him. From then on J. J. was her baby to love and protect."

Like so many Camp Husky dogs, she talks constantly. Randy and Jodi are "absolutely happy" they adopted the affectionate and chatty Sophie.

Heather McMilin and Jennifer Clary Adopt Cooper

Heather and Jennifer remember watching the news broadcasts about the Camp Husky rescue shortly after the death of their special dog, and they continued to follow the story in the newspaper and on the nightly news. As Heather explains, "We had lost our Norwegian elkhound, Dakota, to cancer in August 2008. I was not ready to even think about adoption; Dakota was an incredible soul mate from college, and I needed to mourn him before adopting. Then on the Friday morning right before Christmas, I saw a news report about two litters of puppies that were shipped from Camp Husky to the Western Montana Humane Society. I knew right then that I was ready. I got up Saturday morning and told my partner it was time, and we headed out to see the puppies. I just knew Dakota was telling me it was time."

The women took their eleven-year-old black cocker spaniel named Reece along with them to pick out a puppy. Folks at the shelter introduced the women and Reece to Cinnamon's litter. After two hours they decided to adopt the biggest and most laid-back of the puppies, who also seemed the most compatible with Reece.

Heather stated, "While in the room, we picked a name for the puppy we had chosen. We picked the name Cooper, having no idea at that time what his actual name was. Then when we filled out the paperwork, the individual assisting us said, 'So you would like to adopt Cooper!' We were floored to learn that we had picked the same name they had given him. We took it as a sign that we had selected the pup that was meant to be with us; however, there were five other folks who had put in a request to adopt Cooper. We went home, and an hour later we received a call from the shelter saying they had decided to give Cooper to us because we had spent the most time and effort to make sure that the puppy we chose would be compatible with our other dog. We picked him up Sunday morning." And thus Cooper ended up living with Heather, Jennifer, Reece, and two cats named Spud and Peyton.

"As a puppy, Cooper had his big brother, Reece, teaching him the ropes, as well as a group of friends and their dogs socializing him. We went on dog walks and he played hard with the other dogs. He went to doggie day care and played hard there as well; we ended up taking him out of doggie day-care groups. While his mentor, Reece, has passed away, Cooper has some dog friends with whom he tends to be submissive. One of Cooper's best buddies is a rescued dachshund named Prince. It's a riot to see them play!

"Cooper loved our two cats when he first met them," said Heather, "and even now, as an adult, he continues to play with them, although he now towers over them in size.

"Cooper also *loves* people, a little too much considering his size." The enthusiastic dog had a tendency to show his affection by jumping on Jennifer and Heather when they returned home from work, or on children he wanted to play with, so his devoted owners wisely enlisted a dog trainer to help them deal with this and other issues. The trainer has helped greatly.

Heather described Cooper as "definitely a Belgian Tervuren." Like his sister Sophie, Cooper is a talker. "He definitely talks, especially when he gets wound up. He comes in and yells at us and tells us it's time to do something."

Valkyrie (a.k.a. Tesla) Is Adopted by Robert and Meta Halverson

Tesla was another of the beautiful puppies from Cinnamon's litter adopted right before Christmas from the Humane Society of Western Montana. After hearing the story of the dogs on the school bus, the Halversons of Turah, Montana, wanted to adopt one of these dogs because they have a special fondness for both Siberian huskies and German shepherds. Also, in the winter of 2008–2009, the Halversons were losing their very special companion dog to old age and illness. The couple wanted to adopt a Camp Husky puppy to help them cope with the imminent loss of their cherished companion.

Only four of Cinnamon's ten puppies remained when the Halversons chose a puppy "with a unique-looking gray face but with the black-and-tan saddle typical of German shepherds." The couple renamed their puppy Valkyrie, but the name does not seem to fit the playful dog, who loves to socialize with all the neighbor dogs as well as with people. When their older dog passed, Robert and Meta adopted a young Labrador retriever mix as a companion for Valkyrie.

The Halversons have an outdoor kennel with an insulated dog house to keep their dogs comfortable during the severe Montana winters. Both dogs completed a basic obedience class. Meta said that "Valkyrie has been an easy dog since puppyhood. She was easy to housebreak and quick to learn basic obedience."

The best part of Valkyrie's day is probably the long walk she enjoys every evening when Meta arrives home from work. The Lab and shepherd behave very differently on these walks. While the Lab runs off exploring far ahead, Valkyrie stays close to Meta, displaying the instinct to protect so characteristic of German shepherds. "Valkyrie is a great companion dog and also very protective. When I hike with the dogs, Valkyrie is always there with me, and I feel safe. Once when I was walking down a logging road and the Lab was far ahead as usual, Valkyrie started growling, something very uncharacteristic of her. I knew from her behavior that she was aware of some danger in the woods. She is an astute dog, so I paid attention to her warning and headed home right then."

Django (a.k.a. Nova) Is Adopted by Christy and Alan Bradley

Nova was a pup with a failed first adoption who would find a great home about four months later than his littermates. Christy and Alan Bradley had a husky–border collie mix and an Australian shepherd until March of 2009, when the former died. Their second dog, Hogan, was grieving for the dog that had died. Worried about the way Hogan was moping around the house, Christy decided to go by the Humane Society of Western Montana in Missoula and just take a look. The workers showed her several puppies. When she saw Nova, Christy was impressed by his low-key behavior and the way he looked at her. "He was friendly, but not super friendly. He was the calmest of all the dogs at the shelter and just looked at me like he knew he was meant to be ours. All the other dogs were jumping around and barking and he was sitting upright watching me." Her intuition told Christy that she should adopt this dog. Her husband, Alan, would require a little more convincing.

The shelter folks suggested that Christy bring Hogan to meet the puppy in order to determine if the two would be compatible. "When they met at the shelter, Nova was interested in Hogan and wanted to be friends, but Hogan was much more interested in running around sniffing everything."

In April of 2009, the Bradleys and Hogan took the puppy home. Christy said that their puppy was about five months old when adopted, so they think he was adopted earlier and it didn't work out. No doubt they are correct, because the Camp Husky puppies had arrived in Missoula before Christmas and all were quickly adopted. It seems likely, therefore, that Nova lived with another family for a few months before being returned to the shelter. I know of three of our dogs displaced from their first homes by the financial crisis of 2008–2009, when those who adopted lost their jobs and homes. That might have been the case with this pup.

The Bradleys chose a unique name for their new puppy. They named him Django after Django Reinhardt, the Belgian French jazz guitarist of Roma (Gypsy) parentage who achieved fame in the 1930s. Obviously, the Bradleys enjoy jazz.

Christy said that "Django took to Hogie right away and started cuddling up with him." Three years later, when I first interviewed the Bradleys, they reported that "the two dogs are best buddies and can often be seen cuddled up under a tree. Django and Hogan play a lot and get plenty of exercise running around our three-acre fenced yard during the day when we are at work, but in the evening they are in the house with us."

When they first brought him home, Django was about half the size of Hogan; however, he grew to be a much larger dog. Django weighs about 110 pounds even though he is skinny. He has the long and lean look of a German shepherd. His coat is a light tan color, and he is long haired. Django has enjoyed good health, and the Bradleys can't remember him ever being sick. They sent me a photo of Django as a puppy with his big brother, Hogan, towering over him. In a picture taken four years later, a mature Django towers over Hogan. When Django moved into the Bradley household, he soon discovered that the animal that ruled inside the house was the family cat, Ares. "The cat is king, and the dogs know it and treat him as such." Django is affectionate and submissive toward the cat and his humans. The cat likes to tease both dogs by running and charging at them. In 2014, a fourth animal joined the family, a kitten named Scarlet. No doubt Ares will train her in how to rule over dogs.

Just about one year after Christy and Alan adopted Django, three wonderful children joined the Bradley household. Alan and Christy adopted four-year-old twin girls, Wynter and Kaely, and their two-year-old brother, Hakaru. Christy described Django as "awesome with the kids. He is gentle and submissive with the children. He loves to hang out with them when they are playing outside. He follows them around and is very relaxed with them. He loves to roll over and have them scratch his belly."

Django is friendly and well behaved with people in general, but "sometimes people meeting him for the first time are intimidated by his size." For example, when the eight-year-old daughter of Christy's friend visited the house for the first time, the child became frightened when Django walked up to her and one of the twins. The twin told Django to sit, and he did. Assured by the twin that Django was gentle, the other child relaxed.

Christy said that "Django is an excellent companion. He and Hogan are members of our family. Django is such a blessing. He is submissive and sweet natured." Shortly after adopting him, Christy took Django to a puppy class offered at the Humane Society of Western Montana, where he enjoyed learning new skills and basking in the extra attention from Christy.

Like Cinnamon's other puppies, Django is a talker, especially when his owners come home from work and he is happy that the family is together once again. Django's first adoption failed, but now the sweet-natured dog has a great life, with Hogan to learn from, a cat to play with, and three delightful children to love. It is pretty obvious that Django's mission is to give love and affection, and he could not find a better family.

Update: Hogan passed away in 2014, leaving Django moping around and grieving for his best friend; however, Django is bonding well with the new kitten, Scarlet. Each of the Bradley children shared their feelings about their special dog.

"It is cute when Django and our little kitten, Scarlet, touch noses through the window screen. He is very gentle with her, and she loves him."—Kaely

"I think Django has talent because once when I was feeding him, he stood up on his hind legs and walked backward. It was funny because he is so big."—Wynter

"Django is my favorite pet, and I love him. He is playful with me and he is a sweet dog."—Hakaru

Casey Drummond Adopts Japhy (a.k.a. Sparkle)

Sasha's puppies were named Disco, Glitter, and Sparkle. In December 2008, a young man named Jordan presented his girlfriend, Casey Drummond, with a very special twenty-first birthday present: Sparkle the puppy. Casey had admired Jordan's dog and expressed a desire to have one of her own. Knowing Casey had experience working with sled dogs, the young man thought that a Camp Husky puppy would be ideal for her. Although Jordan and Casey are no longer together, she said that her Camp Husky puppy is "the best birthday present I ever got."

About five months after adopting Sparkle, Casey graduated with a degree in English from the University of Montana. This may explain why she renamed her dog Japhy after the poet with a penchant for the simple life and Zen Buddhism in *The Dharma Bums*, Jack Kerouac's 1958 beat-generation novel.

Casey has had varied experience with dogs, growing up with Lab mixes in Boise, Idaho, working summers conditioning sled dogs for mushers, volunteering at the Iditarod in Alaska, working for a business that takes dogs out for group hikes, and working for a veterinarian. When I first interviewed Casey, she and Japhy were living in Missoula and preparing to move to Bozeman, where Casey would be taking science courses at Montana State University to qualify for admission to a veterinary medical college. Casey is currently completing her third year of veterinary studies, and Japhy is often her practice patient.

Japhy weighs seventy-five pounds and is "super healthy." When Casey had genetic testing done on Japhy, she was surprised to learn that her dog was pure German shepherd with no sign of husky heredity, which would indicate that her father was one of our many white German shepherds. Casey and Japhy completed an obedience class in Missoula, and Casey has gone on to teach her dog a number of tricks such as twirling around while giving a high five. Japhy is a strong believer in tricks for treats. Like so many Camp Husky dogs, Japhy also likes to talk. She talks whenever Casey comes home from school or work.

Although Japhy is devoted to Casey and is an obedient dog that has not been destructive or a nuisance barker, living with Japhy has led to some challenges for Casey. While Japhy gets along well with other dogs, she is distrustful of men until she gets to know them. She tends to be standoffish and protective of Casey, both common characteristics of German shepherds. When Casey first took Japhy to Boise to meet her parents, Japhy was suspicious of Casey's father until he made an effort to win the dog's trust. Now the two are bonded.

Casey had two difficult experiences with Japhy in the first couple of years. First, a landlord in Missoula had a negative attitude toward German shepherds and told Casey that she had to move. Japhy was very attuned to Casey's emotions by then, and sensing how upset Casey was over the forced move, her dog stayed "glued" to her.

The worst time Casey had was when Japhy ran away while in the care of someone else. While Casey was out of town, Japhy went on a group dog walk with a company that Casey used to work for, and what should have been a fun outing turned out badly for Japhy. The man who was leading the hike yelled at Japhy when she and another dog got in a spat, and the timid Japhy just ran off. Luckily, Casey came back that very day, so she was able to begin searching only a few hours after Japhy disappeared. Casey spent several hours in the woods that night searching the area where Japhy had last been seen. Worn out, discouraged, and distraught at the thought of losing her beloved dog and never knowing what happened to her, Casey was about to give up her search for the night when suddenly Japhy came running to her on that dark night. After ten hours alone in the woods, Japhy was as distraught as Casey. The two "spooned all night," grateful to be reunited.

While they were living in Missoula, Casey and Japhy had the opportunity to meet Japhy's mom, Sasha, and her owners. "We first ran into Sasha hiking on the Waterworks Hill, and knew her right away." Casey met several other Camp Husky dogs while living in Missoula and observed that they all had a special quality that made them stand out.

Japhy has had to adapt to four new homes as she and Casey went from Missoula to Bozeman and then to Logan, Utah, and, finally, to Pullman, Washington, where Casey will complete her last two years of training at Washington State University College of Veterinary Medicine. In all her moves, and living as a single woman, Casey has appreciated both the companionship and protection that Japhy has provided her. Japhy has the German shepherd quality of being "cautious around new people but able to warm up quickly to dog people. She is very intelligent and protective. I never thought protection would be a quality I would have sought out in a dog, but as a single girl who lives by herself, I love it. Japhy is my protector, and I could not be more grateful."

During the 2014 spring break from veterinary college, Casey and Japhy visited friends in Missoula and later dropped in to visit me. I can attest that Japhy is a good-natured and well-adjusted dog with a very devoted owner. Japhy has been a big help and emotional support as Casey has progressed through her rigorous studies. "Japhy continues to be the best friend a girl could ask for, and she's very tolerant when I poke and prod her constantly as I try to learn anatomy and palpitation."

As a teacher myself, I know that Casey will be a superior veterinarian, not just because she is an intelligent, hardworking, and conscientious student, but because she has a far deeper appreciation than most people—and I dare say, most veterinarians—of the powerful bond of love that can exist between a person and a dog. Casey's animal patients and the people who love them will all benefit because their doctor bonded with an angel.

As of spring 2016, Casey is finishing her third year of veterinary studies and is looking forward to beginning her senior year of clinical work. While a student in Logan, Casey adopted another dog. "I adopted a male German shepherd named Santiago," she told me, "who was in need of a foster to get him out of an overfilled shelter. Santiago and Japhy pretty much hit it off right away, so I didn't foster for long. Santiago and Japhy are great companions and enjoy playing together. The love and affection of these two dogs motivates me to keep doing all the hard work involved in veterinary studies, and they give me an excuse to get outdoors for exercise. Japhy is starting to slow down at age seven, and she has much more white in her face now.

"Wherever we go, people still ask me if Japhy is a wolf. Her health is good but she has had progressive urinary incontinence over the past couple of years. I've been treating Japhy with acupuncture while working on my acupuncture certification (for animals). The treatments are helping her a lot. She still loves to get outdoors to splash in mud puddles, chase bunnies, and play with Santiago. Japhy is a very special dog, and the story of the dogs on the bus is the most unique dog story I have ever heard. I'm glad that I'll have a book to remember the dog who has kept me safe these last seven years as I set out into the world and pursued the goal of becoming a veterinarian. Japhy relieves my stress as I study for very difficult exams, and she continues to provide unconditional love and wonderful companionship every day. I can't even describe how incomplete my life would feel if Japhy were not in it. I don't think another dog will ever be able to touch my life the way she has."

Barley (a.k.a. Disco) Is Adopted by Jeff Gailus

Sasha's puppy Disco was not as fortunate as his sister Sparkle. From what I have learned, he did not have good or reliable owners, and he lacked proper socialization and care in his first three years. Thus, this white German shepherd ended up back in the Humane Society of Western Montana in 2012.

While I was writing this book, I got an urgent e-mail from Cindy McIlveen about a Camp Husky dog named Barley. Cindy, like most of us who worked at Camp Husky, can easily recognize our distinct dogs. I learned from Casey Drummond that Barley was actually Sasha's male puppy, Disco. Casey had seen Disco as a puppy when she adopted his sister Sparkle. Casey recognized Barley as Disco later when he was returned to the Humane Society of Western Montana, and she went to visit him before Cindy fostered him in 2012.

Cindy then went to visit Barley, got him out of the shelter, and fostered him until she found a permanent home for him with Jeff Gailus of Missoula. Barley was one of sixteen Camp Husky dogs that found forever homes with good people who appreciate them, thanks to Cindy.

Jeff, a writer, university teacher, and grizzly-bear expert, described Barley as a "sweet and gentle giant of a dog who has become a permanent and important part of our family." Jeff shared what he learned of Barley's early experience and his issues: "He's got a few issues, mostly fear and anxiety around other dogs and some people (mostly men), but my wife and I love him and are glad to have been able to give him the loving home he deserves. Apparently, he was adopted out to someone here in Missoula, who then passed him on to a second owner who chained him in the backyard. Barley ended up back at the Humane Society after this guy was sent to jail. Barley flunked his adoption assessment, so the Humane Society

215

here was unwilling to adopt him out. Cindy McIlveen took him into her home until she could find a suitable home for him, and that is how Barley ended up with us. He has come a long way since we adopted him, and gets better by the week. With us, he's playful, affectionate, super smart, and never devious or malicious."

CHAPTER 9

I Have a Family Now

Many of those I interviewed for this book were single men or women, ranging in age from early twenties to over ninety, who lived alone but formed families with their Camp Husky dogs. Many dogs also lived with and bonded with cats or other dogs in these homes. Many couples who adopted had young children or teenagers at the time. Some of the youngest couples had babies after adopting their dogs. Many of those who adopted had grown children, and their Camp Husky dogs have bonded with grandchildren or even great-grandchildren. This chapter features fourteen Camp Husky dogs in a variety of these family situations.

Ollie, the Dog That Loves Backpacking and Winter Sports

Christine and Stephen Handler were living in Missoula and looking to adopt a puppy when they heard on the news that Camp Husky dogs were available for adoption. The young couple drove to Butte on Thanksgiving Day 2008 and selected, from among the many available puppies, "a little red fur ball" with a husky mom named Ethel and a white German shepherd father. There were only three pups in Ethel's litter, and two were in the animal hospital with kennel cough when the Handlers chose their puppy, filled out the paperwork, and gave her the name Ollie. Once Ollie was weaned, a volunteer drove her to the Handler's house. The volunteer told the Handlers that Ollie howled all the way from Butte to Missoula. When she arrived at her new home, Ollie was fourteen pounds of rambunctious and mouthy puppy, but she grew into eighty-five pounds of energy, making her perfectly suited to be the companion of a young couple who enjoy hiking and being active in the outdoors. From the time she was a little puppy, Ollie enjoyed backpacking trips with Christine and Stephen in Montana. Initially, she was so small that Christine carried her in her backpack. She soon became an old hand at backpacking. "From Ollie's point of view there is nothing like coming across a lingering patch of mountain snow on a hot July day," said Christine.

Ollie has backpacked with her family in the Bob Marshall Wilderness of Montana, the San Juan Mountains of Colorado, and the Sycamore Canyon of Arizona. Now, at age seven, Ollie still spends lots of time enjoying winter sports with Christine and Stephen. "Ollie adores winter snow, and recently Christine taught her skijoring. It's pretty obvious that Ollie has the husky attitude when it comes to winter sports," said Stephen. "When we are getting ready to go skijoring, Ollie cannot contain her excitement—she's bouncing off the walls, howling, and yelling until we get moving!"

In addition to all the other fun things they do, Stephen and Christine take Ollie on weekly runs with their human and dog friends, as Christine explains. "Ollie can't contain her excitement when she gets to run with her dog friends…she's a pack animal at heart. (Although sometimes she may think herself a bit more of the alpha of the pack than we'd like.)"

Ollie has enjoyed lots of adventures and adapts well to change. In her first four years, Ollie and her family moved from Missoula to Flagstaff, Arizona, back to Missoula, and then to Houghton, Michigan, where they met Katie and Rick Donovan, who were among the important volunteers at Camp Husky. Katie was surprised and happy to find a Camp Husky dog so far from Butte.

As this book goes to print, Ollie and her family are still living in Houghton, in the upper peninsula of Michigan. Life in a small city suits Ollie. Christine described her as "a people-loving dog." Ollie is "loving and affectionate" toward Christine and Stephen, as well as their friends, and she enjoys walks in the city, where there are lots of people to greet. "Ollie's favorite days," said Christine, "are going to the farmers' market or any kind of street fair where she gets to be greeted by all of her adoring public. She draws quite a crowd some days, and most people stop us to say how beautiful she is, and many others ask if she is a wolf or wolf hybrid."

Stephen told me that "Ollie has a couple of interesting personality quirks. Not only is she protective of us, she is protective of children when she is around them. If she sees a child jump off a dock into a lake or swing on a swing set, she howls and acts as though she is concerned they will get hurt. And whenever we are running with a group of friends and dogs, she acts as though it is her responsibility to take care of the whole pack. If the one group splits into two, she doesn't like it and runs back and forth to keep an eye on both groups. Her other peculiarity is her talking. Ollie is not a barker, but she is a talker. She makes a huge ruckus when we get home from work—a weird whine/howl for a good five minutes!"

Stephen and Christine have been devoted dog owners, taking Ollie to obedience classes when she was young, seeking advice from trainers when they needed it, making sure she gets lots of exercise, and finding dog friends for her to play with, especially her best friend, a springer spaniel named Chester.

In the spring of 2013, Ollie had surgery for a partial cruciate ligament tear. Although Christine and Stephen found it challenging to keep Ollie still and inactive for a few months, she recovered well. Ollie was one of three Camp Husky dogs that needed this surgery.

Ollie has enjoyed a great life with Stephen and Christine, and this couple credits Ollie with "keeping us active and entertained for the last seven years. We are so thankful we very impulsively chose to drive to Butte and adopt Ollie. We don't know what we'd do without her now."

Apollo (a.k.a. Moose #13a) Lives with Kirby and Jonathan Rowe of Colorado

Just a few months after getting married, Jonathan and Kirby Rowe adopted Moose, the largest pup in one of the first litters born at Camp Husky. Apollo was only ten weeks old and weighed twenty-two pounds when adopted. Kirby was on winter break from college when the couple adopted Apollo, so she had time to form a special bond with the pup during the first few weeks.

Apollo joined the other family dog, Zeus, who is a black Lab. The two dogs soon became best buddies. While Zeus is "calm but moody, Apollo always appears happy and energetic."

The young couple and their two dogs relocated to Colorado shortly after Kirby graduated from Montana Tech. Apollo was thrilled to welcome a new member of the family in 2011, when Jonathan and Kirby brought home their son, Logan. Three years after Logan's birth, Kirby described the relationship between their little boy and their Camp Husky dog: "From the time we brought our baby boy home, Apollo instantly claimed Logan as his new best friend and hasn't left his side since. Apollo is happy to have a playmate with the same amount of energy as he has."

Now the two dogs enjoy playing together in their big backyard but are most happy inside the house with Logan, Kirby, and Jonathan. "They can come and go as they like with a doggie door, and they definitely prefer being indoors with us," said Kirby.

Kirby described her hundred-pound Camp Husky dog as "a giant teddy bear. He loves to cuddle with me. Apollo is a very sociable dog that likes people, but he is protective of me and Logan as well. While he is not a barker, Apollo does make funny, talking sounds." (Apollo is the smiling dog at the bottom of the front cover.)

Bear and Katie in Great Falls

While Priscilla, one of our mother dogs, was giving birth to a litter of puppies, an eight-year-old girl in Great Falls was reading about Camp Husky on the Internet and dreaming about having a dog. Katie's parents, Tammy and Robert Evans, had agreed that their youngest child was ready to have a dog, and Katie wanted one of the Camp Husky puppies. The family drove to Butte, and Katie picked out her puppy when Priscilla's litter was only twelve days old. Seven weeks later, Katie was able to take her puppy home. She named him Bear.

In the beginning, Bear needed a lot of special nurturing from Katie and Tammy because he was scared of everything. Puppy kindergarten and visits to the dog park with Katie helped him gain confidence. Tammy said that in the early months, Bear was like the famous dog Marley: sweet and affectionate but very difficult to train. "He would do anything for a treat, but he flunked obedience class. He just wanted to play with the other dogs the way he does at the dog park."

When still a puppy, Bear developed a problem with his right front elbow, causing him to limp. A veterinarian recommended a nutritional approach consisting of liquid glucosamine, vitamins E and C, and fish oil. Tammy kept Bear on the nutritional regimen for several months, and eventually the lameness disappeared. Bear grew to be a healthy eighty-five-pound adult. The pure-white coat he had as a puppy gradually turned into shades of gold with white "husky stripes." Tammy and their veterinarian estimate that Bear is about three-quarters German shepherd and one-quarter Siberian husky.

After adopting Bear, the Evans family was inspired to help other dogs by becoming a foster family for homeless dogs through the Great Falls Pet-Paw-See program. Through this great program for cats and dogs, the Evans family has fostered and found homes for forty dogs since adopting Bear! Tammy explains that Bear was a big help with the fostering process. "He went up to each new arrival with a warm and friendly greeting; however, we became concerned because Bear showed increasing sadness each time a foster dog left for a permanent home. When Bear formed an especially close relationship with a very energetic border collie named Toby, we decided to adopt Toby for Bear's sake. The two dogs are great buddies, and Bear has been a calming influence on Toby." When Bear talks and howls like the typical Camp Husky dog, Toby tries to imitate the older dog but with little success.

Growing up together, Katie and Bear have developed a close and special bond, as Tammy explained in our interview: "Bear has an exceptionally sweet nature and is always loving toward dogs and people alike and very protective of Katie. Katie and Bear enjoy walks in our urban neighborhood, and Bear's friendly disposition has made him a favorite in our neighborhood as well as with our friends."

A few months after Bear moved in with them, Tammy and Robert did not have to worry about young Katie when she was off on a walk or playing in the neighborhood, because Bear was always watching out for her. His protective instincts are not limited to his family. Katie has a girlfriend who owns a miniature pinscher, and the two girls enjoy taking their dogs to the dog park for exercise. A few years ago, Bear and the pinscher were playing at the park, when a group of large dogs came running their way. Although the dogs intended no harm, Bear realized they could trample his little friend, so, like a linebacker, Bear placed his large body in front of the miniature pinscher to block the pack of dogs and protect his friend. Katie's scared little puppy had grown up to be her brave and loyal friend.

Update in August 2015: Katie is now a teenager, Bear is a mature dog of six and a half, and the two are more bonded than ever. Katie and Bear also have the new hobby of agility competition. Katie trained Bear, and he is very good. Bear is one lucky dog to have been adopted by Katie and her parents. To see pictures of Bear and Katie in competition, go to our Facebook page. Bear is the featured dog at Camp Husky 2008 Butte Montana.

Bill and Sharon Miller of Butte Adopt Bobbie (a.k.a. Bob)

In Edinburgh, Scotland, there is a famous statue of Greyfriars Bobby, a dog so revered for his loyalty to his master that he was honored with a royal visit from Queen Victoria. The Camp Husky pack has its own Bobbie, an equally loyal dog. Bill Miller learned about Camp Husky from the *Montana Standard*, and applied to adopt a puppy in early November 2008. At the time, Bill and his wife, Sharon, were retired and had one pet, Skippy, a Shetland sheepdog. Bobbie (Bear's brother) was approximately eight weeks old when Bill brought the pure-white German shepherd puppy home. The puppy was fortunate to have a large yard to play in and an enthusiastic Skippy to play with. The puppy and older dog soon became best friends and enjoyed playing together from the start. Initially, Skippy, at twenty-five pounds, outweighed the puppy, but Bobbie grew into a very large and long dog weighing ninety pounds. Sharon notes that "Bobbie is careful to never hurt Skippy even when he drags Skippy around in play." However, Bobbie tries to imitate Skippy by jumping onto Sharon's lap, which is a problem given his size.

The Millers take good care of their dogs, and the dogs have returned the love. Bobbie and Skippy enjoy apples for treats, and according to their veterinarian, Dr. Cornelius, both are quite healthy. Rather than taking out-of-town trips requiring them to board their dogs, the Millers prefer to do a lot of camping in the summer and take the lucky dogs with them. Also, both dogs enjoy riding in the car with Bill on his errands around town.

Sharon described Bobbie as "gentle and very affectionate with Bill and me. While his bark and size sometimes scare friends and strangers alike, he is very gentle with our three-year-old great-granddaughter."

Bobbie does not talk like most of the Camp Husky dogs. But he does have a most interesting trait: he likes to watch television and will howl at certain commercials. He especially likes the commercial for GEICO insurance with the green lizard, and he will howl enthusiastically when that particular commercial is aired.

The Millers are glad they adopted Bobbie even though he was rather destructive as a puppy. His biggest fault is that he can be bullheaded. When I first interviewed Sharon, she said how safe she felt because of her Camp Husky dog. "Bobbie is very protective when strangers come to the house, and I feel safe when Bill is away and I am alone with Bobbie."

In the fall of 2014, I received a note from the Millers describing how Bobbie had protected Bill and stopped a robbery. "One afternoon when Sharon was in Florida visiting relatives, a couple of men tried to rob us. I was in the house with Bobbie and Skippy and did not hear anything due to my hearing loss, but Bobbie suddenly started going crazy, alerting me that something was wrong. At first, I thought my grandson might be in the yard, but it was two men breaking into our property! It was Bobbie who alerted me and Bobbie who prevented the robbery!" Sharon's premonition that Bobbie would protect her proved true. She had left her home and husband in good hands when she traveled to visit relatives.

Cindy and Bill Hanley of Butte Adopt Lucy

Cindy and Bill were not planning on adopting a dog when they went shopping in December 2008 at the Quality Supply Store in Butte. But when they saw the adorable puppies there and talked with Camp Husky volunteers, they decided to adopt one (another adoption that can be credited to volunteer Barb LeProwse and her friends).

The sweet little puppy the Hanleys chose grew into a large, beautiful dog with a coat of blond, fluffy fur. The Hanleys describe Lucy as "timid and standoffish with strangers but highly affectionate with the family, even needy sometimes." Like Bobbie in the earlier story, Lucy loves children. "Lucy is especially good with our grandchildren. She is gentle and affectionate with our three-and-a-half-year-old grandchild. Lucy is a really good dog, both playful and energetic." Lucy gets to play with other Camp Husky dogs when she visits at All about the Dawg, the doggie day-care facility run by a former Camp Husky volunteer. "We *love* Lucy," say the Hanleys.

Lucky and the Ashpole Family

Lucky, a long-haired husky-shepherd cross, was adopted by a couple with two young daughters. Lucky's family lives on forty acres outside of Butte. David and Karen Ashpole describe their family dog as "gentle, loyal, and playful. Lucky has never tried to bite anyone and has never been anything but a good companion to our family. Lucky has always been especially good with our daughters, who were about eight and twelve when we adopted him."

Duke Lives on a Farm in Eastern Montana with the Harrington Family

Debbie and Shawn Harrington were Butte residents when they adopted a male puppy they named Duke on December 31, 2008. Duke is typical of the Camp Husky dogs. He is pure white, weighs about seventy-five pounds, and is a talker. For the first two years of his life, Duke was a loving companion to Debbie, a nursing student at the time, and her husband, Shawn, then retired. The couple already had an adult poodle named Carl when the puppy came to live with them.

While Duke lived with Debbie and Shawn in Butte, the couple frequently babysat their second son's baby girl, and Duke was always gentle and protective of the young child. "Once, when the baby was about eighteen months old, she was out in the front yard with Duke and Carl. They were all fenced in; however, our granddaughter was trying to open the gate and get out. That is when we learned how very protective Duke can be. He created a racket to get my attention," recalled Debbie, "and when I looked out, I saw him jumping up and down all concerned about the baby trying to open the gate."

When Duke was two years old, Debbie graduated with her RN degree and took a job in Great Falls, Montana. At that time, the couple's eldest son and his wife adopted Duke. They live on a farm near Glendive, Montana, with their little boy, so Duke has another child to love. Debbie reports that Duke is good with her grandson. The big dog also gets along well with all the farm animals, including horses, cows, and three Siamese cats.

Rusty (a.k.a. Faith), a Puppy for Goldie

The following is Janet Foster's account of how one of our white German shepherd puppies, Faith, was adopted by Janet and her husband, Bill, of Anaconda. Although Faith (renamed Rusty) passed away before this book was finished, she had a great life and will never be forgotten by the family who loved her.

"In late spring of 2008, my husband and I adopted a one-and-one-half-year-old white Siberian husky–Akita cross named Goldie; the volunteers at Pintler Pets (a volunteer-run, no-kill shelter in Anaconda) gave her this nickname because her eyelashes are the golden color of wheat. Goldie's quiet demeanor and gentleness was deceiving because she could also be hyper and mischievous; we couldn't even keep her in the yard! Not knowing what else to do, we asked our veterinarian at the Amherst Animal Hospital, and he suggested, or rather prescribed, a puppy for Goldie to calm her down. We weren't quite sure that we wanted another dog, despite what the veterinarian said, so we waited to see if things would change on their own.

"By early winter nothing had changed; if anything, Goldie was even more exasperating. One evening, while watching the local news, we heard that a bus full of more than a hundred huskies had been seized and the dogs, many of them pregnant females, would eventually need homes. Since we're avid proponents of adopting and rescuing dogs, this was just the push we needed to fill Goldie's prescription; we were hoping for one of the puppies. For months we waited and followed the story until finally it was announced that adoption was open to the public.

"After arriving at Camp Husky, a volunteer named Tara showed us around and asked us questions like which sex would we prefer, age range, temperament, and so on. Once we told her our story about Goldie and our preference for a spayed female no more than a year old, she took us straight to the last two remaining puppies from a litter born on the bus. These puppies were approximately six weeks old when they were taken from the trailer with their mother and were about six months old when we met them. Both were females with short white fur, long snouts, long gangly legs, and huge paws. One of them had a floppy ear and a white spot on her nose the shape of a martini glass. Their nicknames were Faith and Hope because the volunteers had faith and hope that someone would adopt them soon.

"Tara led us and the puppies to the yard where we could visit with them for a bit so we could make our choice. Several times, Faith, the one with the white spot on her nose and one floppy ear, tried to crawl into my husband's jacket while he was squatting to pet her, and then she threw a fit when we put them back in the kennel and turned to leave. That made my husband decide he wanted Faith.

"A waiting period was required to fulfill our request that she be spayed, which gave us time to prepare our home for a puppy. The day we arrived to pick Faith up, she was literally handed to us by another volunteer named Samantha. Faith was just back from the vet's office after surgery and was not quite awake yet. Bundling her up in my arms, we went straight to the car and drove home. I sat with her in the back seat as she slowly woke up from the anesthesia.

"As Faith grew, so did her fur. Eventually it grew to a total length of four to six inches, and it framed her head like a lion's mane. As her fur grew longer, it also changed to a cream color with a strip of rust-colored fur from the top of her ears, down the length of her back, and halfway down the top of her tail—hence the name Rusty. The top of her fur might be long, but the undercoat is short, thick, and as fluffy as a pillow.

"While our big Camp Husky puppy brought us the usual frustration of coping with chewed socks, shoes, picture frames, and a remote, as well as the challenge of house training, our patience paid off as she matured. Rusty closely bonded with us and never strayed far and always immediately returned when called. She grew to be very, very protective of us, viciously barking at people and other dogs that came too close. But when we were alone with her, Rusty was loving and gentle, even when she played. Rusty was an exceptionally smart and sensitive dog, and she seemed to understand when one of us was sick, and she tried to offer comfort in her own way. She would bring all her toys to us and lie at our feet.

"When Rusty was a young adult, we tried a dog obedience class with Samantha Collier (the same volunteer who handed Rusty to me when we were finally able to take her home from Camp Husky), but Rusty scared everyone in the class except Samantha. Samantha kindly volunteered one-on-one training with us at no extra cost. Although we declined, Samantha was gracious enough to offer tips on how to handle Rusty's somewhat aggressive personality. With Samantha's tips, Rusty quickly learned how to sit, walk on a leash, say hello in her best imitation of Scooby-Doo, and take food gently from a hand. It was harder to stop her from jumping up on us in her excitement to see us when we get home, but she kept improving. It's hard to teach a dog not to be that happy to see family members when they return home.

"To give our dogs the exercise they needed we walked them on a trail on the outskirts of Anaconda to avoid scaring people. That way we could take them off the leash and let them chase each other through the grass. Rusty was fast; we clocked her at twenty-five to thirty miles per hour, but she couldn't turn on a dime like Goldie. It was funny to watch Rusty's head pop up above the grass looking for her pal after Goldie made one of those sharp turns.

"By the time she was three years old, Rusty stood about thirty-six inches from the floor to the top of her head (not including her ears); she was thirty-six inches long (not including sixteen inches of tail), and she weighed seventy-two pounds, twice the size of Goldie.

"Every morning around 5:00 a.m., Rusty would come into our room to wake us; our alarm is usually set for 5:30 a.m. Both dogs insisted on their cuddle time before we started our day; otherwise Rusty would pout or be mischievous and not be sorry for her minor infraction, or if it was a weekend, she would vocally demand our attention all day. Rusty was the biggest lap dog we've ever owned. I joked that Rusty was a three-lap dog since it truly did take three laps to hold her.

"We love our big baby, for that is what she was to us. All she wanted from us was our attention, which we gladly gave, and couldn't get away with not giving since she was very good at insisting. The good news was that Rusty had the effect on Goldie that the vet said she would, and now they both had a best friend for life, and so did we!

"We did a lot of things with our dogs, but they had the best times fishing and camping with my husband. One summer, after Rusty turned five years old, my husband took her, Goldie, and our newest pup, Little D (a Bospin half Boston terrier and half minipinscher) camping and were gone about ten days. They came home on a Wednesday night. That night when I got home from work, I wasn't greeted with the usual enthusiasm from Rusty, but there was some spark and a tail that wagged so hard I thought it might fall off. I just thought that she was tired. The next night's greeting from Rusty was the same as the night before; no 'herro' in Scooby-Doo fashion, and she didn't jump up and down with excitement. In fact, she didn't even get up. I insisted that my husband take her to the vet Friday morning. It didn't take long for the vet to determine what was going on. She was dying from an autoimmune disease; she only had days, if that, to live. There was nothing the vet could do for her.

"We decided not to let her suffer, so my family gathered around her for her final moments. As the light slowly left her eyes, I kept repeating the greeting I always said back to her every day, 'Herro, big baby, herro.' Then she smiled and was gone.

"Although we miss Rusty very, very much, we have no regrets despite our short time with her. We know that we gave her a good life and we would do it all over again even if the outcome was the same. We know she was as happy and content with us as we were with her. And that feeling has not gone away in the years since her passing, and I don't think it ever will.

"We will never forget how gentle Rusty was with our not-so-gentle granddaughter. Nor will we forget the time when Little D was first learning how to lock her jaws and clamped down on Rusty's tail as Rusty swung around in a circle trying to get Little D off, or how she stood over and licked Little D until she was able to stand again after she let go of Rusty's tail. Nor will we forget the sound of her hello. Thank you, Camp Husky, for the best dog we have ever had!"

Becky Johnson Adopts Pearl (#60c)

Becky Johnson—associate professor of mathematics at the Great Falls College of Technology, Butte native, and Montana Tech graduate—was celebrating Thanksgiving with her mother in Butte when the two women decided to do something to help the dogs at Camp Husky. The next day they showed up at Camp Husky with blankets, bags of dog food, and their checkbooks. When a volunteer named Tara took their donations, Becky asked about adopting a puppy. Tara suggested a puppy that she was fostering at the time, and on December 17, 2008, Becky took home an eight-week-old puppy to live with her and four cats.

Becky named her puppy Pearl, and it is a perfect name, not only because the white German shepherd's fur is the color of a pearl but also because the love, protection, and devotion she has shown toward Becky and the cats is priceless. Becky described Pearl as "very loving toward people she knows and very protective but never aggressive. For example, Pearl can be playing enthusiastically with other dogs at the local dog park, but she always has an eye on me. If Pearl notices a strange dog coming near me, she will run over and stand between me and the other dog, being friendly toward the other dog but making sure I am safe."

Pearl's protective instincts are not limited to people. From the time she was a puppy, Pearl decided that the four resident cats were her responsibility, and she takes that responsibility very seriously. Every time she comes into the house after being out in the backyard or enjoying an outing with Becky, Pearl checks on the cats first thing. "She locates each cat, gives it a few sniffs to make sure it is well, and then moves on to the next cat. Naturally, the cats did not like this routine at first, but now grudgingly accept it. The youngest cat, Missy, gives Pearl no end of aggravation because of Missy's constant efforts to escape from the house."

Most people who have a close relationship with a dog find themselves wondering how their dogs can understand so much about their thoughts and needs without fully understanding human speech. Pearl, for example, understands that her cats belong in the house and that Becky is upset if one of them gets out the door and escapes. Three of the cats are no problem because they are quite content to stay indoors; Missy, on the other hand, is always alert to any opportunity to sneak outside. Frequently, when Becky opens the back door and has her arms full of groceries, Missy will run out before Becky can stop her. That is where Pearl takes over. She will catch the cat, take hold of her scruff, and gently carry her back into the house. Once Missy escaped into the backyard without being seen by Becky as she left for work. That evening the next-door neighbor Jamie told Becky that she had spent twenty minutes watching through the chain-link fence as the ever-vigilant Pearl herded the cat and prevented her from climbing the fence and escaping from the backyard. No wonder Pearl was exhausted that evening! It would have been far easier to protect a herd of sheep than one frisky young cat.

Pearl normally spends weekdays outside in the backyard, where she has a doggie-door entrance leading into a section of the garage with a soft bed. There she can rest and stay warm in cold and stormy weather until Becky comes home from work. Late one afternoon in July 2012, Becky drove into the garage after teaching summer school and shopping for groceries on the way home, and she was a little surprised when Pearl was not waiting for her in the garage. After carrying in the groceries, Becky went out to look for Pearl in the backyard and saw that someone had opened the gate and let Pearl out. Expecting to see Pearl exploring the neighborhood, Becky stepped through the gate. To her horror she saw her beautiful dog lying motionless in the street with blood all around her head! After a quick check, Becky determined that Pearl was alive but seriously injured. She pulled Pearl out of the street to protect her from the traffic and then ran to the next-door neighbor for help. Jamie suggested using her truck, and the two women transferred the injured dog into the back of the truck and to an emergency veterinary clinic.

From the moment she realized Pearl had been hit by a car, Becky kept asking herself, "How could I bear losing Pearl? She is my best friend. She is always there for me. How could I stand losing her unconditional love and her happy spirit?" The veterinarian assured Becky that there was every reason to be hopeful because Pearl was conscious. As it turned out, the collision had broken a leg and three ribs and knocked out three teeth. Although she was obviously in pain when Becky came to visit her the next day, Pearl's eyes lit up and her tail thumped. Pearl has recovered from her injuries, and Becky now has a chain and padlock on the gate so that no one can open it.

Like most of the Camp Husky dogs, Pearl is a talker. Whenever she greets Becky, Pearl has something to say. The question, "Do you have a story?" is all it takes for Pearl to start a monologue. Sometimes it sounds like "Why did you have to stay at work so long?" or "What are we doing tonight?" Becky doesn't always understand what Pearl is saying, but "she is adorable. Pearl is also very smart and, in obedience class, gets a rating of eight, with ten being the very best possible." When Becky says, "I want a hug," Pearl rubs the side of her face against Becky's cheek. "Pearl has been a phenomenal influence on my life," said Becky. "She is an amazing dog, and I was hysterical when I thought I might lose her."

When Becky isn't working, she usually has Pearl with her. Among Pearl's favorite activities are walks, trips to the dog park, and visits to Petco. Becky takes Pearl to Petco for her grooming needs and likes to give her a summer cut for the hot weather since this dog has the very heavy coat typical of a shepherd-husky mix. Pearl is well behaved during grooming but much prefers shopping for treats and toys.

Update in August 2015: Becky took a teaching position at Montana Tech and is back in her hometown of Butte. She reports that "Pearly has adjusted well to her new home. Our house sits on three lots and Pearl has unlimited access to a huge yard. Her grandma (my mom) regularly spoils her. She bakes bones for Pearly, which are one of her favorite treats. Our mailman even throws a daily dog biscuit. We are also starting to take advantage of Butte's new dog park. Pearly is healthy, happy, and enjoying life. One of our cats passed away in 2013, so Pearly now has only three cats to mother, but she remains very affectionate and protective toward her cat family and me."

Gwenie Is Adopted by Jay and Janet Cornish of Butte

In February 2009, the Cornish family adopted one of the last puppies born at Camp Husky, coming into the world on November 19, 2008. Like several of the Camp Husky dogs, Gwenie had trouble digesting food as a puppy until Janet and Jay did some research and found a low-fat food that Gwenie tolerates well (and likes very much). Gwenie was a destructive puppy, chewing everything—shoes, furniture, and so on. Luckily, she soon outgrew that behavior. After attending a puppy class, the young dog obeyed simple commands quite well. "She is a great companion: very playful and very affectionate," said Janet.

Jay and Janet had a well-behaved older dog named Lucy and a cat named Tigger when they brought home a Camp Husky puppy. Both animals proved to be very tolerant of the rambunctious puppy. Janet described the relationship between the dog and cat: "I think the most humorous aspect of our life with Gwenie is observing how she plays with our very tiny cat, Tigger. Tigger is a male tabby Manx and weighs about seven pounds, while Gwenie weighs nearly eighty pounds! One day, as I looked out the window to our backyard, I noticed Gwenie was playing with something, dragging it across the lawn. All of a sudden it dawned on me that the 'toy' was Tigger! I raced outside just in time to see Tigger take off at warp speed for the safety of the weeds across the alley. Despite the seemingly unfair odds, Tigger often eggs Gwenie on, complaining if she does not engage him in play. A typical encounter includes Tigger taking a swipe at Gwenie with his tiny paw. Then Gwenie responds by putting Tigger's entire head in her mouth. Tigger simply pulls back and sinks his teeth into Gwenie's muzzle. Both make some ungodly noises, and then they begin the entire exercise again."

With Tigger for a playmate and the calm and well-behaved Lucy for a role model, Gwenie has a good life. Janet, a group facilitator and corporate trainer, can often be seen walking Lucy and Gwenie on the trail below the Montana Tech College. When I asked Janet and Jay if they are glad they adopted their Camp Husky puppy, they responded with enthusiasm: "Yes! Gwenie has a very strong presence in our lives. She is our friend and companion and her sheer size makes her a very big part of our home. We love her!"

Sasha (a.k.a. Lady #45) Is Adopted by Tom Susanj of Butte

Lady was an adult German shepherd with pretty white eyelashes and a white, cream, and tan coat. Having never been socialized, this lovely dog was unsurprisingly skittish and fearful at Camp Husky. However, she had three volunteers who helped her find a wonderful forever home. Tim was the first to give lots of extra attention to Lady. When Camp Husky closed, she was one of the dogs fostered by Cindy McIlveen. Next, Kacie Raybould found her a home with musician Tom Susanj of Butte in the summer of 2009.

Tom described his dog, now named Sasha, as "intelligent, friendly with people, playful, and submissive rather than aggressive." Other than being "a little scared" of other dogs, Sasha is an easy companion. Tom and Sasha live alone with no other animals, and the two enjoy a close bond. Tom was one of several people I interviewed who reported that their dogs have a strange "smile" when happy. This smile looks like a snarl to some folks, but the owners know their dogs are happy and expressing affection rather than anger.

Tom provides Sasha with lots of attention and rituals they both enjoy, like walks and playtime. Tom has taught Sasha to walk off leash and to stop before they cross the street. Sasha is kept safe with a fenced backyard. Apart from digging in the yard, she is a well-behaved dog. Like several of the Camp Husky dogs, Sasha had a bout of stomach problems when first adopted, but with Tom's good care, her digestion improved, and she has been healthy ever since.

Buddy (#9) Is Adopted by the Hackman Family

Lee Hackman works for Gilboy's Towing Company and was the driver on duty on the night of October 7, 2008, when the police took custody of the bus and trailer full of dogs. Lee hauled the bus and trailer to the animal shelter, and he hauled the bus full of one hundred dogs to the Anselmo mine shaft building the next morning. Like all those who saw the dogs on the bus that first night or next morning, Lee was "shocked by the filthy and disgusting condition of the bus and cages where the dogs were kept. As a tow truck driver I have seen a lot of sad things, but what I saw that night was an atrocity."

Lee believes that the bus broke down in Butte for a reason. "Butte is the most dog-loving town on the planet. We cherish our dogs." Lee was so moved that night by the distress and plight of the dogs on the bus that he decided then and there that he would adopt one of our huskies as soon as they were available, although he already had a nice dog.

When asked how he chose Buddy, an older dog that was very popular with volunteers, Lee said, "Buddy found us. He seemed to be smiling at my wife and me when we walked by his cage." Lee described Buddy as a perfect dog. "We loved him to death. He was the best." Buddy was a contented member of the Hackman household for eighteen months, playing with the other dog, roaming the property, and guarding the household—until tragedy struck. Like so many dogs in our community and elsewhere, Buddy was terrified of the firecrackers that go off from afternoon to late at night for nearly a week around the Fourth of July. Unbeknownst to Lee, Buddy had sought to escape the terror of the firecrackers by crawling under the motor home. When Lee attempted to move it, Buddy was so badly injured that he had to be euthanized. Sarah and I remember Buddy as one of the sweetest dogs at Camp Husky. Lee described him as a big dog with "the perfect disposition," a dog that always seemed to be smiling. "He was the best."

Gus (#59) and Basil (a.k.a. Kahlua #62) Are Adopted by Auguste and Suraya Lockwood of Seeley Lake

The Lockwoods, a couple from Seeley Lake in northern Montana, had four female huskies and wanted to adopt one or two male huskies "to be wrestling companions for our female huskies after our male wolf cross, Paiute, passed away." The couple knew nothing about Camp Husky when they drove to the Humane Society of Western Montana in Missoula in the winter of 2008. Auguste and Suraya were introduced to two young adult "husky" dogs sharing a kennel. Gus and Kahlua were brothers from Camp Husky and were so bonded that they needed to go to the same home. "We observed that Gus really needed his brother Kahlua," said Suraya. The couple kept the name Gus but changed his brother's name to Basil.

Gus is the larger of the two dogs and weighs about eighty pounds. He looks more like a German shepherd, and his back end shows the breed's characteristic downward slant. Basil has a more square shape and has much black coloring. Both dogs were underweight when first adopted. They have since achieved an ideal weight and are very healthy.

Unlike the female huskies, the new arrivals showed no natural talent for pulling a sled, and the couple soon realized that the dogs had more German shepherd than husky characteristics. Neither Gus nor Basil talks, although the female huskies do. Auguste said that the brothers are good guards but not aggressive. The Lockwoods are glad they adopted Gus and Basil, and they describe their Camp Husky dogs as very sweet and affectionate.

When Gus and Basil had been with the Lockwoods for little more than two years, the roof of the house caught fire, and it might have been disastrous had it not been for one of the huskies, Monkey, who ran upstairs and woke the couple, alerting them to the fire. Although the upper half of the geodesic dome house burned down, the Lockwoods and their seven dogs all escaped uninjured. "It was quite a challenge to rebuild," said Suraya, "but I am happy to say that we are back in the dome home with the poopers."

In the fall of 2015, I received the following update from the Lockwoods: "Basil unfortunately passed away after Christmas 2014. His legs just suddenly stopped working. We brought him to the vet and were told that the problem was not neurological, so we took care of him and carried him in and out until it came time to have to put him down. He spent his last days comfortably, with his buddy Gus right next to him. He is buried back of our house with our other much-loved pets. When you last spoke with us, Auguste and I had seven huskies. We are now down to two. It has been very strange having only two. We plan on adopting another husky eventually. The two huskies we have left are Gus and Monkey, the husky that alerted us about the fire. Gus and Monkey are both German shepherd–husky mixes and are together all the time. Monkey is fifteen and Gus has taken the role of being her nurse, always cleaning her eyes and keeping her active by wrestling. Gus is a real sweetheart and a true gentleman. He is quite big, nearly one hundred pounds. His nickname is Goofball. He now spends most of his time napping next to Monkey inside the house.

"Thanks again for sharing Gus and Basil's stories. They are both much loved and Basil is very much missed."

CHAPTER 10
Volunteers and Their Dogs

M any of those who volunteered at Camp Husky adopted one or two dogs. I have already introduced some dogs adopted by volunteers in previous chapters. This chapter introduces fifteen additional dogs adopted by volunteers. In most cases volunteers took home dogs with health or behavior issues or older dogs that were less likely to be adopted. Two of these dogs were fostered and later adopted by a volunteer because they were too sick to remain at Camp Husky and needed special care. Three were adopted by volunteers who feared that no one else would take them because they were very timid and afraid of people. I adopted one such dog myself. In other cases, volunteers just developed a relationship with a special dog while volunteering at Camp Husky.

Sarah DeMoney Adopts Flippy
On the first night of the rescue, among the dogs taken from the trailer was a litter of puppies about fourteen weeks old that had been in a cage with both their parents. The parents were representative of the majority of Camp Husky dogs in that they both appeared to be purebred long-haired white German shepherds. The mother was solid white like the majority of Camp Husky dogs, and the father had a coat that one might describe as white mixed with apricot, also very typical of Camp Husky dogs. These parents were also typical in that they were larger than most modern-day German shepherds; the size and weight of these dogs—100 to 120 pounds for males and about 85 pounds for females—was more in keeping with

German shepherds of the past, like the famous 1920s movie-star dog named Strongheart.

The puppies and parents taken from the trailer and housed at the Chelsea Bailey Animal Shelter on the night the rescue began remained there for about two or three weeks, but the director disliked all the dogs, and she wanted them removed as soon as possible. Thus, the pups and their parents arrived at the Anselmo mine yard, placing an even greater burden on the volunteers. These new arrivals were housed on the first floor, while the dogs from the bus were on the second floor. Since volunteers were given very little time to prepare for the arrival of these dogs and puppies, they were too overwhelmed to notice that a half-starved mother dog still nursing puppies was about to give birth to another litter. In an effort to get her puppies to stop nursing so she could prepare for the upcoming birth, she got a little too aggressive, and one pup ended up with a broken jaw.

Samantha Collier was using her vacation time to volunteer at Camp Husky when the puppy, aptly named Hope by volunteers, was injured, and it was Samantha who saved her life. When Samantha and the other volunteers discovered the injured puppy, Samantha got the animal-services director to drive her and the puppy to the veterinary clinic under contract with animal services. The veterinarian who examined the puppy said that "she should just be euthanized." The animal-services director said nothing, but Samantha got angry. "No, you won't kill this puppy. You haven't even tried to help her," Samantha told the veterinarian. Because Samantha was there to defend the puppy, her jaw was repaired. Samantha took little Hope home with her rather than leave her to recuperate at the clinic.

Since little Hope needed a lot of special care, Samantha took her to work with her at the YMCA. Here Hope met Sarah DeMoney, who later fostered and adopted her. Sarah tells how the white German shepherd puppy that Samantha saved came to be part of her family: "While I was working at the YMCA, Sam Collier brought in a puppy from the rescue that was injured. All of us in the office oohed and ahhhed over the puppy, named Hope, and Lacey Cleveland and I took her into one of the showers to clean her, as she was pretty stinky. After her shower, we bundled her in towels, and I held her on my lap while I worked and she slept. Hope was about five months old when her jaw was broken, and Sam brought her to work where she could be watched and then took her home each night to care for her.

"On the third day of having Hope in the office, Sam asked if I could take her home for 'just one night' as she had an engagement to attend. Of course, I gladly said yes! I took her home and introduced her to my husband, three teenage sons, two dogs, and one cat. Almost immediately, my husband renamed her Flippy as one of her ears did not stand up. In anticipation of Flippy being at our home, we had purchased her a bed and puppy food. As Flippy's jaw was taped closed, so it would heal, we had to use the blender to pulverize her food so she could lap it up without using her jaw.

"The following morning I brought her and her bed to work with me. She lay right behind my desk and would follow me around the building as I conducted my work. Our office at the YMCA had one wall of windows that overlooked the swimming pool, and when I went to teach my water exercise classes, Flippy sat by the window watching and whining until I returned to the office. Flippy was, without a doubt, *my* dog—I kept her as a foster dog, and as soon as we could legally adopt her, we did.

"Flippy joined Ed, a Rottweiler-malamute mix; Fisher, a golden Lab mix; and Tazo, a red-tipped Siamese cat with crossed eyes and a broken tail—all rescue animals. Ed was very patient, and he did his best to teach Flippy correct behavior such as no barking, no running in the house, and no accidents in the house. He was the yard and house monitor and would nudge or scold Flippy if her behavior was not to his liking. Fisher was Flippy's playmate! Where Ed was the disciplinarian, Fisher was the mischievous older brother that taught Flippy how to check the yard's perimeter while barking, how to dig holes, and how to wrestle outside and in the house. And our cat, Tazo, became Flippy's best friend. Tazo sees himself as a small dog and was raised by Ed since he was seven weeks old and just two pounds. He loved that Flippy was closer in size to him than the other dogs. Tazo taught Flippy the art of being gentle. Since Flippy grew to seventy-five pounds and taller than the other two dogs, she had to learn how to play with Tazo while being gentle. Even today, nearly seven years later, Tazo and Flippy play together, and Tazo lies on the floor near Flippy during nap times and cuddles up to her when it is a chilly day.

"Flippy came with some PTSD; she did not like strangers, especially males who wore hats. Whenever my sons' friends came over, they had to immediately remove their hats. She didn't like strangers; we put a treat jar near the front door to have our guests give her a treat upon entering our home to train her that guests were OK. Petting her head has been a big no; she does not like to have a hand come toward her head. Instead we suggest that she is petted on the rump, which she loves. To this day, Flippy will greet a new guest skeptically, look them over, and then give them the house rules rather vocally—not barking, but talking with head movements and eye contact. We have a harness for her for walking, which she enjoys and seems to be calmer when wearing it. Each day when I return home from work, Flippy tells me all about her day, and she will pause and wait for my reaction and then continue speaking. She also argues with me; if I tell her no, she will sometimes argue and shake her head at me, wait for me to respond, and then retort. We have had many a fun time guessing what she is trying to tell us.

"Both of our beloved older dogs had passed on when my oldest son moved back home with his dog, Magnus, an emotional support dog. Magnus has been a visiting dog at nursing homes, loves children, and is a calming force. He has been Flippy's therapy dog as well. When Flippy would begin to become agitated, Magnus would calm her down. Because of the relationship Flippy has with Magnus, her remaining fears and anxieties have lessened considerably.

"We, especially me, love Flippy. She is very intelligent and caring toward her family. Flippy came without an instruction book; we had to work to understand her and her to understand us. It was a total family effort (human and animal family members) to assure her she was safe and loved. None of us can imagine a time without her."

Samantha Collier Adopts Gigi (#63), the Great-Grandmother of Camp Husky

Gigi, among the oldest female dogs at Camp Husky and showing signs of numerous pregnancies, was probably the great-grandmother of many of our puppies. Gigi was also among the dogs most frightened of people. Soon after the dogs moved into the Anselmo, Gigi escaped and got outside. Volunteers searched for her with no luck, but the next morning when Katie Donovan arrived to start the early-morning shift, there was Gigi at the door. Her desire to be back with her pack overcame her fear of people.

Realizing that this dog needed extra care and attention, Samantha took her home as a foster around Thanksgiving 2008. Gigi lived contentedly with Sam until she died six years later at about age fifteen, an exceptionally long life for a German shepherd–husky mix. Gigi had the face of a traditional black-and-tan German shepherd but the body of a husky. She maintained a healthy weight of between seventy-five and eighty pounds, just a little lighter than the average Camp Husky female.

Accustomed to a very large pack, Gigi enjoyed playing with other Camp Husky dogs that Sam fostered in the winter of 2008–2009, and later with dogs that boarded at Sam's country home. Gigi especially enjoyed long hikes with Sam and the many dogs from her doggie day care. Gigi loved playing in water and running into creeks.

While she remained very shy with strangers, Gigi loved Sam and her partner, Tracy. Sam described Gigi as very gentle and said, "She had the greatest smile. She was also so happy to see Tracy and me when we came home from work. She would smile and talk to us. We knew she was saying, 'I am so happy to see you.'" Gigi is gone, but she passed on her gentle nature and her tendency to smile and talk to many of the Camp Husky dogs descended from her.

It is not surprising that Sam chose to adopt one of the dogs that needed the most emotional support. Sam had a special gift for working with dogs at Camp Husky, and later several of the Camp Husky dogs, including this author's dog, benefited from the basic obedience class that Sam taught. Tracy wrote me about the relationship she observes between Sam and the many Camp Husky dogs that currently board at their country home. "Sam babysits a large number of dogs with her doggy day-care business and among them are many Camp Husky dogs, and these huskies have a unique way of relating to Sam. I witness this every time one of the huskies comes to this house! These dogs are *very* attached to Sam, following her around the house, watching every move she makes. When Sam has to leave the house to pick up or deliver a dog, I always stay with the dogs until she returns. The amazing thing is that every single husky in the group will howl when Sam leaves. They pace the floor until she returns, and then each runs up and rubs against her, and only then do they calm down. It is only the Camp Husky dogs that go through this ritual. I have told Sam many times that these dogs seem to know the role Sam played in saving them. It makes me proud that they love her so much." I have to note that my own Camp Husky dogs also react very positively to Sam when she comes to my home. My dog, Hector, was one of the dogs fostered by Sam in the early days of Camp Husky.

The Schwartz Family Adopts Ginger (#20) and Her Son, McCloud

One day at about noon in early October 2008, Pat Schwartz was taking a walk past the Anselmo when he saw volunteers walking Camp Husky dogs. It was then that Pat decided to join the volunteer effort, and soon his wife, Christine, and the couple's three teenagers were all volunteering on weekends. In addition, this family decided to help by fostering two dogs until adoptions could be started. They chose a mother dog named Ginger and her adult son, McCloud. The family chose large adult dogs, knowing it would be easier to find homes for puppies than adults, and they chose to keep the names that volunteers had given the two dogs. Once the Butte-Silver Bow government acquired legal custody of the Camp Husky dogs, the Schwartz family was able to officially adopt Ginger and McCloud. They were among the first families to adopt.

Both German shepherds have been healthy since they moved in with the Schwartz family. Ginger weighs about seventy-five pounds, and McCloud is much larger at one hundred pounds. Pat described both dogs as gentle, affectionate, and playful with the whole family. Pat enjoys taking the dogs out into the countryside where they can run off leash. "They are good dogs and obey well," said Pat. "However, they obey a little faster when my wife, Christine, gives the command."

The dogs have a fenced yard to play in, and they especially enjoy digging holes. "They have pretty much destroyed the yard, but it is their space, so we don't mind," said Pat.

Debbie Kane Adopts Molly (a.k.a. Lady)

Debbie Kane was one of those who responded to the first call for volunteers, working every Saturday and Sunday, although she already had a demanding full-time job. Debbie usually worked on a team with two other women, Jocelyn Dodge and Barb LeProwse, organizing kennels and setting up the maternity ward. About one hundred puppies were born at Camp Husky, so working in the maternity ward was very challenging for volunteers, as Debbie explains: "We did our best to provide the pregnant dogs and new mothers with whatever help we could give them. It was especially challenging keeping the mothers and newborns warm when there was no heat at the Anselmo hoist house. We used blankets to cover the sides of the kennels so that the mothers could feel safe, and we also put clean blankets or comforters on the cement every day to keep the mothers and pups warm. With about three litters of puppies born every week, the maternity ward required enormous work. We were so busy and working so hard that I did not have time to actually visit with the many people working at Camp Husky, but I remember being impressed by a high-school coach who came in from West Yellowstone to volunteer on weekends. I never learned his name."

While working with pregnant dogs, Debbie got to know a large white dog named Lady. "Lady was pregnant when she came off the bus, but sometime later, her puppies died inside her, causing her to become septic. Volunteers did not realize anything was wrong until Lady became very sick. Then an operation was performed to remove the dead puppies. After two weeks at the veterinary hospital, Lady was returned to Camp Husky. It was around Thanksgiving time, and we had just moved into our new building with heat on Arizona Street. Lady was still very weak and still sick from the infection. At that time many of our puppies were coming down with kennel cough, and I feared that Lady would be at risk in her weakened condition. Also, with so many mothers giving birth, we needed to make room for the puppies. That is why I took Lady home with me. Later, I changed her name to Molly."

It took a little while after her adoption before Molly realized that the Kane home was her home, as Debbie explained: "At first, Molly would jump over our fence, but once she realized that we were her family, she was contented to stay home and in her yard." Molly's efforts to escape may have been driven by a desire to return to the large dog pack at Camp Husky, the only family she had known.

Debbie explained that "Molly has always been sweet with a gentle disposition, but she was so afraid of people" when Debbie took her home.

"She would not let my husband or our friends touch her for an entire year! Eventually, Molly overcame her fear of people, and now she will even let strangers pet her." In addition to being afraid of people in general, Molly was also upset by any sudden and fast movements, no doubt a result of the trauma of life on the bus with a disturbed man.

While it took time for Molly to bond with her human family, she bonded right away with the family's miniature cocker spaniel and cat. The three animals sleep next to each other on their beds; however, Debbie observed that her little dog's fast movements triggered anxiety in Molly.

By Christmastime 2008, Debbie had to back away from volunteering because of year-end work required for her job at Northwestern Energy Company. Debbie was so committed to Camp Husky that she recruited some friends to take her place. While she could no longer work at Camp Husky, Debbie continued working hard to help the dogs. She joined the fundraising team that Barb LeProwse organized. Through that group, Debbie played a critical role in raising money and finding homes for many of our dogs.

Update: Molly passed away from leukemia in September 2014. Thanks to Debbie and her husband, Molly was able to grow old in a safe and loving home.

Megan Maes of Anaconda Adopts Puppy Kai

Megan Maes was a twenty-one-year-old facing a rigorous senior year as a petroleum-engineering student at Montana Tech when she learned about Camp Husky through one of her professors. Although very busy, this young woman committed to working three hours every Sunday. Megan had an unusual reason for volunteering. When eight years old, she had been attacked by a pit bull, and her injuries required medical treatment and stitches. That trauma left Megan fearful of dogs in general. She decided that volunteering at Camp Husky would not only be a way of helping the dogs and the community, but it might help her to overcome her fear.

When Megan spoke to me from her home in Edmond, Oklahoma, she recalled her volunteer experience: "Although it made me sad to see how Brode had mistreated the dogs, volunteering turned out to be a fun thing. I remember many of the dogs I walked, especially one black-and-tan

German shepherd mother dog named Star and two white German shepherd brothers named Mr. Smith and Mr. Jones. There were two men, Tim and Monte, who were awesome in handling the dogs, and they did a really good job of showing me how to work with the dogs. The dogs were anxious and fearful in the early days but they were not mean at all. We were so busy working that I didn't have time to be afraid of the dogs. There was a rule that we had to carry a leash at all times so we would be ready if a dog got loose. The work was intensive. Many of the dogs were sick, and that created all the more work for those of us cleaning kennels.

"Volunteering was often mentally and emotionally exhausting. The condition of many of the dogs brought tears to my eyes. Other times it was actually fun to just sit with and comfort a frightened dog in his kennel. I had never been in a kennel with a dog before the Camp Husky experience."

Megan is proud of the way the people from the local communities supported Camp Husky. "I felt that I was part of this outpouring of support from the community for these poor mistreated dogs." The Camp Husky experience convinced Megan that dog hoarding is a serious problem, causing untold suffering for animals and enormous burdens for communities. "Hoarders don't understand the harm they do. They really need psychological help."

One of Megan's favorite jobs at Camp Husky was caring for the moms and puppies. It was through this work that Megan bonded with a sweet but very skinny puppy born to a beautiful long-haired, yellow-colored German shepherd. While volunteering, Megan heard talk among volunteers that a vet had suggested euthanizing this particular puppy, named Kai, because she suffered from an autoimmune problem affecting her mouth. Megan decided to adopt Kai and, with proper medication, the beautiful dog has thrived.

Megan took Kai to her parents' home in Anaconda, where the family has four acres of land. Megan's parents, Kris and Laurin, had a golden retriever puppy at the time that was only one month older than Kai, and the two puppies became best buddies. The two older cats were not friendly toward the puppies, and while there is peace between the cats and dogs, there is no particular affection.

After arriving at the Maes home, Kai was timid and resisted taking walks with Laurin and the golden retriever puppy, choosing instead to stay close by the house, where she felt safe. Gradually, Kai overcame her fear of leaving the house and meeting new people. Now, said Kris, "Kai enjoys going for walks and is friendly and outgoing. She is great with everyone and has a nice personality. Her sister is jealous because Kai gets so much attention when out walking with people petting her and admiring her beauty. Kai also gets along well with dogs of all sizes."

Laurin described Kai as "a happy dog and very loyal to the family. Actually, she is the smartest dog we have ever had." Megan agrees that Kai is unusually intelligent and good at problem solving. She has respect for the family and is good with her golden retriever sister.

Megan described Kai as "well behaved. I love her. She is so good. Just awesome." When Megan graduated in May 2009 and took a job in Oklahoma, she made the painful decision to leave Kai with her parents rather than uproot her. Megan is now married, and she and her husband have adopted a shelter dog.

Dana Cotton Adopts Lizzie

Dana Cotton was teaching at Montana Tech when she decided to volunteer at Camp Husky. "While volunteering at the Anselmo," said Dana, "I fell in love with many of the dogs. I was working there when the pups were available for adoption in the winter of 2008, and I adopted a female from a litter with a beautiful red-coated mother—I had noticed one crawling all over all of her brothers and sisters. When I picked her up, she let out a ridiculous grunt that melted my heart, and man, she was stinky!" That was Dana's Lizzie, named after Queen Elizabeth of England. As an adult, Lizzie continues to grunt and still behaves in a humorous manner. "Lizzie is hilarious. She is always playful, loving, and needy! She is a singer when she knows you're listening, and she is always talking." One of Dana's favorite activities is to "get Lizzie singing by talking to her in my best doggie voice. I just love it!"

Dana enrolled her Camp Husky puppy in a training class where "she did great." However, training Lizzie was a challenge in two ways. The puppy was slow to catch on to potty training, and she liked to chew and destroy Dana's shoes and belts. Crate training helped with the former problem, and she grew out of the latter problem.

When Dana adopted Lizzie, she had a six-year-old shelter dog named Smokey (Labrador–Bernese mountain dog mix) and two cats. Like some of the other Camp Husky dogs, Lizzie, as a young puppy, bonded with the good-natured Smokey before bonding with Dana. "Smokey was the most important soul in her life at the beginning. He let her chew on his ears, tug at his tail, paw at his face, and cuddle up on him to sleep. It was precious to watch their bonding."

Smokey was Dana's first dog, and in comparison, Lizzie was much easier to train than Smokey had been. While Smokey was patient and affectionate toward the puppy, he was occasionally "a naughty influence as well" in the first few years of their relationship. For example, Smokey was "a fence jumper and runner," and he tried to pass this on to Lizzie. Dana said that "since Smokey was my first dog, I learned a ton from him. Compared to Smokey, Lizzie is a dream!"

Lizzie is timid with strangers in spite of Dana's efforts to help her develop confidence. "Even though I have worked with her extensively, she can still be wary of strangers; however, it doesn't take long for her to warm up to someone." Lizzie has "a sweet demeanor" with people once she gets to know them, and she especially likes children. "She is amazing with kids. She's just so big that the little ones often end up being toppled over while playing with her."

Dana credits her friends, their children, and their dogs as positive influences in socializing Lizzie. Thanks to Smokey and her other dog friends, Lizzie has learned to get along well with dogs of all sizes. Although most dogs she plays with are much smaller than Lizzy, she is generally submissive with them, as Dana explains: "There have been a few dogs that have dominated her so much that she just avoids them. She's so incredibly submissive. She will cry at the slightest bump or if her doggie playmates get too rough—even though she outweighs and towers over her friends."

When Lizzie was about a year old, Dana accepted a new job as assistant professor of education at the University of Montana in Dillon. At her new home, Dana fenced the yard for the dogs and scouted out some "awesome trails nearby" for weekend adventures. All the pets acclimated well to their new surroundings.

When asked if she is glad she adopted a Camp Husky dog, Dana responded, "Absolutely is an understatement. Having Lizzie in my life has just been so much fun." Dana is an outdoorsy person who enjoys running, hiking, and boating, and Lizzie is a great companion on these adventures. "Lizzie is the biggest river dog most boaters have ever seen; yet she perches herself on the side of the boat and relaxes with the best of them. Lizzie is a huge part of my life. She makes me laugh all the time, and I appreciate her obedience so much. I am also just mesmerized by her beauty. She is a natural phenomenon on four very long legs! As an adventure dog, she gets out there a lot, and I often find myself convincing others that Lizzie is not going to take their heads off, and I always put her in her orange vest to let folks know she is, in fact, my beautiful dog." Update: Smokey passed away in February 2015, and Lizzie has been grieving the loss of the beloved big brother she depended on for more than six years. Dana noticed a definite change in Lizzie after they lost Smokey. Not only was Lizzie sad, but she seemed to take on more responsibility. "As the only dog now, Lizzie has become more protective of me," said Dana.

Twin Sisters Volunteer and Save Two Very Shy Dogs

Cathy Decker and Christy Stack are twin sisters reared in Waterloo, Montana, who now live near each other off dirt roads in the community of Walkerville, outside of Butte. Although both women had other animals at home and full-time jobs, they were among the most reliable and hard-working volunteers at Camp Husky, working Saturday and Sunday shifts from October through April when Camp Husky closed. By mid-March 2009, fewer than twenty dogs remained at Camp Husky, mostly hard-to-adopt adult dogs afraid of people. The sisters would each take one of our "unadoptable" dogs home with them.

Christy Stack Adopts Christy (a.k.a. Nippy)

Nippy was a beautiful German shepherd–husky puppy with sad eyes that could melt the heart of any dog lover. She had the black-and-tan coloring of a German shepherd with a cream-colored face and dark nose and eyes, but she also had the smaller stature, shorter legs, and long fur of a husky. "We estimated that Nippy was only about four months old when she was taken off the bus. She had the sweetest face, and kindness showed in her eyes," said Christy. "But she was terrified of people, especially men. I can't help thinking that Brode did something that caused her to be terrified of men. We will never know for sure."

As mentioned earlier, the routine at Camp Husky was for two volunteers to take the two or three dogs in a kennel for a walk, while another volunteer cleaned the kennel. However, a few of the dogs were so traumatized when they came off the bus that we could not put leashes on them without further traumatizing them, so we allowed them to stay in their kennels where they felt safe. This was the case with the two dogs that Christy and Cathy would adopt. "Unlike her cage mates, Nippy made it hard for volunteers to put a leash on her or take her for a walk," explains Christy. "This frightened dog got her name because she would try nipping through the wire of the kennel when volunteers got too close."

By mid-March, we were down to about sixteen dogs at Camp Husky, and we were very concerned about finding homes for these hard-to-place dogs. "One Saturday in March, while working as a team with my sister and Cindy McIlveen, I said, 'We have to change Nippy's name. No one will adopt her when they see her name on the kennel.' When I came in Sunday morning, Nippy had a new name on her cage. Cindy and Tim had given her my name because this dog was by then my special project at Camp Husky. I had taken on the task of trying to socialize her because I could see that she really was a good dog. I would look into those kind but frightened eyes and ask her if she wanted to go for a walk. She was just too afraid to leave her kennel. By the end of March, I knew no one would adopt her, and we would soon have to leave the building, so I decided to take Christy home with me. Later, Tim said that he knew I would take Christy."

Christy the human had to give some thought to how she would take Christy the dog home and introduce her to her other dogs. "We loaded my truck with one of the kennels no longer needed at Camp Husky and set up the kennel in our yard with an igloo inside." Two other dogs lived with Christy and her partner, Glen. When their good-natured male Rottweiler mix named Bart went up to the kennel to investigate the new arrival, Christy acted afraid, although Bart was friendly toward her from the very beginning.

On the second day with Christy and Glen, Christy the dog climbed on top of her igloo and was able to jump out of the kennel. She ran under the neighbor's shed, and Glen and Christy could not coax her out. "Glen and I put food in Christy's kennel and set a trap for her. We fixed it so that when she went in to eat the food, the door would drop and trap her. Sure enough, it worked. The next morning, Glen covered the top of the kennel so that Christy could not climb out."

After spending about a week in her kennel, Christy had overcome her fear of the household dogs and was ready for her first walk on a leash. "I put a leash and harness on Christy and let my other two dogs run free as we walked down the dirt road. Christy quickly bonded with my two older dogs, especially Bart. It was obvious by week two that Christy saw Bart as her pack leader, and I could see that she felt safe whenever she was near him. Soon I was able to let Christy walk off leash. She would stay close to the other dogs on our walks, and she even followed them into the house at night to sleep. She was well behaved in the house. She had her corner of the living room where she would lie quietly, never making any kind of fuss.

"Christy was just a frightened puppy when I took her home," said Christy. "Little by little, she gained confidence. First she bonded with our dogs, then with me, and finally with Glen. Glen had reservations about keeping her at first because Christy was so afraid of men, but eventually she accepted him and he developed a real affection for her. She was an exceptionally well-behaved dog apart from her fearfulness. She was quiet, never tearing things up or acting up in the house." In 2012, Christy and Glen lost their female dog, Brandy, to old age. Only a year later, old age caught up with Bart as well, and the couple had to euthanize that fine dog. "These losses were just as painful for Christy as for us. Christy was a dog that needed the support of other dogs. Although Christy was always a quiet dog, she howled all night in terrible grief following Bart's death. I stayed up all night just comforting her. Somehow she knew he would not come back." Thanks to Bart and their owners, Christy the dog had learned to trust humans and feel safe in her home by age five. The kind but frightened dog had found a home at last.

After Bart died, Christy liked to be at Cathy's house, hanging out with her dogs. She was not vehicle savvy, and she ran out into the road, and a neighbor in a pickup truck ran into Christy. The poor dog was so badly injured and in such excruciating pain that she had to be euthanized. "I still have a broken heart," said Christy when I interviewed her in the summer of

2015. "Although Glen and I miss her terribly, we are comforted by the fact that Christy had a good life with us and she knew she was loved."

Cathy Decker Adopts Pinkie

Like Christy, Pinkie was a husky-shepherd mix with the smaller stature and shape of a husky. This special dog has a beautiful red-and-cream-colored coat, but her most distinguishing feature is her large pink nose, thus her name. Like Christy, Pinkie was a half-starved puppy forced to endure the horror of the bus trip with no opportunity for socialization with people. Some volunteers remember seeing her come off the bus "a frightened, very skinny puppy with filthy and terribly matted fur." Since Pinkie was far more afraid of people than most of the Camp Husky dogs, volunteers were never able to walk her until Cathy Decker started working with her.

In the last two months of the camp, when there was less work to do, Cathy had time to give Pinkie lots of individual attention. With great patience, Cathy worked to socialize Pinkie and get her comfortable with a leash. The breakthrough came one day in April 2009 when Cathy took Pinkie for her first walk, and that was when Cathy knew she needed to adopt this special dog. Pinkie did not take to her new home immediately—all she wanted was to return to her pack at Camp Husky, as Cathy explains: "Pinkie escaped from our house and ran back to Camp Husky on two occasions, trying to return to her original dog pack. Tim called me the first time, and I took her home. The second and last time she ran off, all the dogs were gone and Camp Husky was closed. Luckily, Tim was there sweeping and cleaning the place up one last time. Before I put her in the car, I let Pinkie go through the building so that she would understand that her pack was gone. She never tried to run away again, and soon she bonded with my family and our dogs and cats.

"Pinkie has made great progress in adapting to family life. She is bonded with Magnum, a Lab mix, and the two dogs enjoy playing together. She has become a normal, affectionate dog, and she likes to be brushed and actually comes up to us now, asking to be petted. She even lets visitors pet her. The dog that was terrified of a leash now loves to go for walks on a leash."

The animal-services director had arranged for some people who claimed to be trainers and dog evaluators to come to Camp Husky for a day. I was there that day and was not at all impressed. When a dog stands with his back to other dogs, and he is generally surrounded by dogs, this is not a calm situation in which to evaluate a dog. This author lost all respect for trainers/evaluators who see a dog for a short time in a bad space and then declare that he is not adoptable. Those evaluators were worthless in this author's opinion because the very dogs they failed went on to adapt very well to family life, including Pinkie. Cathy remembers that "the evaluator flunked Pinkie as well as Mufasa, a dog my sister and I had walked for weeks. He labeled them as unadoptable based on seeing them for only a short time. I worked with Pinkie for weeks and knew what she was really like. With patience and love, she has become a completely different dog from the pathetically skinny, dirty, abused, and terrified creature that came off that bus."

Both Christy and Pinkie developed pannus. The eye disease is not uncommon with German shepherds living at high altitudes. So far, this author knows of six Camp Husky dogs with the disease. Fortunately, it can be treated with medication. Christy and Cathy proved that even very shy and unsocialized dogs labeled as unadoptable can in fact become loving family members when they have a patient and compassionate owner and a good dog to mentor them.

Kelsey Estabrook Adopts Wiley #27 (a.k.a. Peanut)

Kelsey was a Montana Tech student working part time and living with her parents on twenty acres outside of Butte. As busy as she was, Kelsey volunteered for ten days at the Anselmo location, walking dogs and even helping with vaccinations. It was during this time that Kelsey adopted an older puppy named Peanut, changing his name to Wiley. Interestingly, Peanut was a cage mate of Pinkie's and looked very much like the dog Christy. When I interviewed Kelsey, Wiley was still living with her parents while Kelsey continued her studies at the University of Montana in Missoula. Kelsey was paying for her dog's care, and she visited him frequently. "I am his mama. He is the sweetest and most gentle dog you could imagine."

When asked why she volunteered at Camp Husky, Kelsey said, "I love dogs. We had another dog named Sadie, a Saint Bernard–Akita mix, and a little dog that was much older. About ten months before I started volunteering at Camp Husky, our little dog died and Sadie was very sad." That was one of the reasons that Kelsey adopted Peanut.

Kelsey did not think it was right to buy a dog when so many Camp Husky dogs needed homes. Mary Ann Maguire, an animal-services employee, helped Kelsey with the adoption process. Because Mary Ann is a friend of Kelsey's aunt, Kelsey was able to bypass the screening process. At that time, Peanut and a young female named Pumpkin were the only puppies that had been spayed and neutered and were ready for adoption. Pumpkin was a sweet dog with a deformed leg resulting from a bad break left untreated when she was with Brode. Kelsey and her parents are very active and needed a dog that could run and keep up, so she chose Peanut. (Pumpkin would later find a permanent home not far from the Camp Husky location.)

Kelsey's first order of business upon adopting Wiley was to have him groomed. Initially, Wiley was afraid of everything, including the open spaces outside, and he would run into the house and hide. Kelsey got a metal dog crate and put it in her bedroom. Wiley was not housebroken when she brought him home, so Kelsey took him for regular walks on a leash because the timid dog would not walk with her and would run back to the house if not on a leash. (This may seem strange until you consider that older puppies like Wiley were probably born on the bus and went outside at Camp Husky only when walked by volunteers, and even then, they were always close to the building in an enclosed area.)

Initially, Wiley appeared distant and standoffish toward Kelsey. However, a short time after adopting him, Kelsey left Wiley at the house with her parents and went for an overnight visit to her aunt's home. Wiley apparently missed Kelsey a lot, and when she came home, he ran up and licked her face. Kelsey believes that the puppy was acknowledging her as his pack leader. This event marks the point where Wiley started making rapid adjustments to his new home. "His learning curve was high from then on. He started playing with Sadie, and they became like two peas in a pod." Though the puppy soon grew bigger and faster than his dog pal, he nevertheless remains submissive to Sadie.

"Although he was still a puppy when I brought him home, Wiley didn't act like a puppy or display the happy, affectionate, and playful nature one expects from a puppy. But all that changed once he felt at home with us and knew he had a family. I really believe Wiley now realizes how good he has it. Now, he is very affectionate and likes nothing better than to sit on my lap, or if I am not there, he is happy to cuddle up to either of my parents." Kelsey and her parents named Wiley after Wile E. Coyote.

As Kelsey described him, Wiley is timid with new people but well behaved with groomers. "He acts afraid of strangers but never aggressive." He likes puppies and is sweet and gentle with them, but he is still scared of adult dogs. When I interviewed Kelsey, she said that Mary Ann Maguire had come to dinner recently and was impressed by Wiley's progress. Kelsey believes that Sadie was the key to Wiley's recovery. "He loves Sadie." The puppy needed an older dog to socialize him just as Christy needed Bart, and Pinkie needed Magnum in the previous story.

Wiley now has a great life with people who treasure him, as well as an older dog to mentor him; however, there is some sadness. Wiley, like the two dogs in the previous story, also developed pannus, an eye disease that can lead to blindness. Kelsey said the disease is more common in high altitudes and perhaps the bright snow of the Highlands area where her family lives may have aggravated the condition in Wiley.

Wiley likes to run alongside when Kelsey's mother, Tammy, goes for a bike ride. Before, he would turn around and run home if he saw neighbor dogs. Now, he stays with Tammy and is not as afraid. While many Camp Husky dogs are vocal, Sadie is the vocal dog in this household. Wiley is not a barker, but he does howl sometimes. (Kelsey recalls working at the Anselmo when one dog would start to howl and they would all join in.) Once afraid to go outside, Wiley now likes being out of doors. In spite of his vision problems, he is a lucky pup that found a great home.

Debbie and Bill Bajovich Adopt Jenna (a.k.a. Jenny #1b), an Awesome Puppy

Debbie and Bill Bajovich read about Camp Husky and the need for volunteers in the *Montana Standard* and showed up to help out. Bill could help out for only a few days as he was a US Postal Service employee at the time, but Debbie became a regular volunteer. "The conditions for the dogs at the Anselmo were deplorable, although the volunteers were doing their best," recalled Debbie. "It broke my heart to see all those dogs needing loving homes. At the same time, we were very proud of Butte for taking on the rescue. The people of Butte took responsibility to help those animals, rather than just ignoring the suffering dogs as other communities had done, and we were glad to be a part of that effort."

Debbie described her Jenna as awesome. Jenna is a favorite with Debbie and Bill's granddaughter, who chose the name. "Jenna has tons of energy and is very fast. On one of her many hiking trips with Bill, Jenna almost caught up with a deer." Jenna enjoys camping with Debbie and Bill. She stays right beside them. She is a well-behaved dog; however, she does not care for little dogs. Their normal evening ritual is for Jenna to lie on the bed for about thirty minutes before going to her own bed on the floor. Like so many of the Camp Husky dogs, Jenna talks.

Cindy McIlveen Adopts Jack

Jack was a young adult Belgian Tervuren–husky mix that got off to a bad start when the dogs were taken from the bus. Volunteers had removed all the dogs from the bus, with one exception. The animal-control officers arrived on the scene when the work was almost completed that first day of the rescue, and according to those I interviewed, one of these men decided to take the last remaining dog off the bus.

Like most of the dogs, Jack was naturally frightened by the whole experience of strangers taking the other dogs off the bus. Then, to make it much worse, the animal-control officer did something none of the volunteers had done. He used a snare pole and tore the dog's mouth, inflicting a serious wound requiring veterinary care and stitches. Unfortunately, the first human after Brode that this frightened young dog came in contact with was someone who terrorized him and inflicted considerable pain and injury. While the wound the animal-control officer inflicted would heal in time, the emotional damage would prove much harder to heal. It would take the love and devotion of four special volunteers to undo most of the emotional damage that one officer did to Jack that day. (I know of no other dog injured that day. In fact, I have many photos of volunteers gently caressing and comforting frightened dogs as they came off the bus.)

Those of us who volunteered knew that Jack had problems, and his kennel was off-limits for ordinary volunteers like this author, and so it was very heartwarming when I visited Cindy's home three years after Camp Husky closed and saw for myself the progress Jack had made. There were about six people sitting in Cindy's backyard, including former volunteer Katie Donovan, who had flown in from Michigan. Jack enjoyed playing with the other dogs and demonstrated no particular fear of people. That might not seem unusual to most folks, but for those of us who volunteered at Camp Husky, it was a little miracle. The dog that had the worst odds of adapting to family life because of the cruelty he had experienced was alive and in a secure and loving home, all because of the devotion of some special volunteers, who never lost faith that he could be saved. This is Jack's story as told by Cindy McIlveen, and it starts with a volunteer named Tim.

"Tim was a resident of the Butte Pre-Release Center who was completing a correctional program after serving a prison term for drug-related offenses. From the first day he volunteered at Camp Husky, Tim found his mission. He loved the dogs and dedicated the next eight months of his life to ensuring that each of our dogs found a home. He was a dedicated, hardworking man who was something of a dog whisperer."

Tim was kind to all the dogs, but as Cindy observed, he formed a special bond with Jack, our most fearful and aggressive dog. "If you got too close to Jack when you were cleaning his kennel, he would snarl and lunge at you. Clearly these were only warning signs, as he was an eighty-pound dog that could have done damage had he wanted to. I recall that some visitors to Camp Husky in the first month of operation assumed that we would be euthanizing Jack. I told them that there is always another option, and we would not be resorting to that. I hoped that was true, but in reality none of us volunteers had the time to devote solely to rehabilitating a single dog, so all we could do for Jack was to clean his kennel and give him fresh water and food. For three long months Jack did not go on a single walk or even leave his kennel.

"I recall one day when something startled Jack so much that he actually climbed up his kennel wall and onto one of the high rafters in the ceiling of the Anselmo. Of course, the person who would rescue him was Tim.

Putting on a pair of thick gloves and fully expecting to get bitten, Tim scaled up the wall after Jack. Placing Jack's welfare before his own, and risking a fall that could have been fatal, Tim grabbed hold of Jack and carried him back down the wall. The ordeal ended well, and Jack did not bite Tim. After that incident, rehabilitating Jack by earning his trust became a top priority for Tim.

"Tim spent every spare moment he had just sitting in the kennel with Jack, doing nothing but talking to him. Each day Tim would move a little closer. After Jack became accustomed to the patient man sitting very close to him, he allowed Tim to put a hand on him. With some pointers from a dog trainer from Bozeman named Troy, Tim learned how best to put a leash on Jack and teach him to walk on a leash."

I remember one Saturday in the spring of 2009 when someone shouted for all of us volunteers to stop what we were doing and look outside. A happy sight awaited us—Jack was frolicking in the snow with Tim, and Jack was smiling! Someone caught that breakthrough moment on film. Tim's patient attention for several months had overcome Jack's fear of humans so that the dog could play with him.

Cindy also remembers receiving a phone call from a volunteer that Saturday afternoon, telling her to get to the camp as soon as possible. "I was there within an hour, when I walked out back I couldn't believe what I saw. Jack and Tim were out back in the fenced yard rolling around together playing. Jack had finally let down his guard and allowed Tim into his life. It was as if Jack just let go and surrendered to Tim's love. Tim's tremendous patience and dedication finally paid off, and Jack had a human friend for the first time. For the next few months, Tim was the only person Jack trusted, but he was able to get out of his kennel and enjoy a walk every day. We could all see how happy Jack was whenever Tim was close to him.

"That day when Tim won Jack's trust was a turning point for me. I knew in my heart that if we could save Jack, then we could save them all. We spent the next three months finding new homes for the dogs. So, when only the last few seriously troubled dogs were left, and Camp Husky closed, Jack and his new human friend Tim came home with me. We got permission from the Pre-Release Center for Tim to stay at my house so he could take care of Jack and the other fourteen dogs that ended up at my house. All of the dogs were eventually adopted except Jack. Jack had lived in my house for a month and still would not let me pet him. I could sit on the couch with him, but if I got too close he would either snap at me or run away and hide."

Jack and Susie (chapter 6) were just two of the fourteen hard-to-adopt dogs that had no place to go after Camp Husky closed in April 2009, and they ended up at the home of Cindy McIlveen. Later, Mufasa (chapter 6), Jake (chapter 6), and Barley (chapter 8) would join the ranks of dogs temporarily fostered by Cindy. I recall one weekend in the summer of 2009 when Cindy had some dog trainers from Helena come to help her and Tim with socializing Jack and Susie. I can still recall good-natured Mufasa watching all this commotion from an upstairs window. Cindy found good homes for all the Camp Husky dogs she fostered.

Later that summer, after the last of the Camp Husky dogs found good homes, Tim and Jack moved into their own place. About the same time, Cindy quit her job with Butte-Silver Bow government and found temporary employment working as a geologist on oil rigs off the coast of Africa. Later, she took a job in Houston. Cindy hired Carl Brien, a college student and Camp Husky volunteer, as house sitter and pet sitter for her two older dogs while she was away working.

In the meantime, Tim was losing the battle with his addiction, as Cindy explained. "After a few short months of his new life and without the structure of the Pre-Release Center and his work at Camp Husky, Tim was once again overcome by his addiction. I got a call one day at work in Houston and learned that Tim had been arrested and would be going back to prison. I caught a flight back to Butte that afternoon. Later that evening when I got into Butte, Carl, my pet sitter, went with me to Tim's house and helped me coax Jack into a crate to take back to my house. I knew then that I was not going to put this poor dog through any more human traumas in his life, and thus he became a permanent member of my household that night. Now I just had to convince this dog to trust me as he had trusted Tim and to let me touch him. I remembered how Tim had won Jack's trust, and I tried to behave the same way. For the better part of two days, I sat on the floor reading a book in the bathroom where I kept Jack. Each hour I moved a little closer to him until at one point I was actually leaning up against him. By the next day, I was walking him on a leash, petting him, and giving him big hugs. Carl was hesitant at first to take on responsibility for Jack in my absence, but Jack was changing daily, and he accepted Carl almost immediately.

"Carl and I worked very hard with Jack over the next year. Jack escaped out of my yard once and remained at large for several days. I heard rumors of a wolf in uptown Butte, so I knew he was still in my neighborhood. I would see him in the alleys, and he would let me get about ten feet away and then bolt again. But he never went far from my house. Carl and I set live traps for him, but he was way too smart for that. Carl had heard about how Tim would lie in the yard at Camp Husky and Jack would pounce on him, so Carl decided to try that with Jack. Carl went across the street from my house and laid down on his back in a vacant lot. Watching from inside my house, I saw Jack bounding out of the alley. When Jack saw Carl, he ran across the street and was on top of Carl in seconds. Now, many people might have found this a bit terrifying but not Carl. He rolled around and played with Jack for a few minutes before clipping the leash he had in his pocket to Jack's collar. Carl has been Jack's best buddy ever since."

Cindy decided that she needed to leave Butte both because she had work in Houston and because she feared that Jack would not be safe in Butte. She feared that if he should get loose while she was away working and was picked up by animal control, he would be in real danger because of the hostility of the animal-shelter director toward Camp Husky dogs. Carl wanted to continue his studies at a university, so he ended up moving out of town with Cindy. Nearly seven years later, Carl continues to take care of Jack and the other dogs when Cindy travels for work.

"Jack is the true embodiment of Camp Husky," said Cindy as she reflected on her experience at Camp Husky and Jack's story. "Socializing Jack and the whole Camp Husky rescue seemed like impossible challenges at the time. Both required extreme patience, tremendous human resources, and many, many hours of hard work. In the end, the single most important factor in the success of Jack and Camp Husky proved to be the loving, caring, kindhearted individuals involved. Many people showed us that a seemingly hopeless situation can be turned around with a little faith and a lot of hard work and determination. Between Camp Husky and Jack, I experienced a couple of the most difficult years of my life, and I would do it all again in a heartbeat. Those wonderful dogs and amazing volunteers changed my life forever. I am lucky enough to get a reminder of them all every night as I curl up with Jack at my side."

Merlena and Monte Moore Adopt Zeva and Sunshine

While volunteering at Camp Husky, Monte and Merlena initially worked in the nursery. As they cared for the moms and pups, they made a decision to adopt a puppy. In January 2009, they took home a little husky-shepherd mix named Zeva. The puppy was only five weeks old when she went to live with Merlena and Monte. The Moores had three female Chihuahuas that took little interest in the puppy, but Zeva liked the toy dogs, and to this day is protective of them. When Merlena is gathering up the little ones to take them outside or for a trip to the groomers, Zeva always checks to make sure Merlena has not left one of them behind. Zeva, now over eighty pounds, is careful not to step on her three little friends, each between three and four pounds. As a puppy, Zeva was rambunctious and needed a playmate, but the Chihuahuas would have none of that.

When I interviewed him, Monte recalled how he and Merlena ended up adopting a second Camp Husky puppy. "I was working at the camp one day in March 2009 when we volunteers received a phone call informing us that one of our puppies was being abused and badly neglected by the man who adopted her. The call was from a neighbor reporting that this poor puppy was left outside all the time even on the coldest days and not even fed most of the time. In fact, neighbors were throwing food over the fence to keep her from starving." Volunteers took immediate action to gain possession of the puppy and bring her back to Camp Husky. Monte described the puppy named Sunshine as "pitiful looking and way too thin when we volunteers got her back. Her long fur was badly matted as well. By this time, all our puppies had either been adopted or transported to other shelters around the state. With only large adult dogs remaining at Camp Husky, four-month-old Sunshine was without a suitable playmate. That night I told Merlena how Sunshine had been abused and neglected by her owner, and we decided to adopt her. After all she had suffered, we wanted to make certain that Sunshine would have a good home, and Zeva needed a playmate.

Thus the two Camp Husky pups grew up together and had a very good life with Monte and Merlena. Monte walked the dogs daily and trained both dogs to lie down when they got in the car so that they would be well behaved on the long trip to and from California each year. Both dogs spent a lot of time with Samantha Collier at All about the Dawg as well. In 2011, I spent several hours at the day care interviewing Samantha about Camp Husky. I took my own Camp Husky dog along, and he had a great time playing chase with Zeva and Sunshine.

Sunshine and Zeva grew into very large, healthy adults with long and thick fur. Merlena knew that both pups had white German shepherd mothers but was curious about their fathers since the dogs are different in appearance and temperament. Genetic testing revealed that Zeva is three-quarters German shepherd and one-quarter Siberian husky. Sunshine, on the other hand, tested pure German shepherd. Zeva has a cream-colored coat that is even heavier than Sunshine's, and she seems to tolerate the cold much better. Zeva has an exceptionally beautiful face with husky markings that reflects what Merlena described as a "sweet and gentle personality. Sunshine, on the other hand, has a white coat with a light apricot color mixed in. Both dogs are friendly, but Sunshine is needier when it comes to attention, and she is a quiet dog. Zeva is the talker."

Both dogs lived happily with the Moores until the fall of 2012. Monte was approaching his eightieth birthday and in failing health when he and Merlena asked my husband and me to adopt Sunshine. Sunny joined our household and gets along exceptionally well with our other Camp Husky dog. It was a very sad day for all of us who knew him when Monte died in June 2013. All of us who worked beside him at Camp Husky can attest that Monte was an exceptionally skilled, hardworking, kindhearted, and generous man. Sunshine is a daily reminder for me of a wonderful man who kept the rescue going and touched many people with his kindness and positive personality. Without the Moores, Sunshine would never have been rescued, because Camp Husky would not have been operating. The Moores' generosity and Monte's long hours of labor enabled the last of the dogs, including Sunshine, to find homes. With our love of dogs, and especially Sunny, Merlena and I have become good friends as well.

Zeva and the other dogs have helped Merlena to cope with the loss of a devoted husband. Merlena also misses Sunny, who used to follow her from room to room. Luckily, Merlena and Sunny get to see each other frequently. Sunshine has had some serious health challenges in 2015—an autoimmune condition affecting her red blood cells. In addition to good veterinary care, Merlena and I decided to try acupuncture, Chinese herbs, and lots of steamed vegetables. Merlena has been taking Sunny to acupuncture, veterinarian, and grooming appointments, while I am trying to finish this book and teach my classes. One could say that we two women share custody of Sunshine. The good news is that Sunshine's blood is back to normal now, and she is much more energetic.

Sunshine is a very loving and well-behaved dog. Monte and Merlena did a good job of training her, and she is a perfect match for my Hector. Hector is shy and submissive while Sunny is outgoing and a bit domineering toward him. The good news is that Hector does not mind. He loves his Sunny and rarely gets upset even when she runs and pounces on him while he is sleeping. At about ninety-five pounds (when she is healthy) Sunshine is among the larger Camp Husky females. She is longer, taller, and about fifteen pounds heavier than Hector. Hector is more compact and runs much faster than Sunshine. Now, with her energy back, Sunny is once again dominating Hector, and he doesn't mind at all.

Roberta and John Ray Adopt Hector (a.k.a. Ace #33)

Photographs were taken of some of the dogs on different parts of the bus before they were unloaded. One photo shows approximately ten puppies of about four to six months of age hiding together in one corner of the bus. Among all the white pups in that photo, one can see a black-and-tan German shepherd, probably Susie, and one black male. Volunteers named the male puppy Ace because he was solid black with just a little white in the middle of his chest, the classic Belgian sheepdog. Ace was one of two surviving puppies born to a purebred Belgian sheepdog, the only one at Camp Husky, and sadly, this gentle mother was among the dogs Brode chose to take with him when he was released from jail. I noticed this mother dog because I was familiar with the Belgian sheepdog breed, having adopted one in the past. The Belgian sheepdog mother was initially kenneled with her female pup. After Brode took her mother away with him, the female pup was boarded at Samantha Collier's country home.

Later, this same puppy would find a good permanent home with a family in Deer Lodge, Montana. I have another Camp Husky photo of Ace playing with a pure-white puppy. I believe that puppy was Snowflake, a sweet and affectionate dog that found a loving home with a woman named Jennifer Heintz. A few years later, Jennifer told me that Ace's little playmate grew up to be a wonderful dog, especially gentle and loving toward children.

As I volunteered at Camp Husky, I walked dogs and cleaned kennels when I had completed my regular job of washing dishes. Two of my favorite dogs to walk were Ace and his cage mate, Rudy (chapter 7, "Adventure Dogs"). Many volunteers remember this pair because they were very easy to walk and exceptionally well behaved. Rudy was a big, beautiful, long-haired Belgian Tervuren–shepherd mix, while Ace was much smaller and plainer looking. While Rudy was self-confident and friendly to both dogs and people at Camp Husky, Ace was shy, reserved with people, and scared of the big dogs. It was obvious when one walked the pair that Rudy was the leader and that Ace depended on him for a sense of security. When adoptions started in December, both puppies were about six months of age. I was not surprised when the vivacious Belgian Tervuren was one of the first to be adopted. After Rudy left us, I noticed that Ace was acting very depressed. Other dogs got excited and showed interest when a volunteer came by their cages; however, Ace just kept his head down and never looked up. He was still well behaved and easy to walk but very sad. Although Ace had a sweet face and was a very gentle and well-behaved dog that never soiled his cage, I feared he would not find a home because he was afraid of people and depressed by the loss of Rudy. I told my husband about Ace, and we made the decision to adopt him. We took him home a few days before Christmas, and we knew from that first day that we had chosen the right dog for us. Our only regret was that we could not offer a home to a couple more of the hard-to-adopt dogs.

We changed his name to Hector, after the noble and courageous defender of Troy as told in Homer's *Iliad*. Ace was so timid that we felt he needed a bold name. Adopting Hector had been more of an emotional/intuitive decision than a rational one, but it is a decision we have never regretted even for a moment. At the time, we had two older German shepherds—Greta, ten, and Rodman, thirteen. Both dogs had found a second home with us some years before. Rodman's health was failing. We got acupuncture treatments for him to help with joint pain, but we did not expect him to live more than a few weeks. When we first took Hector home, he was terrified of Rodman and Greta, but within three days, he felt very comfortable and safe with both dogs.

Hector and Rodman developed a very close bond. Whether Rodman was outside in the yard or in the living room, Hector would be right beside him. Although it was difficult for Rodman to walk by then, he took on the role of fathering Hector. We had adopted Rodman from a young man, a former basketball player in Vancouver, Washington, who could no longer keep his dog. I still feel sad when I think about how much that young man must have missed the dog he drove all the way to Montana. I know Rodman missed him. Before Rodman joined our family, my husband and I had become a sort of informal shepherd rescue. Rodman was a good-natured dog that liked nothing better than playing with his ball. In the last year of his life, he found his mission in caring for the frightened puppy. Rodman would grab Hector by the neck and pull him down in a show of discipline while Hector wagged his tail in delight. Within a few weeks, they were father and son, completely devoted to each other. Rodman slept a lot, and Hector was contented to just snuggle up beside him. John and I are convinced that Rodman lived another year only because he knew how much the frightened pup needed him.

My husband and I did not socialize Hector—Rodman and Greta did that for us! While Hector bonded quickly with those two old dogs, it took ever so long before he warmed up to John and me. Knowing how frightened he was of people, we made a point of being extra gentle with Hector and keeping our voices warm and friendly. Even so, it was more than three months before Hector would approach us. We both remember one April evening, almost four months after he had joined our family, when we were sitting in the living room talking, and Hector walked up and stood by John's chair. That was the first time he approached one of us. From that evening on, Hector was John's dog. Even after he was comfortable with us, Hector was inclined to hide when new people came to the house. For the first year, he would hide beside Rodman or behind Greta; now he is happy to greet visitors. He especially loves our pet sitter, Shirley. She is the only person Hector will kiss.

About a year after we adopted Hector, Rodman died, and a few weeks later Hector was unable to walk. He had an ACL tear in both hind legs. Our veterinarian said that there was only one veterinary surgeon in the state who could do the complex and expensive surgery. Hector needed the surgery or he would have to be euthanized. Both our veterinarian and the surgeon in Bozeman remarked that Hector was among the gentlest dogs they had ever encountered. Although it obviously hurt him as the veterinarians handled his hind legs, Hector never growled or showed any aggression toward them.

The surgeon warned us that the surgery would not work unless we were very careful with the postsurgical care. For many weeks, Hector had to have maximum rest, and he was restricted to two five-minute walks a day. John and Greta took on the care of Hector and did a splendid job. John took Hector outdoors twice a day for just five minutes and took care of the bandages, while Greta took on the job of staying with Hector the rest of the time and keeping him calm both day and night. Greta, who never had puppies, was a natural mother. We could not crate Hector because something about his experience on the bus had left him terrified of crates. With Greta beside him, Hector was content to rest quietly in the living room. After a few months, he was completely healed thanks to John, Greta, and an excellent surgeon. Now, more than five years after that surgery, when we watch Hector run, we know that we had picked the right dog for us. They were all equally wonderful dogs, and I would have loved to have any one of them living with us, but the black puppy needed Rodman and Greta, and he needed the surgery and aftercare that we could provide. I believe he was meant to be with us.

As Greta grew older, it was harder for her to play with Hector, although she tried to keep up with the energetic younger dog. As Greta was turning thirteen and was in failing health, I worried how Hector would manage without her. Greta was all that a German shepherd should be, and we had come to depend on her to take care of Hector. For example, he did not tear things up when alone in the house because he felt safe with Greta there. We probably waited longer than we should have to euthanize Greta because Hector needed her, and we did not want to lose her. She had been a mother to Hector and, like Rodman, had helped the puppy gain confidence. I held Greta in my arms as she passed, and I hope she knew how much we loved and appreciated her.

Then Sunshine came into our lives. Hector and Sunny are opposite in most ways but very compatible. Sunshine is very friendly with everyone. When in the house, she is always close to me, following me from room to room, as she did with Merlena. Hector, on the other hand, remains shy and usually prefers to rest under a small table in the dining room when I am writing upstairs or cooking in the kitchen. It is always a treat when Hector comes up to us asking for affection. Sunny plays rough with Hector, but he doesn't seem to mind. He loves to play chase with her. It has been my experience that German shepherd bitches dominate when they live with male dogs, and that is certainly the case with Sunny and Hector.

Sunny acts like the typical German shepherds I have known except that she has more facial expression. Like so many Camp Husky dogs, Sunshine bares her teeth to smile and crinkles her ears when she is being extra loving toward John or me. Hector, on the other hand, has most of the characteristics of Belgian sheepdogs: sensitive, easy to train, and eager to stay close to home. His husky side shows in his tendency to talk to us, especially when we return from work. Sunshine wags her tail to welcome us home, but Hector dances in a circle and talks up a storm. The only other time Hector talks is when he wakes John up at exactly 4:45 each morning. First, Hector nudges John. If that doesn't work, he starts talking directly into John's ear in order to wake John but not me. When John is out of town, Hector never tries to wake me. He allows me to sleep in as late as I like. Although John complains about being forced to get up earlier than he would like, we both love our Camp Husky dogs. The Camp Husky dogs are unique and magical beings, and we feel privileged to share our home with two of them.

CHAPTER 11
Lessons from Camp Husky

D ogs have been a part of my life from the very beginning, and the most important lessons I learned about courage, love, and morality, I learned from dogs and other animals. The first dog I knew was a medium-sized terrier mix named Daisy. My father was driving home from the hospital in Huntington Park, California, on the day I was born, when he saw a skinny, dirty, pathetic-looking young dog wandering in the street. My dad stopped and took her home, even though the last thing he needed was another mouth to feed on his modest salary as a night watchman at an aircraft plant. My father had a lot on his mind when he rescued that homeless mutt: the country was engaged in World War II, and Dad's beloved younger brother in his early twenties, whom he had coached to be one of the top tennis players in the country, was in a hospital slowly dying. In spite of all he was going through, my father showed compassion for the dog, and it paid off for our family. Daisy was a sweet, quiet, and companionable member of the family, far better behaved than the four rowdy little girls to whom she always responded with patience and gentleness.

My first understanding of how heroic dogs can be came when I was in elementary school; my mother read a newspaper story about a collie dog in our town saving a family from a house fire. As I recall, the dog was in the backyard while a young couple and their baby slept indoors. Smelling smoke and unable to rouse her family by barking, the desperate dog used all her strength to crash through the sliding glass doors that separated her from the family she loved. The collie woke the parents so that they could escape the fire with their baby. As the couple stood outside watching the house go up in flames, and the fire engine arrived on the scene, their loyal dog collapsed, having bled to death from the deep wounds she sustained breaking through the glass door. Daisy performed no such heroics, but still I mourned her death after eleven years of friendship. As I thought about our missing family member, I had an uncomfortable awareness that Daisy had been morally superior to me and that I fell far short when I compared her virtues to my own.

About four years later, my sisters and I were alone in our isolated country house, without a telephone and a mile from the nearest neighbor, when a motorcycle gang roared up the dirt road and started circling our house. My sisters and I were terrified. Luckily, we had two dogs at that time, a German shepherd and a greyhound-shepherd mix. Those two dogs fought valiantly, biting at the gang members' legs and preventing them from getting off their bikes, with no thought to their own safety.

While we lived in that rural area, I had, unfortunately, ample opportunity to see how cruel humans can be toward animals. Our nearest neighbors had two fine horses, and both were shot while in their stalls. Hunters also shot one of our dogs. And, most traumatically, I discovered a coyote caught in a trap. Just as acts of kindness touch one forever, acts of brutality against children or innocent animals haunt one forever.

In my kitchen there is a picture of a black dog standing on a mountaintop looking toward the heavens. It was drawn with colored pencils by a little boy as a tribute to the dog who saved his older sister's life. The dog was named Cato, and he taught me a powerful lesson about love, courage, and the oneness of all life.

Cato was a black German shepherd with brown legs. He was quite large and an exceptionally swift runner. Cato was my parents' companion until they moved from their house in Hemet, California, to an apartment in Butte, Montana. Then Cato moved in with my husband and me and our German shepherd, Mandy. Both dogs were well trained, with AKC obedience titles. Mandy, however, was trained to babysit and track my nieces and nephews, who frequently visited during the summers. Mandy was very bold and afraid of nothing, while Cato was so timid that he once dropped flat on the ground when a miniature poodle growled at him. It was the summer of 1992 when I took two children, eight-year-old Kristen and nine-year-old Joe, on a camping trip that would forever change me. I had no premonition of danger as I cooked our dinner on the camp stove and tucked the children into their sleeping bags. After all, Mandy was lying between them in the cozy little tent, and I had every confidence that she would keep them safe. Mandy came from a long line of police dogs, and no one but the five of us was in the little campground that night. We were alone and safe, or so I thought as I fell asleep with Cato beside me.

Dawn was breaking, and I was sleeping soundly in the back of my station wagon, when Cato awoke me. Somehow, without barking, he communicated to me that there was danger. I looked out the window and saw a herd of cattle, at least thirteen. A careless rancher had allowed them to wander into the campground; something had startled them, and now they were stampeding. I registered two facts in an instant: the cattle were heading straight for the tent where the children were sleeping, and I could not save the children. Cato motioned for me to open the door, and I obeyed. Then I watched in absolute terror as Cato, a city dog, ran straight for the tent. When he got in front of the tent, he made eye contact with me as if to say good-bye, and then he ran straight toward the approaching cows. I watched helplessly, knowing that Cato would be crushed to death and then the children would be killed, but when he was about three feet away from the lead cow, that cow turned, and the others followed. Cato, who had never been around a cow before that day, calmly escorted the cows out of the campground with no sign of aggression toward them; then he returned to me, sat down, and started shaking so badly that I feared he would die of a heart attack. That dog had been absolutely terrified, yet he put his life on the line for the children and Mandy.

As I sat there in the campground and the children continued to sleep peacefully, I looked at Cato and realized that I owed that dog a debt I could never repay. Had it not been for his keen intelligence in sensing and evaluating the danger, and his willingness to sacrifice his life for others, a horrendous tragedy would have occurred on my watch. That experience changed my whole perspective on how we humans relate to animals. I was now convinced that neither I nor any human is superior to any animal and that idea led me to conclude that it is morally wrong to abuse animals in any way. We are never justified in harming any creature to serve our own ends, no matter how deeply ingrained that practice is in most human societies.

From that day on, I became painfully aware of all the ways we humans inflict cruelty on animals. For example, there is a bird sanctuary near our home, where my husband and I liked to walk our dogs on leashes. Among the birds were snow geese. One spring and summer I witnessed an amazing act of altruism on the part of a male goose and his mate. They had no young ones that spring, but they adopted a very small female duck (mallard) and her many ducklings. The male goose would stand guard over the little ducklings and their mother, while his mate helped keep the young ones from wandering off. By keeping the baby ducks safe, the geese were sacrificing time they needed to feed and put on fat for the winter. Two years later, these two special snow geese and all their brethren were slaughtered in the sanctuary by a man with a gun.

About a year after Camp Husky closed, I once again encountered senseless violence aimed at birds. I was walking home from work when a man and woman called my attention to an injured raven near my house. It was obvious that the bird could not fly. I telephoned my friend Noorjahan, and she helped me to capture the bird. Noorjahan kept the bird at her home until John and I could drive it to the Flyaway Wildlife Center in Helena, where they rehabilitate injured birds, since I could not find a local veterinarian to treat it. The next day I received a telephone call from the folks at the center informing me that the veterinarian treating the raven had found a bullet in the bird. Someone with a rifle had shot the bird in an urban area where children frequently walk. The bird will never be able to fly again, but it will live out its life in a good place; however, I am haunted by the fact that his mate was watching over him when we caught him—she followed us to Noorjahan's home and watched from a tree as we put her mate in our car to drive to Helena. No one can convince me that the female was not mourning her mate.

Cruelty toward animals is all too common and reflects the dark and sadistic side of human nature. In just the last few weeks, there have been three stories in the news of disgusting violence toward animals. There was a story of a dentist from Minnesota who paid $50,000 to have a lion named Cecil lured away from the safety of a national park in Zimbabwe so that this violent man could kill the animal. A second article told of a man in Missoula who beat his mother's fifteen-year-old German shepherd to death. Finally, there was an article about an Idaho man who stabbed his black Lab while it was chained to his truck. When I read about the German shepherd, I could not help but remember Butte's first police dog, Kato, who took a bullet defending a police officer. When I read about the Lab, I thought of my friend Shirley's father and the black Lab that pulled him to safety when, as a little boy, he fell into an icy lake and was unable to swim. As these stories exemplify, we humans are capable of greed, destruction, and extreme cruelty. I have never seen that darkness in animals, and perhaps that is why I am convinced that we humans are not morally superior to dogs, cats, or any other animals.

While that dark side is all too common with humans, I believe there is also a part of our nature that is wise and compassionate, calling to us to extend compassion to all living things and to realize our oneness with all life. Albert Einstein, the greatest genius of modern times, saw that human progress must go hand in hand with compassion: "Our task must be to free ourselves by widening our circle to embrace all living creatures and the whole of nature and its beauty." Mahatma Gandhi, one of the moral giants of the twentieth century, said, "The greatness of a nation and its moral progress can be judged by the way its animals are treated."

The story of the dogs of Camp Husky illustrates both the compassionate side of human nature and the dark side. Most of the dogs encountered compassionate people who saw how wonderful they were, but from the very beginning there were those people who were blinded by prejudice and their own demons, who projected their own darkness onto the dogs, and who argued for euthanizing all the dogs on the bus. There were some individuals who wanted me to present in this book what one volunteer called "the Disney version" of the Camp Husky story; they wanted me to leave out the facts about the dogs that were killed because of the animal-services director and some shelter operators. I know as I am finishing this story that it would be so much easier to write a sanitized version of what happened, but it would not be the truth. Animals suffer because many people lack compassion and because even more people want to turn a blind eye to animal abuse in its many forms. I made every effort to be factual and tell the truth as I have come to know it, and I chose to tell the bad as well as the good, knowing that many will say that I am not diplomatic, sensitive, or fair to good people. I am not judging the people; I judge their actions.

The dogs that were killed in Dillon were every bit as wonderful, brave, and good as my Cato. I volunteered at Camp Husky because of Cato, and I owe it to him to tell the truth about all the dogs. The eighty-one dogs you have read about in this book are proof that there were angels on the school bus.

After more than five years of research, I have come to the conclusion that the primary reason both the Butte and Dillon animal shelters, as well as some veterinarians in both towns, were so hostile toward our Camp Husky dogs is breed discrimination. Had the bus full of dogs been some other breed, such as cocker spaniels, Doberman pinschers, or even pit bulls, I believe no one would have said, "They should all be killed." I believe those that were euthanized by a shelter or met with violence, like the gentle Hunter, were the victims of an ignorant and cruel bias. Our dogs were Siberian huskies, German shepherds, and husky-shepherd mixes, as well as three types of Belgian shepherds, and it was precisely because they were these breeds that some of our precious dogs were killed.

The husky has a long tradition of invaluable service to humans in Alaska and other far-north regions. It is impossible to calculate how many men and women have survived treacherous journeys through snowstorms only because their teams of huskies had the intelligence, fortitude, and courage to bring their humans safely to their destinations. In chapter 5, "Dogs with a Mission," a nurse told how she had depended on a team of huskies to lead her safely from one Eskimo village to the next in the worst winter conditions so that she could minister to the medical needs of villagers.

Although they cannot pull a sled through a frozen wilderness, German shepherds are the most versatile of all dogs in their service to humans. Whether as war dogs, police dogs, tracking dogs, or family pets, dogs of this breed are known for their keen intelligence, ability to think for themselves, courage, and steadfast loyalty. Many years ago I met a man who had worked as a dog trainer during World War II. He told me that the army tested different breeds of dogs but found that only German shepherds or German shepherd mixes could be depended on to lead a group of soldiers through a mine field or carry a message through enemy lines. I will always remember his words: "Other breeds will understandably panic under a barrage of gunfire, but the German shepherd will make it through enemy lines even when wounded. Only death will stop him from performing his duty." The first American dog to go into combat in World War II, the most decorated dog of that war, and the canine equivalent of Audie Murphy, had much in common with our Camp Husky dogs. Chip was a mix of German shepherd, husky, and collie who single-handedly captured four German soldiers who were firing on Americans from a pillbox. Although wounded in that first action, later the same day, this mutt (who looked like some of our Camp Husky dogs) captured ten Italian soldiers! As remarkable as Chip was, his intelligence, courage, and strongheartedness was matched by many other German shepherd war dogs from the 1940s to the present time. Thousands of soldiers returned from World War II, the Korean War, the Vietnam War, and our current wars because of courageous German shepherds (and now Belgian shepherds as well). German shepherds were also the first seeing-eye dogs and drug-detection dogs and are currently among the favorite breeds for search-and-rescue work.

I find it a sad irony that two breeds that have served humankind in such selfless ways were discriminated against simply because they resemble wolves. It is precisely because they are so genetically close to wolves, as opposed to most other breeds, that these dogs have such intelligence, courage, and loyalty. Just as the leaders of a wolf pack, whether male or female, will sacrifice themselves to save their packs, countless huskies and German shepherds have done the same to save their human packs.

One of the gentlest beings I ever knew was a German shepherd–wolf hybrid. This animal lived with my husband and me and other dogs for twelve years. I never once saw him even growl at a person or another dog. Even when he encountered a mouse, he showed no desire to harm the little creature. Once, when some of my family members were in the woods about to enjoy a picnic, a baby black bear ran up and jumped on the picnic table with mother bear coming up behind. I told everyone to stand still. My niece, who was holding her baby boy, was standing closest to the mama bear. My wolf dog, Duke, was on the other side of her. The smart dog made eye contact with me and then looked at the baby in my niece's arms. I am convinced he was telling me that he would protect the baby if necessary. Duke never once moved or looked toward the baby bear or mother bear. After about twenty minutes, the mama and baby bear walked away peacefully. That encounter had a happy outcome, and no creature was harmed, because of a wolf's wisdom.

There are those who look at an old-growth forest in awe and feel fortunate just to see it and know that it exists and is enriching the total ecosystem in wondrous ways. There are other humans who look at that same forest and think how they could make a quick buck by destroying it, with no concern for the harm their actions will cause to the environment on which human and animal life depends. There are those who look at a homeless cat and want to offer food and safety, and there are others who want only to throw a rock at the poor creature. This dark side of human nature, destructive toward nature and cruel toward animals, is all too common, but it is not just the animals that suffer.

The wisest humans have realized that we are one with all life. Thus, when we cut down an old-growth forest, pollute a river, or inflict cruelty on animals or fellow humans, we are ultimately harming ourselves. Such acts of destruction and violence empower the dark side of our nature. Today, in the twenty-first century, more than ever before, our survival may well depend on the willingness of humans to see that we are one with all life and that the violence we inflict on a dog, a cat, a pig, or a wolf, we inflict on all of humanity. Every act of cruelty and violence to an animal or a human diminishes all of us, while every act of love and compassion ennobles all of us.

I once encountered a magnificent coyote when out hiking alone. We stared at each other for a while, and then I sat down on the ground, just enjoying being in the presence of this delightful being. I didn't want to threaten him in any way or end that sense of oneness I was experiencing. Later, I realized that by being totally nonthreatening to the coyote, I might have made him more vulnerable to human cruelty. I said a little prayer that the beautiful animal would be able to live out his life without encountering a human with a gun or, worse still, a trap. Every time I encounter a wild creature in the woods, I feel privileged. Just encountering a moose, a coyote, or a fox is a magical experience, and I always feel sadness at the thought that their lives may be cut short by a human.

Many people have encountered a dog, a coyote, a wolf, or some other animal; looked into that animal's eyes, and experienced a sense of oneness with that animal and all life. Philosopher Martin Buber understood this type of deeply meaningful communication: "An animal's eyes have the power to speak a great language." Sarah DeMoney's sister Dale discovered the truth of Buber's words when, as a young woman, she encountered a wolf in Yellowstone Park. Dale, a hospital administrator from Seattle, never forgot those few moments when a wolf spoke to her soul without uttering a sound. Some years later when she was dying of cancer, Dale asked her family to scatter her ashes in the place where she had looked into the eyes of a wolf.

Some may say that compassion for animals is just impractical sentimentality, but I would argue that unless we end our cruelty to animals in all its many forms, we will never stop inflicting cruelty on each other, and we will ultimately destroy ourselves. Saint Francis of Assisi knew a lot about man's inhumanity to man, and he also realized that there is a strong link between cruelty to animals and cruelty to humans. "If you have men who will exclude any of God's creatures from the shelter of compassion and pity, you will have men who will deal likewise with their fellow men," said the saint. Modern research supports what St. Francis said. I once attended a conference where experts explained that where there is animal abuse in a home, there is a high probability of spouse or child abuse. Also, most serial killers get their start inflicting pain on animals.

A new acquaintance told me a wonderful story about the Lab-Chow dog her family had when she was a child. When the little girl started school, the dog accompanied her and the other neighborhood children as they walked to school in the morning and waited at the school until the children went inside. Somehow this intelligent dog knew when school was out and would be waiting outside the school yard to walk about ten children home. The dog learned to do this on her own. This gentle dog was naturally a favorite in the neighborhood, but one day an older boy went into her yard and deliberately hurt her, causing her to bite him in self-defense. Animal control was about to seize the dog and kill her when the injured boy's mother stopped them, saying that the dog was innocent and that her son must have done something to cause the dog to bite him. How many parents would have the wisdom and compassion to speak the truth in that situation? When the dog died some years later, the boy, now a young man, cried and admitted that he had hurt the dog. His mother's integrity and truth telling helped the boy to develop compassion and overcome the dark side of his nature, and, as a result, I am certain he has enjoyed better relationships with people as well as animals.

Compassion for animals can make us more compassionate toward people, and ultimately, compassion for animals can make the world a kinder place for all of us. I learned that lesson at an early age. When I was five years old, I ran into the street chasing a ball. I was hit by a car, but I was not badly injured or killed only because the man who was driving was an exceptionally kindhearted individual who always drove well under the speed limit in residential areas for fear that he might hit a dog or cat. His compassion for animals saved my life.

Anatole France, the writer and philosopher who won the 1921 Nobel Prize in Literature, said, "Until one has loved an animal, a part of one's soul remains unawakened." By saving the dogs of Camp Husky, the volunteers enabled the dogs to pass on love to many people, from babies to the elderly, and even saved some human lives. Just as the villagers who allowed the wolf to live in peace with them were ultimately saved and taught unconditional love by that wolf, those of us who labored to save the dogs of Camp Husky also received far more than we gave. Our souls were awakened. We were touched by angels.

About the Author

Roberta K. Ray holds a PhD in speech-communication from the University of Southern California and is a professor at Montana Tech of the University of Montana-Butte, where she teaches communication courses.

An environmentalist and animal rights activist, she volunteered at Camp Husky and was inspired to share the dogs' remarkable stories in her memoir *Angels on a School Bus*.

She currently lives in Butte, Montana, with her husband, John, and their three dogs.

Made in the USA
Lexington, KY
21 March 2017